The
RISE
of
AMERICAN
DEMOCRACY

VOLUME I

THE CRISIS OF THE NEW ORDER
1787–1815

Books by Sean Wilentz

The Rise of American Democracy: Jefferson to Lincoln (2005)

The Rose & the Briar: Death, Love and Liberty in the American Ballad (ed., with Greil Marcus, 2004)

David Walker's Appeal to the Coloured Citizens of the World (ed., 1995)

The Kingdom of Matthias (with Paul E. Johnson, 1994)

The Key of Liberty: The Life and Democratic Writings of William Manning, "A Labourer," 1747–1814 (with Michael Merrill, 1993)

Major Problems in the History of the Early Republic, 1789–1848 (ed., 1992)

Rites of Power: Symbolism, Ritual, and Politics since the Middle Ages (ed., 1985)

Chants Democratic: New York City & the Rise of the American Working Class, 1788–1850 (1984)

The
RISE
of
AMERICAN
DEMOCRACY

VOLUME I
THE CRISIS OF THE NEW ORDER
1787–1815

Sean Wilentz

W. W. Norton & Company
New York London

For information about permission to reproduce selections from this book, write to
Permissions, W. W. Norton & Company, Inc., 500 Fifth Avenue, New York, NY
10110

ISBN-13: 978-0-393-93006-1 (pbk)
ISBN-10: 0-393-93006-8 (pbk)

The Library of Congress has catalogued the one-volume edition as follows:

Wilentz, Sean.
The rise of American democracy : Jefferson to Lincoln / Sean Wilentz.—1st ed.
p. cm.
Includes bibliographical references and index.
ISBN 0-393-05820-4 (hardcover)
1. United States—Politics and government—1783–1865. 2. Presidents—United
States—History—18th century. 3. Presidents—United States—History—19th
century.
4. Politicians—United States—History—19th century. 6. Democracy—United
States—History—18th century. 7. Democracy—United States—History—19th
century. I. Title.

E302.1.W55 2005
973.5—dc21

2004029466

W. W. Norton & Company, Inc.
500 Fifth Avenue, New York, NY 10110
www.wwnorton.com

W. W. Norton & Company Ltd.
Castle House, 75/76 Wells Street, London W1T 3QT

1 2 3 4 5 6 7 8 9 0

A NOTE ON THE COLLEGE EDITION

The three-volume College Edition of *The Rise of American Democracy: Jefferson to Lincoln* has two chief goals. First, many students and teachers, as well as many general readers, are mainly interested in one or two phases of the long history covered in the larger work. Publishing each of the book's three major parts as separate volumes allows those readers to focus on their period or periods of special interest. Second, many readers prefer a version without the elaborate scholarly apparatus of the original, but with pointers on further reading. The College Edition includes a list of select additional titles pertinent to each volume, while it eliminates the endnotes in the full edition. Not a word of text from the larger work has been omitted.

To enhance continuity, brief synopses of events covered earlier in the general work appear in volumes II and III.

—S.W.

To P.B. and L.W.
& to all my dearest

CONTENTS

LIST OF ILLUSTRATIONS

MAPS

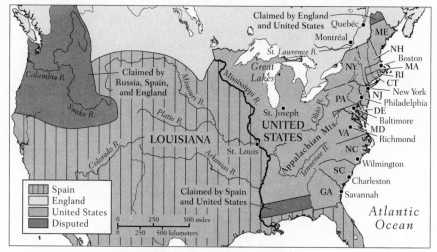

NORTH AMERICA, 1783

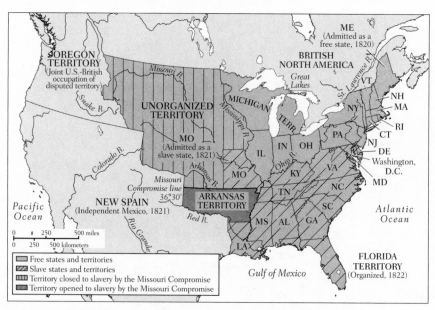

THE MISSOURI COMPROMISE, 1820

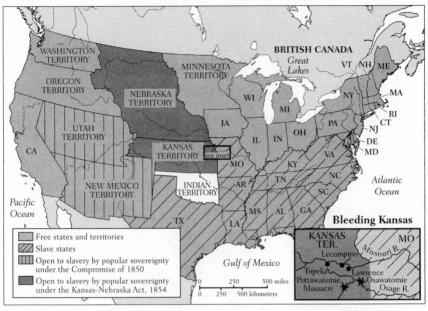

THE KANSAS-NEBRASKA ACT, 1854

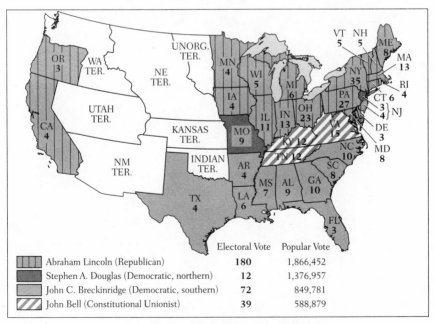

		Electoral Vote	Popular Vote
	Abraham Lincoln (Republican)	**180**	1,866,452
	Stephen A. Douglas (Democratic, northern)	**12**	1,376,957
	John C. Breckinridge (Democratic, southern)	**72**	849,781
	John Bell (Constitutional Unionist)	**39**	588,879

THE ELECTION OF 1860

PREFACE TO VOLUME I

The simple title of the general work from which this volume is drawn, *The Rise of American Democracy*, describes the historical arc of the overall subject. Important elements of democracy existed in the infant American republic of the 1780s, but the republic was not democratic. Nor, in the minds of those who governed it, was it supposed to be. A republic—the *res publica*, or "public thing"—was meant to secure the common good through the ministrations of the most worthy, enlightened men. A democracy—derived from *demos krateo*, "rule of the people"—dangerously handed power to the impassioned, unenlightened masses. Democracy, the eminent political leader George Cabot wrote as late as 1804, was *"the government of the worst."* Yet by the 1830s, as Alexis de Tocqueville learned, most Americans proclaimed that their country was a democracy as well as a republic. Enduring arguments had begun over the boundaries of democratic politics. In the 1840s and 1850s, these arguments centered increasingly on slavery and slavery's expansion and led to the Civil War.

The change was astonishing, but neither inevitable nor providential. American democracy did not rise like the sun at its natural hour in history. Its often troubled ascent was the outcome of human conflicts, accommodations, and unforeseen events, and the results could well have been very different than they were. The difficulties and the contingencies made the events all the more remarkable. A momentous rupture occurred between Thomas Jefferson's time and Abraham Lincoln's, in which the elitist presumptions and institutions of the infant republic gave way to far broader conceptions of popular sovereignty and to new forms of mass political participation, in and out of elections. The polity that emerged contained the lineaments of modern democratic politics. The rise of American democracy is the story of that rupture and its immediate consequences.

Democracy is a troublesome word, and explaining why is one of *The Rise of American Democracy's* larger purposes. A decade before the American Revolution, the early patriot James Otis defined democracy in its purest and simplest form as "a government of all over all," in which "the votes of the majority shall be taken as the voice of the whole," and where the rulers were the ruled and the ruled were the rulers. As fixed descriptions go, this is as good as any, but its abstractness, of course, begs explication. Since the Revolution, citizens, scholars, and political leaders have latched onto one or another particular aspect of government or politics as democracy's essence. For some, it is a matter of widened political rights, usually measured by the extent of the suffrage and actual voting; for others, democracy means greater opportunity for the individual pursuit of happiness; for still others, it is more of a cultural phenomenon than a political one, "a habit of the heart," as Tocqueville put it, in which deference to rulers and condescension for the ruled give way to the ruder conventions of equality.

All of these facets are important, but I think we go astray in discussing democracy simply as a form of government or society, or as a set of social norms—a category or a thing with particular structures that can be codified and measured. Today, democracy means, at a minimum, full enfranchisement and participation by the entire adult citizenry. By that standard, the American democracy of the mid-nineteenth century was hardly a democracy at all: women of all classes and colors lacked political and civil rights; most blacks were enslaved; free black men found political rights they had once enjoyed either reduced or eliminated; the remnant of a ravaged Indian population in the eastern states had been forced to move west, without citizenship. Even the most expansive of the era's successful democratic political reforms encompassed considerably less than half of the total adult population, and at best a bare majority of the free adult population.* But to impose current categories of democracy on the past is to block any understanding of how our own, more elevated standards originated. It is to distort the lives of Americans who could barely have anticipated political and social changes that we take for granted. It is to substitute our experiences and prejudices for theirs.

By democracy, I mean a historical fact, rooted in a vast array of events and experiences, that comes into being out of changing human relations between governors and the governed. Stopping history cold at any particular point and parsing its political makeup negates that historical flow and stifles the voices and activities of actual people attempting to define the operations of government. Only over an extended period of time is it possible to see democracy and democratic government grow out of particular social, intellectual, and political contexts.

---

* This is based on the figures gathered in the federal census for 1850, which show that 44.5 percent of the adult population (twenty years and older) and 51.0 percent of the free adult population were white males. Noncitizens and Indians are not included in the calculations. The numbers are crude indicators, but the main point of comparison with the present is obvious.

Democracy appears when some large number of previously excluded, ordinary persons—what the eighteenth century called "the many"—secure the power not simply to select their governors but to oversee the institutions of government, as officeholders and as citizens free to assemble and criticize those in office. Democracy is never a gift bestowed by benevolent, farseeing rulers who seek to reinforce their own legitimacy. It has always to be fought for, by political coalitions that cut across distinctions of wealth, power, and interest. It succeeds and survives only when it is rooted in the lives and expectations of its citizens, and continually reinvigorated in each generation. Democratic successes are never irreversible.

Since Tocqueville, there has been a long tradition of scholarship devoted to understanding the democratic rupture that the general work describes. The rise of American democracy engaged the attention of great historians now forgotten by the general reading public (Dixon Ryan Fox, J. Franklin Jameson), as well as such acknowledged giants as Charles and Mary Beard, Frederick Jackson Turner, Richard Hofstadter, and, most recently, Gordon S. Wood. But modern study of the subject owes the most to Arthur M. Schlesinger Jr.'s *The Age of Jackson*, published in 1945. Before Schlesinger, historians thought of American democracy as the product of an almost mystical frontier or agrarian egalitarianism. *The Age of Jackson* toppled that interpretation by placing democracy's origins firmly in the context of the founding generation's ideas about the few and the many, and by seeing democracy's expansion as an outcome more of struggles between classes than between sections. More than any previous account, Schlesinger's examined the activities and ideas of obscure, ordinary Americans, as well as familiar political leaders. While he identified most of the key political events and changes of the era, Schlesinger also located the origins of modern liberal politics in the tradition of Thomas Jefferson and Andrew Jackson, and in their belief, as he wrote, that future challenges "will best be met by a society in which no single group is able to sacrifice democracy and liberty to its interests." Finally, Schlesinger examined and emphasized the shattering moral and political dilemmas that an expanding southern slavery posed to American democracy, leading to the Civil War.

Since *The Age of Jackson* appeared, a revolution in historical studies has focused scholars' attentions on groups of Americans and aspects of American history that held minor interest at best in the historical profession in 1945. That revolution has altered historians' views of every detail of our past. The tragedy of Indian removal; the democratic activities of ex-slaves and other free blacks; the ease and sometimes the viciousness with which some professed democrats, North and South, championed white racial supremacy; the participation of women in reform efforts (and, in time, in electoral campaigns), along with the ridicule directed at the fledgling woman suffrage movement; the liberal humanitarian impulses that informed important strains of supposedly "conservative," pro-business politics; the importance of ethnicity and religion in shaping Americans' political allegiances—each of these, either ignored or slighted sixty years ago, has generated an enormous scholarly literature.

Yet if the social history revolution has profoundly changed how historians look at the United States, it has not diminished the importance of the questions *The Age of Jackson* asked about early American democracy. On the contrary, it has made those questions—especially about democratic politics, social class, and slavery—all the more pertinent to our understanding of the dramatic events that led from the American Revolution to the American Civil War. Some important recent works have attempted to raise those questions anew, and bridge the so-called new style of history with the older. The most ambitious of them have reinterpreted the connections between society and politics before 1860 as part of a larger market revolution that swept across the country. But these admirable studies have generally submerged the history of politics in the history of social change, reducing politics and democracy to byproducts of various social forces without quite allowing the play of politics its independent existence and importance. *The Rise of*

American Democracy offers a different interpretation of these connections and with a greater focus on the vagaries of politics, high and low.

The general work's subtitle, *Jefferson to Lincoln*, reaffirms the importance of political events, ideas, and leaders to democracy's rise—once an all-too-prevalent idea, now in need of some rescue and repair. Thomas Jefferson, more than any other figure in the early Republic, established (and was seen to have established) the terms of American democratic politics. Abraham Lincoln self-consciously advanced an updated version of Jefferson's egalitarian ideals, and his election to the presidency of the United States caused the greatest crisis American democracy has yet known. By singling out Jefferson and Lincoln, I certainly do not mean to say that presidents and other great men were solely responsible for the vicissitudes of American politics. One of the book's recurring themes is how ordinary Americans, including some at the outermost reaches of the country's formal political life, had lasting influence on the exercise of power. But just as political leaders did not create American democracy out of thin air, so the masses of Americans did not simply force their way into the corridors of power. That Jefferson and not John Adams was elected president in 1800–01—a fact that nearly did not come to pass—made a vast difference to subsequent political developments. So did the presence of other public officials, elected and unelected, from the top of American public life to the bottom. Featuring Jefferson and Lincoln in the subtitle of the larger work is a shorthand way of insisting on what ought to be a truism: that some individuals have more influence on history than others. The title, by referring to a broader history, insists that they cannot make history just as they please, constrained as they are by a host of forces and persons beyond their control and anticipation.

The Rise of American Democracy can be read as a chronicle of American politics from the Revolution to the Civil War with the history of democracy at its center, or as an account of how democracy arose in the United States (and with what consequences) in the context of its time. Either way, the general work has a few major themes. One, given special attention in the first volume of the College Edition, is that democracy, at the nation's inception, was highly contested, not a given, and developed only piecemeal, by fits and starts, at the state and local as well as the national level. A second theme, taken up in the second volume, is that social changes barely foreseen in 1787, chiefly the rapid commercialization of the free labor North and the renaissance of plantation slavery in the South, deeply affected how democracy advanced, and retreated, after 1815.

Third, Americans perceived these social changes primarily in political terms and increasingly saw them as struggles over contending ideas of democracy. Americans of the early nineteenth century lived in a different mental universe from ours with regard to politics. Above all, they inherited from the Revolutionary era a republican perspective that regarded political institutions as the foundation of social and economic relations, and not the other way around. Certain kinds of societies appeared more conducive than others to a just and harmonious government. Americans sharply disagreed about which societies were superior. But if order and happiness abounded, they believed it was because political institutions and the men running them were sound: disorder and unhappiness stemmed from unsound institutions or from the corruption of sound institutions by ambitious and designing men. Across the chasm of the Civil War, the era of high industrialism, and the conflicts of the twentieth century, we are more likely to see economic power and interests as the matrix for politics and political institutions. For Americans of the early Republic, politics, government, and constitutional order, not economics, were primary to interpreting the world and who ran it— a way of thinking that can wrongly look simplified, paranoid, and conspiracy-driven today.

A fourth theme concerns the constancy of political conflict: democracy in America was the spectacle of Americans arguing over democracy. If the word became a shibboleth for new and emerging political parties and movements, it did not on that account become degraded and bland. Precisely because opposing groups claimed to champion the same ideal, they fought all the harder to ensure their version would prevail. There was no end to the possible qualifying labels Americans could devise to illustrate exactly what sort of democrats they were—not just with separate major- and third-party labels (Democratic, Whig, State Rights, Know-Nothing, and so on) but with the blizzard of names for factions within the parties that always bemuse uninitiated readers: Loco Foco, Barnburner, Hunker, Silver Gray.* In part, these labels connoted patronage connections for political insiders. But in an age when elections came to be conducted more or less year-round, they also reflected beliefs and deep commitments above and beyond party machinations—while for a radical such as William Lloyd Garrison they were craven and sinful, and for a corrosive skeptic such as Herman Melville they inspired ambivalence and dread.

Fifth, the many-sided conflicts over American democracy came, in the 1840s and 1850s, to focus on an issue of recognized importance since the Republic's birth: the fate of American slavery. Throughout the decades after the Revolution, but with a hurtling force after 1840, two American democracies emerged, the free-labor democracy of the North and the slaveholders' democracy of the South—distinct political systems as well as bodies of thought. Although they often praised identical values and ideals, and although they were linked through the federal government and the national political parties, the two were fundamentally antagonistic. The nation's political

---

* From 1856: "Thus every party and sect has a daily register of the most minute sayings and doings, and proceedings and progress of every other sect; and as truth and error are continually brought before the masses, they have the opportunity to know and compare. There are political parties under the names of Whigs, Democrats, Know-nothings, Freesoilers, Fusionists, Hunkers, Woolly-heads, Dough-faces, Hard-shells, Soft-shells, Silver-greys, and I know not what besides; all of them extremely puzzling to the stranger, but of great local significance." Isabella Lucy Bird, *The Englishwoman in America* (London, 1856), 422–23.

leaders suppressed those antagonisms, sometimes in the face of powerful protests and schismatic movements, from the 1820s through the early 1850s. By 1860, the conflict could no longer be contained, as a democratic election sparked southern secession and the war that would determine American democracy's future.

The work's final theme is implied in the others: the idea of democracy is never sufficient unto itself. Since the Second World War, and even more since the great democratic revolutions of 1989–91, the world has witnessed the continuing resilience and power of democratic ideals. So swiftly have former tyrannies turned into self-declared democratic governments that the danger has arisen of taking democracy for granted, despite its manifest fragility and possible collapse in large parts of the globe. As the early history of the United States shows, the habits and the institutions of modern democracy are relatively new in the larger span of history. Their breakthrough, even in the most egalitarian portions of the New World, required enormous reversals of traditional assumptions about power and legitimacy. As those habits and institutions began taking hold, different American social orders produced clashing versions of democracy, generating enmities so deep that they could only be settled in blood. Thereafter, democratic ideas, both in the United States and elsewhere, have had to be refreshed, fought over, and redefined continually. The rise of American democracy, from Jefferson's era to Lincoln's, created exhilarating new hopes and prospects, but also fierce conflicts and enormous challenges about what democracy can be and should be. Along with democracy's hopes and prospects, its conflicts and challenges persist. So do its vulnerabilities.

This first volume of the College Edition of *The Rise of American Democracy*, entitled *The Crisis of the New Order*, takes the story from the era of the Revolution through the War of 1812. While helping design the Great Seal of the United States in 1782, Charles Thompson incorporated the following motto from an eclogue by Virgil: "Novus Ordo Seclorum." Translated roughly as "A New Order for the Ages," this phrase optimistically expressed the prevalent belief that the Declaration of Independence heralded a new historical epoch. Yet as early as 1787, Americans found themselves hard at work framing a new constitution to replace the Articles of Confederation. Under the new framework, fresh conflicts arose over foreign as well as domestic affairs that raised anew an issue debated fervently during the War for Independence: how democratic should the new American republic be?

The

RISE

of

AMERICAN

DEMOCRACY

VOLUME I

THE CRISIS OF THE NEW ORDER

1787–1815

PROLOGUE

On pleasant evenings in the middle of the 1830s, Noah Webster, then in his eighties, would return home from his daily walk around New Haven, sit in his front-porch rocker, pick up his newspaper, and moan. The latest political dispatches told Webster that the republic he had loved and fought for had gone to the devil, a democratic devil in the shape of Andrew Jackson, and the future looked bleak. Webster's wife, upon hearing his sighs, knew what was coming: a monologue on mob rule, the death of Christian virtue, and the savagery of strange doctrines and slogans ("rotation in office," "the rich oppress the poor," *the spoils belong to the victors*") that had taken the country by storm. Later in the evening, a few of Webster's professor friends from Yale might stop by to listen and nod their heads, forming a mutually admiring circle of dyspeptic learned men. On these occasions, Webster would brighten momentarily. But many of his companions, like himself, had grown old, and the number of Americans like them was too small, Webster feared, to save the republic now.

When the professors did not appear, Webster would rouse himself, scratch down his opinions, and mail them to a few agreeable editors and elected officials. He was still a well-known figure, a veteran political controversialist, die-hard nationalist, and self-made man, a Founding Father of sorts. Although the great dictionary he had published years earlier had not yet found its market, his blue-backed speller had been a rousing success, and trustworthy critics had hailed him as the man who had literally defined the American language. Perhaps his countrymen would heed his wisdom after all. And so he composed his didactic letters, denouncing President Jackson and Jackson's fanatical democratic principles. Webster devised a plan to check the egalitarian tide by raising the voting age to forty-five, dividing the electorate into two classes according to age and wealth, and letting each class choose one house of Congress—an Americanized gerontocratic version of the British Lords and Commons. But his ideas impressed few readers and caused many to snicker, and the old man sank into acrid reveries about his days as a boy soldier during the American Revolution. Had he foreseen what would follow, he told an associate, he never would have enlisted in the patriot cause.

Webster was a political relic in the 1830s, yet around the country, other Americans were also pessimistic. In the summer of 1837, James Kent, the nation's most distinguished legal commentator, journeyed to the spa at Saratoga Springs and joined other gentlemen in discussing the destructiveness of what Kent called "the democracy of numbers and radicalism." In Manhattan, the affluent parvenu and former mayor of New York, Philip Hone, recoiled with horror from the unkempt Jacksonian supporters who ran wild in the streets on election days, and who on one dismal occasion besieged him in his own house with catcalls. Further south, slaveholding planters and officeholders who thought Jackson a turncoat despaired at his popularity with the plain people and voters. "The old 'Warrior Chief' has kicked up a h-ll of a dust throughout the nation," a Tennessean wrote to a North Carolina planter, in 1834, adding that while "most of our friends of N. Carolina are against [Jackson's] 'experiments,' I should suppose that the people of the State were for him." Other southerners despaired that the masses of farmers and the anti-Jacksonians were like aliens in blood.

Jackson's critics were prone to see the sum of the new democratic order in the president's craggy face, and in what Kent called "the horrible doctrine and influence of Jacksonism." But men with longer experience such as Noah Webster knew there was more to it than that. For Webster, Jackson was a reborn Thomas Jefferson, accomplishing what Jefferson had only imagined accomplishing when the philosophizing mood was upon him. Jackson himself, not known for philosophizing, called his political beliefs an extension of "good old jeffersonian Democratic republican principles." And if Jackson came to symbolize a fulfillment of Jeffersonian desires, his path had been cleared long before he took office. The kind of political charisma (and, for many, scariness) he emanated could not have been produced by his military glory and personal fortitude alone. For more than half a century, Americans of all persuasions had been preparing the way for Jackson, or some democratic leader like him.

The mysterious rise of American democracy was an extraordinary part of the most profound political transformation in modern history: the triumph of popular government and of the proposition—if not, fully, the reality—that sovereignty rightly belongs to the mass of ordinary individual and equal citizens. For centuries, throughout the Western world, such political arrangements had seemed utterly unnatural. Since Plato, doctrines of hierarchical authority had dominated political thought, whether classical (favoring the rule of the wise), Christian (favoring the rule of the holy), or some mixture of the two. According to these doctrines, most of humanity was unsuited for public duties more elevated than the drudgery of farm animals. History seemed to support hierarchical theory. The fate of popular government in the ancient Greek city-states and the Roman republic had been tragic. Periodic peasant uprisings and urban disorders, from the late fourteenth century on, persuaded the articulate classes of Britain and Europe that the "people" were dangerously unstable and incapable of rational thought. "The beast," "the rabble," "th' idiot multitude" reappeared with contemptuous regularity in the learned treatises, poems, and plays of the early modern West.

Rebellion, civil war, and regicide in England after 1640 set the beast stirring, allied as never before (albeit testily) with its social betters among the Puritan and Parliamentarian insurgents. Entrenched inside Oliver Cromwell's army and in the London trades—"the hobnails, clouted shoes, the private soldiers, the leather and woolen aprons," the preacher and radical hero John Lilburne said—so-called Leveller agitators proposed not simply the abolition of the monarchy and the House of Lords, but the establishment of a government truly representative of the people, based on an equitably distributed franchise. In smaller pockets of rebellion, more outlandish plebeian prophets—Ranters, Diggers, Seekers—announced diverse visions of communal heavens on earth. But the revolution's leaders kept radical dissenters on the political margins. At the famous army debates at Putney in 1647, Cromwell and his lieutenants squelched any possibility of popular suffrage. Over the ensuing chaotic decade, the propertied and educated few closed ranks against the unreasonable many. With the restoration of the English monarchy in 1660, plebeian radical politics plunged underground, to reappear sporadically in conspiracies, riots, and revels over the century to come.

When democracy broke through again, in the 1770s, it was in the New World, not the Old, as a beleaguered force within the American Revolution. The combustion was not spontaneous. Even before the outbreak of the English Civil War, religious sectarians who preferred flight to New England to life under Tudor monarchy established at least a nominal conception of self-rule by compact, to which some dissenters (such as a group of four Rhode Island towns in 1647) attached the word "democracy." In 1644, the schismatic Roger Williams declared that "the *Soveraigne, originall,* and *foundation* of *civill power* lies in the people." Bits and pieces of the English plebeian radicalism of the 1640s and 1650s crossed the Atlantic and survived to help inspire the American revolutionaries and frighten their opponents over a century later. As the independence struggle with Britain reached a crisis in 1774, the more radical of the Massachusetts towns excoriated George III for aspiring, as the selectmen of Billerica put it, to "the unlimited Prerogative, contended for by those arbitrary and misguided Princes, *Charles* the First and *James* the Second, for which One lost his Life, and the Other his Kingdom." The most popular antimonarchical pamphlet of the Revolution, Thomas Paine's *Common Sense,* contained numerous allusions to old English democratic themes.

The radicalism of the seventeenth century belongs to the genealogy of American democracy. And there were important differences between the colonies and the mother country in political practice. Colonial charters installed property requirements for voting, usually landed freeholds, but in newly settled colonial areas where land was cheap, anywhere from 70 to 80 percent of white adult men could meet the qualification. It was far easier for an American man of middling means than for his British counterpart to hold local and even legislative office. The colonies lacked Britain's encrustation of civil bureaucracies, church sinecures, and military commands. Americans' experience of town meetings (where, in New England, humble men won election to local offices) and of independent, parish-run dissenting churches gave them a strong taste of direct political engagement. Some British visitors and American royalists regarded the colonies as wild egalitarian outposts. A writer in *Rivington's New York Loyal Gazette* flatly blamed the Revolution on the Americans' "democratic form of government." Some later historians, with no royalist motives, have even described

eighteenth-century America as a "middle-class democracy" long
before the Revolution.

Yet the evidence of colonial democracy, and especially of the
differences with Britain, can be highly deceiving. In older settled rural areas of the colonies, as in coastal towns and early
cities, the proportion of eligible voters among white men was
much smaller than elsewhere, as little as two in five. Those proportions probably declined during the years immediately preced-
ing the Revolution, when the rate of property ownership in the
colonies was falling. The famous town-meeting democracies of
New England were often run as means to ratify decisions
already made by local leaders, and to give the air of amicable
consensus. In the mid-eighteenth century, more than previously,
the British monarchy was the wellspring of American political
authority, the bestower of favor and fortune through royal
appointment to the competing "interests" or "connections" of
America's premier gentry families. Within this monarchical set-
ting, rival families or factions might mobilize ordinary voters on
election days, through treats or barbecues or more raucous, even
violent gatherings—but the royalist favorites always remained in
charge. Outside elections, the everyday gulf between noble
patricians and the beastlike people was deep, even among those
fortunate men who had risen out of the rabble. No less than the
established grandees, up-and-coming patriot leaders respected
elaborate codes of social deference. The young George Washington beheld the lesser farmers of Virginia as "the grazing multitude." The ambitious John Adams, perhaps in order to set
himself apart from his humble background, spoke offhandedly
of the "common Herd of Mankind."

Philosophically, the assumption prevailed that democracy,
although an essential feature of any well-ordered government,
was also dangerous and ought to be kept strictly within bounds.
The word itself appeared rarely in pamphlets, newspapers, and
sermons before the Revolution, most often alongside "monarchy" and "aristocracy," as one of the three elements of government, tied to specific social orders, that needed to be mixed and

balanced in accord with the British model. On the other occasions when either the word or the concept of democracy appeared, the context was usually pejorative, connoting, at best, a ridiculous impracticality, especially in large countries. At midcentury, the historian William Smith wrote that "[i]n proportion as a Country grows rich and populous, more Checks are wanted to the Power of the People." John Adams deeply feared that although "the prospect of free and popular Governments" might be pleasing, "there is great Danger that these Governments will not make Us happy," and would be undone by noise, meanness, and ignorance. Even the radical Thomas Paine took care, during and long after the Revolution, to reject the idea of a pure or simple democracy in favor of representation grafted on democracy.

The major claims on democracy's behalf before the Revolution rested on the rising power, in many colonies, of the lower houses of the colonial legislatures, in imitation of the rising power of the Commons in England after the Glorious Revolution of 1688–89. In principle, these assemblies represented the common middling sort, the small farmers, artisans, and petty merchants who made up the great bulk of the colonial free male population. According to one North Carolinian, the assemblies were supposed to act as "Eyes for the Commonality, as Ears for the Commonality, and as Mouths for the Commonality." Yet even though a few members of the Commonality actually sat in the assemblies, the legislators were generally out of touch with their own constituents between elections, and ran their affairs much like the oligarchies that commanded the early eighteenth-century House of Commons under Robert Walpole. Colonial assemblymen would receive petitions and letters from their localities, but did with them whatever they pleased. Otherwise, the people had no formal voice of their own in government. And that was exactly how it was supposed to be—for once the electors had chosen their representatives, they ceded power, reserving none for themselves until the next election. As one New England divine wrote, the electorate did not "surrender so much their right or liberty to

their Rulers, as their Power." There was no sense of any continued exercise of political power by the "people out-of-doors." The
people, as a political entity, existed only on election days.

If the unelected had any other political voice, it came in the
form of extralegal mob violence and crowd disturbances—forms
of protests condoned and even instigated by established political
leaders when it suited their political advantage. "Popular commo-
tions," as John Adams called them, could be dangerous, especially when led by unscrupulous private factions of the insider
leadership, but they were tolerable "when Fundamentals are
invaded." Whether commanded from above or organized on their
own, these tumults affirmed that the mass of ordinary citizens
had no regular, legal, permanent involvement in the making of
decisions, the actual stuff of government and politics. They also
reinforced the traditional image of the people as the rowdy multitude, not to be entrusted with formal power.

Only when the gathering American revolutionary impulses
reached the brink of independence in the 1770s did they begin to
look discernibly democratic in any sense that the Puritan radicals
would have understood. At stake were the Revolution's central
claims about sovereignty and representation. On the one hand,
the patriot movement argued that because Americans had neither elected representatives of their own in Parliament nor any
transcendent common interests with the mother country, the
imperial connection was oppressive. Traditional Tory claims that
the colonists enjoyed virtual representation, with their interests
protected by members of Parliament who embodied the good of
the entire realm, dissolved before American contentions that
those very M.P.'s (as a Georgia clergyman wrote) had no "right to
represent and lay on taxes on those who never invested them
with any such power, and by whom they neither would nor could
be elected." Without popular consent, there could be no just or
legitimate representation. Without that legitimacy, Parliament
had no sovereignty over America.

On the other hand, patriot leaders were dedicated to building
a polity governed by the wisest and best among themselves, who

would selflessly devote themselves to securing the unified public good. Outside the imperial context, they clung tenaciously to the idea of virtual representation when it came to their own ordinary people. Products of the British constitutional system, they shared an assumption that men who lacked an independent estate had "no will of their own," as Sir William Blackstone had written in his authoritative *Commentaries on the Laws of England*. Dependent men were politically unreliable because they could be easily manipulated by their patrons—or, alternatively, might use political power to plunder their patrons. Even Thomas Jefferson, who would emerge as one of the most democratic of the Revolution's leaders, was reflexively suspicious at first. "A choice by the people themselves," he complained to a friend in 1776, "is not generally distinguished for it's wisdom."

The Revolution, by destroying the old forms of monarchical government and virtual representation, opened up lines of argument and ways of thinking that severely undermined hierarchical assumptions. The most hard-headed of the revolutionary leaders understood this and, for the most part, found it frightening. Taken too literally, the axiom that government should rest on the people's consent—especially when mingled with the assertion, made most forcefully in Jefferson's Declaration of Independence, that all men were endowed with equal and natural rights—could provoke disorder and give undue influence to the less-than-wise and the less-than-good. John Adams predicted, with prescience, that loosening voting requirements would mean "new claims will arise; women will demand a vote; lads from twelve to twenty-one will think their claims not closely attended to; and every man who has not a farthing will demand an equal voice with any other, in all acts of state."

To the horror of Adams and others, their fears came to pass, as ordinary Americans, organized in independent committees, conventions, and other associations, raised a democratic clamor even before independence from Britain had been secured. "The people are now contending for freedom," one Massachusetts pamphleteer declared in 1776, "and would to God they might not only obtain, but likewise keep it in their own hands." From all across Revolutionary America, cities and countryside alike, came appeals for a widened suffrage, equalized representation, unicameral legislatures, overhauled judiciaries, and a seemingly endless list of other egalitarian demands.

It was one thing, these city and country democrats pointed out, to speak of establishing a kingless republican government and of vaunting the public good. It was quite another to specify what kind of republics the new American governments, state and national, would be. The *philosophe* Montesquieu, read widely in translations of his *L'Esprit des Lois*, had observed that republics could be of different types, in which either "the body, or only a part of the people, is possessed of the supreme power." (As a Massachusetts writer would put it more bluntly a few years after independence, "Republicks are divided into democraticks and aristocraticks.") And so, in an exuberant exchange of ideas, popular spokesmen, and a small portion of the patriot leadership, argued that the new American governments ought to be as "democratick" as possible—and that any government which lacked the full approval of the people, as one New York committee of radical artisans put it, was guilty of "promoting the selfish views . . . of oligarchy." Faced with this pressure chiefly from below, patriot leaders, embroiled in worsening conflict with the British Crown and its functionaries, found themselves backed into a dilemma that would bedevil Americans long after they won their independence.

How "democratick" the governments produced by the American Revolution actually were was open to dispute then, and still is. But between 1776 and the ratification of the Federal Constitution in 1788, a shift certainly occurred in the ways Americans, at every level of political society, talked and thought about democracy. At the outbreak of the Revolution, the necessity of a mixed government of the different social orders remained a widespread article of faith, except among the most radical patriots. As one of Thomas Paine's critics wrote, "[N]o government was ever purely aristocratical or democratical—owing probably to the unavoidable evils incident to each." Eleven years later, when the Framers met in Philadelphia to design a new federal government, fears of democratic government, or of too much democratic government, were still palpable. Yet when they settled down to repair what James Madison called the "vices of the political system" under the Articles of Confederation, and even more when they defended the new constitution they had written, the leading delegates gravitated to ideas very different from the conventional wisdom of 1776. The new federal edifice would not be a mixed government. Nor would it lodge sovereignty in the newly independent state governments, as the Articles had done. Instead, the people of the United States would be sovereign. In the new plan, according to James Wilson (Madison's kindred spirit at the Federal Convention), "[A]ll authority of every *kind is derived by* REPRESENTATION *from the* PEOPLE *and the* DEMOCRATIC *principle is carried into every part of the government."* Therefore, the Constitution, "in its principles," was "purely democratical"— the very phrase that, before the Revolution, had seemed absurd and treacherous. In words and in feelings, the unthinkable was becoming the desirable.

"A fundamental mistake of the Americans," Noah Webster, not yet a relic, wrote in 1789, "has been that they considered the revolution as completed when it was just begun." Webster's judgment would be borne out over the next few years, when new convulsions hastened the emergence of new forms of democratic politics. As Webster understood, those convulsions and fresh departures were continuations of the upheaval that had started in earnest in 1776.

1

AMERICAN DEMOCRACY IN
A REVOLUTIONARY AGE

In the summer of 1776, three different assemblages of revolutionaries worked in Philadelphia. The famous one, the Second Continental Congress, having sat in continuous session for ten months, voted to dissolve ties with Britain on July 2, and two days later signed a formal Declaration of Independence, written chiefly by Thomas Jefferson. In late June, a Pennsylvania Provincial Conference also set up nearby. The delegates had just been chosen by their extralegal local committees of correspondence and, with the approval of the Continental Congress, displaced the dilatory colonial assembly. Under the Provincial Congress's aegis, and while the Continental Congress was declaring the nation's independence, elections were held for delegates to the Pennsylvania Convention to devise a state constitution. This third group assembled on July 8, and spent the summer at the State House, steps away from the rooms where the Continental Congress was working, inventing a new Pennsylvania commonwealth.

One famous delegate, Benjamin Franklin, was elected to all three bodies and played a leading role in shaping both the Declaration of Independence and the new Pennsylvania constitution. At seventy, Franklin was among the older patriot leaders, and the oldest to sign the Declaration. He was also the most renowned, thanks to his scientific discoveries and "Poor Richard" writings, as well as his long political service. And he was proving to be, in some respects, among the most democratic. Franklin's work at the Continental Congress—as an esteemed delegate, a member of the select committee that helped Jefferson draft the Declaration, and a major contributor to the debates over the new Articles of Confederation—is well known. After independence was declared, he pushed to create a strong federal government run by a popularly elected legislature based on proportional representation. (Few of those ideas got far.) Much less familiar is Franklin's contribution as president of the now-obscure State Convention that drafted and approved the most egalitarian constitution produced anywhere in Revolutionary America.

Under the new state plan, Pennsylvanians would be governed by a legislature with a single house and a twelve-man executive council elected by a broad franchise of taxpaying freemen. Representation of different parts of the state in the legislature would be more equitable than in the past. The Council of Censors would be elected every seven years to evaluate the government and censure any constitutional violations. A formal declaration of rights proclaimed "[t]hat all men are born equally free and independent," and that the state's government would exist for the "common benefit, protection and security of the people, nation, or community, and not for the particular emolument or advantage of any single man, family, or set of men, who are only part of that community." It is unclear how much of a hand Franklin had in actually writing the new constitution. But his ideas and, at times, his style were plainly in evidence, so much so that many people thought he was the sole author. With Franklin presiding, the Convention adopted the new framework at the end of September and put it immediately into effect.

It is not surprising that Franklin's more egalitarian leanings prevailed in the Pennsylvania Convention and not in Congress. The planters, merchants, and professional men who signed the Declaration of Independence—including John Hancock, John

Adams, and Edward Rutledge, as well as Franklin and Jefferson—were notables of wealth and standing, with reputations of high degree, at least in their respective provinces. The group's views on government and democracy varied widely, with Franklin, although hardly a thoroughgoing democrat, standing at the more democratic end. The leaders of the Pennsylvania Convention were very different. Most were Philadelphia artisans and intellectuals of a radical democratic bent, many of them disciples of Thomas Paine, with names unfamiliar to most Americans, then and now: George Bryan, James Cannon, Thomas Young, Timothy Matlack. The majority of the delegates were humble farmers from the rural interior, chosen by the radical leadership because of their adherence to democratic political ideals. "They are mostly honest well meaning Country men, who are employed," the Rev. Francis Allison observed with some disdain, "but intirely unacquainted with . . . high matters." The Convention also had strong political ties to the lower sort in the rank and file of Philadelphia's militia companies.

Franklin was one of the few Americans who could feel perfectly comfortable taking a leading role simultaneously inside the Continental Congress and the Pennsylvania Convention—one group defining a nation, the other defining a state; one with a patrician tone, the other decidedly plebeian. Likewise, he may have been the only Pennsylvanian with the prestige, wit, and political skill to bring together the disparate elements within the Pennsylvania State Convention—men from the city and the country, men who agreed on certain egalitarian principles but were otherwise divided by clashing backgrounds, educations, temperaments, and expectations. A similar pattern appeared in the other new states. American democratic politics originated in both the country and the city, from New England through the South. Democratic hopes, which the Pennsylvanians temporarily fulfilled in 1776, would depend on whether these two political milieux could be united—and on how much influence the country democrats and the city democrats would then have in shaping the new republican order.

THE COUNTRY DEMOCRACY

Land forms "the true and the only philosophy of the American farmer," the French immigrant (and self-styled "American Farmer") J. Hector St. John Crèvecoeur observed in 1782. Speaking as if he were an ordinary native tiller of the soil, Crèvecoeur dissembled shamelessly—at the time he wrote, he owned an estate in the Hudson River Valley—but his appreciation of everyday rural political thought was acute. "This formerly rude soil has been converted by my father into a pleasant farm," he wrote of his home, "and in return it has established all our rights; on it is founded our rank, our freedom, our power as citizens, our importance as inhabitants in such a district." At the end of the eighteenth century, land, and the labor applied to it, provided the ordinary farmer's basis for social respect and civic participation. Getting and protecting claims to the land and its products was the pervasive political imperative of the country democracy.

Country democracy arose from a disparate white rural majority of farmers, whom the Pennsylvania gentleman democrat George Logan referred to collectively as "the Yeomanry of the United States." From affluent incipient commercial farmers who lived near cities or river towns to hardscrabble settlers living just beyond the frontier line, these farmers and their households shared certain broad characteristics. They subsisted primarily on the produce of their own farms and on what they could obtain from exchange with neighbors, although a growing number were engaged in some sort of cash-crop production (chiefly wheat, flax, and livestock in the northern states, tobacco and wheat in the southern states). With land plentiful and cheap labor in short supply, theirs were family-centered operations in which fathers directed the work of legally dependent wives and children—and on some farms, most commonly but not yet exclusively in the South, perhaps a slave or two. Contrary to still-persistent American myths of rural rugged individualism, the yeoman households were tightly connected to each other—and, increasingly, to the outside world.

Descended from transatlantic victims of religious persecution and rural dispossession, large numbers of whom had arrived as indentured servants, the American yeomanry had ample reason to celebrate life in the New World. Compared to anything they could have expected in Britain or Europe, America was a wide-open place of cheap and bountiful land and lightly enforced government—"the poor man's best country," in one commonly used phrase. But all was not flourishing tranquility. Especially in back-country areas, conflicts between and among yeomen, would-be yeomen, great proprietors, and government officials, as well as combat with Indians, led to continual wrangling and sporadic violence, all of which worsened after the Revolution.

Much of the conflict concerned access to the land, as farmers seeking independent land titles found themselves squeezed out by gentlemen who had exploited their political connections to gain large (sometimes huge), loosely defined land grants. Tensions between debtors and creditors were also endemic. During hard times, indebted farmers fell back on the forgiving ethic of a complex barter system and demanded stay laws and other forms of legal relief, while government officials enacted restrictive fiscal policies and creditors demanded the immediate payment they believed rightfully theirs. Excessive judicial fees, burdensome taxes, and the failure of colonial (and later state) governments to keep order against bandits and Indians posed severe dangers to would-be independent householders.

Yeomen battled back, with a vehemence born of fear, prejudice, and insular hatreds—as well as an admixture of egalitarian ideals. The largest of the yeoman rebellions before the Revolution, the so-called North Carolina Regulation, began in 1764. Led by, among others, a mystical preacher and landowner named Hermon Husband, the uprising turned into full-scale war against autocratic eastern gentry rule that ended only when the rebels were crushed by combined colonial and British forces at the Battle of Alamance (near present-day Burlington) in 1771. Earlier, New Jersey yeomen defied land laws that favored their proprietors, and New York settlers rebelled unsuccessfully to gain rights over land that, as one of them put it, they had worked "for nearly 30 years past and had manured and cultivated." Farmers in the Granville District of North Carolina, and the Rocky Mount District of South Carolina, obstructed surveyors and rioted against land speculators. Also in South Carolina, propertied vigilantes, frustrated at government indifference to backcountry brigandage, took matters into their own hands in 1767 and 1768. In central Pennsylvania, the "Paxton Boys," furious at the lack of military backing from the colonial assembly against Indian raids, massacred some government-protected Indians and undertook a menacing march on Philadelphia. (Government officials led by Benjamin Franklin met with the protesters and quelled the unrest.) After the Revolution "Liberty Men" in central Maine, "Wild Yankees" in northeastern Pennsylvania, and "Green Mountain Boys" in western Vermont all challenged local landlords and the courts. The most notorious of these struggles culminated in the New England Regulation of 1786–87 associated with Daniel Shays.

The yeoman disturbances occurred in tension with peaceable efforts to obtain redress from colonial and state governments. Before the Revolution, the worst-afflicted backcountry areas occasionally sent petitions to their legislators on matters other than local grievances, humbly pointing out (as the self-styled "poor industrious peasants" of Anson County, North Carolina did in 1769) that unlike the great men of the colony, "great numbers of poor people" had to "toil in the cultivation of bad Lands whereon they can hardly subsist." But during the Revolution, when yeoman households furnished the bulk of the manpower and the supplies to fight the patriot cause, ordinary farmers exerted political leverage on the new Revolutionary governments as they had never done under colonial rule. Petition campaigns continued, as did the sending of instructions to representatives, but with broad political themes and in plainer, more assertive language. The upsurge in the newly established Commonwealth of Virginia was typical of what happened in other states: after 1776, yeomen farmers swamped the Virginia Assembly with petitions that called for reforms ranging from the easing of debt payments to (in Baptist districts) disestablishing the official Anglican Church.

Owing to larger numbers of ordinary farmers in the state legislatures, the petitioners could reasonably expect their demands would at least receive a hearing. The shift in representation was most pronounced in the northern states, yet even in the planter-led South, the proportion of ordinary farmers doubled from one-eighth of the total in the 1760s to one-fourth in the 1780s. These country democrats also participated in the constitutional state-building process, determined to ensure that they would not succumb to the permanent domination of eastern plantation and mercantile elites.

Nowhere were they more vocal or persistent on constitutional issues than in Massachusetts. Months before hostilities between redcoats and patriots broke out in Lexington and Concord in April 1775, crowds of western Massachusetts farmers shut down the courts in Berkshire and Hampshire Counties in an angry response to the passage of the British Intolerable Acts in 1774. Later in 1775, the eastern Massachusetts patriot leadership, with the hurried advice of the Continental Congress, adopted a revolutionary state charter that was a revamped version of the old colonial charter, but did so without consent from the people. The westerners duly rebelled again, now against their new leaders, reshutting the courts and keeping them closed until 1778 in Hampshire County and until 1781 in Berkshire County.

The Massachusetts rebels—dubbed the Berkshire Constitutionalists and led by the Reverend Thomas Allen, the eloquent, Harvard-educated pastor of Pittsfield's Congregational church—were especially incensed at the continuation of the appointive judicial system. With its arbitrary licensing practices and fee gouging, the system had ruled for many years, according to one Pittsfield petition, "with a rod of Iron." The new patriot legislature tried to ease the situation by sharply reducing legal fees, but by the time the offer arrived, larger democratic concerns had come into play. Above all (as a second Pittsfield petition declared in May 1776), the backcountrymen now upbraided the doctrine "that the Representatives of the People may form Just what fundamental Constitution they please & impose it upon the people." Here was a significant shift, from demands for judicial reform to a call for drafting a wholly new constitution to submit for approval to the voters. After two years of official stalling in Boston and renewed protests in the western counties, the call was finally heeded—first in 1778, when the town meetings rejected a constitution drafted by the legislature, and then in 1780, when they approved a constitution framed by a special state convention.

The final constitution fell short of what the Berkshire Constitutionalists desired, and it did not end extralegal rural unrest against the courts and creditors. The Berkshire men did, however, help establish the proposition that any new American constitution required popular approval, an idea of democratic sovereignty realized nowhere outside Massachusetts until the ratification of the new Federal Constitution in 1787–88. What is more significant, the country democrats articulated a coherent egalitarian politics, prickly about power imposed from afar, insistent on equal legislative representation for all parts of the state, and opposed to property requirements in politics. The only qualifications required for any officeholder (let alone a voter), one town meeting stated, ought to be personal merit and fidelity to liberty's cause: "Pecuniary Q[u]alifications can never give a good understanding or good Heart."

At the center of these country democratic claims were those concerns about the land and control of the land, cited by Crève-coeur. Before the Revolution, there had been periodic outbreaks of popular apprehension that a designing class of royal officials, lawyers, and monied speculators was out to build up its own power and bring the yeomanry, as one phrase had it, "into lord-ships." Similar fears arose on the eve of the Revolution, as they did whenever country democrats felt insecure in the face of increased political centralization, and the imminent possibility of biased legislation and oppressive fiscal policies. The fears persisted into the

1780s and well beyond. In 1786, a Massachusetts writer charged that "the wealthy men of this state"—adherents of the "aristocratical principle"—hoped to "drive out that hardy and independent spirit from among us, and forge the chains for our liberties so strong, that the greatest exertions and convulsions will not break them." One backcountry Pennsylvanian noted in 1788 that his neighbors remained frightened they might yet be turned into "dependents . . . who will be reduced to a sort of vassalage."

Evangelical religion added a spiritual basis to these fearful egalitarian politics. Out of the postmillennialist stirrings of New England's rural Great Awakening—as well as the ministrations of evangelizing Separate Baptists, Methodists, so-called New Side Presbyterians, and untold numbers of more idiosyncratic preachers elsewhere—came a growing cultural divide between the backcountry and the seaboard, where more staid, rationalist Anglicans (later Episcopalians), Congregationalists, and Unitarians held sway. Converts to the evangelical gospel found themselves in a new, direct, and individual relation with God that sliced across hierarchies of wealth and standing but insisted on humankind's utter dependence on the Lord. By contrast, the gentry and urban mercantile elite were apt to regard the evangelical effusions of the countryside, with their strange gestures and ardent prayer, as ignorant, degraded, and dangerous to civic order. James Madison, while fighting to end the persecution of Baptists in Virginia in the mid-1770s, reported with alarm the stories he heard from his fellow gentry about the "monstrous effects of the enthusiasm prevalent among the Sectaries."

The spiritual divisions between the elite and the yeomanry showed up in various ways. The most direct conflicts involved country evangelical efforts to end the formal establishment of religion. (In Massachusetts, for instance, the town of Ashby in rural Middlesex County denounced draft provisions in the 1780 Constitution requiring public financial support for the Congregational churches, citing the past "Rivers of blood which has run from the Veins of Marters" as a consequence of "the authority of Legeslature over religeous Society.") Religious vernacular, as well as religious leadership, also appeared in country democracy's strictly secular fights, involving evangelicals and nonevangelicals alike. Hermon Husband, the North Carolina Regulation commander, had been born in 1724 on a small farm in Maryland, where, under the spur of the Great Awakening, he had a religious conversion that led him first to the Presbyterians, then to the Quakers, and finally to a mystical, ascetic faith all his own. Husband drenched his secular political declarations in evangelical language both original and borrowed, appealing to "King Jesus" on behalf of oppressed North Carolinians. The Congregationalist Reverend Allen, leader of the Berkshire Constitutionalists, invoked Jesus and the Disciples in his political lectures, and called for a new constitution settled on a broad basis of civil and religious liberty. Religious men reappeared prominently among the distressed yeomanry, from the Baptist minister Valentine Rathbun of Pittsfield (Thomas Allen's lieutenant during the Berkshire agitation), to the Baptist New Yorker Melancton Smith, an upstater who had moved to Manhattan, who spoke in the 1780s as a self-styled "Plebeian" and tribune of New York's "respectable" yeomanry, and who had been named in honor of Philip Melancthon, coworker with Martin Luther and German Protestant peacemaker.

THE CITY DEMOCRACY

If land formed the basic philosophy of the country democracy, then philosophy—a mastery of abstract ideas as well as arcane manual arts—formed, in effect, the "land" of the urban democrats, the basis for its civic claims and social status. The city democracy rank and file consisted chiefly of skilled artisans and mechanics, as well as petty merchants, shopkeepers, and other tradesmen—what Thomas Jefferson distinguished as "[t]he *yeomanry* of the city (not the fashionable people nor paper men)." Their intellectual and political leaders included a mixture of Enlightenment-smitten professionals (most conspicuously physicians, clergymen, teachers, and lawyers) and men from undistinguished backgrounds whose skills as political writers and organizers blossomed during the Revolutionary years and after. Beneath both the rank and file and the leadership, sometimes pushing the city democrats to take more forceful positions, were lesser tradesmen, the lower grades of sailors and mariners, and unskilled day laborers; beneath them were the free laboring poor and then the slaves.

The urban population of late-eighteenth-century America was proportionally miniscule. Yet the major seaports were commercially dynamic and growing fast, at a rate far greater than the nation as a whole, and a few of them were emerging as economic powerhouses. Even before the outbreak of the Revolution, Boston, once North America's premier entry port, had slipped behind New York and Philadelphia (now the colonies' leading port) in terms of ship tonnage cleared. This trend deepened after Independence, as the latter two became the shipping centers for their prosperous and rapidly growing agricultural hinterlands, far more productive than New England's rocky, worked-over farming areas. To the south, Baltimore and Charleston also picked up considerable economic ground.

Artisans and mechanics, although of secondary social standing in the mercantile cities, were essential to growth. They supplied the seaport merchants and their households with everything from ships to shoe buckles. They also created local manufacturing economies to supply nearby regional markets with necessities as well as luxury goods. Artisan firms—in most cases tiny, with perhaps one or two employees and a live-in apprentice—were roughly analogous to the yeomen's rural homesteads: headed by an authoritarian father, the master craftsman, who oversaw the labor of his wife, children (including any apprentices), and journeymen employees. The proportion of slaves and other unfree adult laborers, an important segment of the urban artisan workforce as late as the 1750s, dwindled sharply north of Baltimore after the Seven Years' War, as rising city populations opened up new markets in artisan wage labor. Without replicating the elaborate guild systems of Europe, the American artisans cultivated an extended familial sense of what they called "the Trade," of reciprocal rights and obligations among masters, journeymen, and apprentices in a particular craft that would open the way to economic independence to any individual who mastered the requisite manual and business skills.

Artisan realities did not always match the ideal. At the top of the trades, master craftsmen often found themselves entangled in credit arrangements with their merchant customers that belied their supposed independence. At the bottom, a large number of lesser artisans, including shoemakers and clothing workers, eked out a scant living and, in hard times, fell into destitution. Just as there was stratification among the trades, there were early signs of divisions within trades between masters and journeymen employees, exacerbated by the growth of readily available pools of cheap wage labor. A handful of craft strikes and other job actions broke out in other seaports over the next quarter century, presaging greater labor conflicts to come.

The main source of plebeian discord in the eighteenth-century cities, however, was not between or within trades, but between artisans of all ranks and the merchant elite. For several decades before the Revolution, propertied enfranchised artisans played significant and at times crucial roles in deciding urban elections. Stifling their deep prejudices about laboring men as "the rabble," competing factions of merchants reached out for their support, and thereby invented many of the tools and techniques that would later become essential to democracy's expansion: the naming of political "tickets"; organizing political caucuses, through taverns and volunteer fire companies; substituting public nomination meetings for private nominations; using a growing seaport newspaper press for (increasingly vitriolic) political appeals; political pamphleteering and the rise of a new subclass of pamphleteers. All these innovations contributed to a curious transformation of urban politics well before the Revolution, popularizing existing techniques of electioneering, but still under the firm control of the mercantile elite.

A more fundamental transformation began during the Stamp Act crisis, and developed with a growing intensity from 1774 to 1776, when the artisans started nominating and electing their own men to office. Invigorated by their involvement in extralegal committees and demonstrations, and dismayed by the hesitation of some merchants and the opposition of others, anti-British artisans and tradesmen developed a sense of themselves as a distinct political interest. "If we have not the Liberty of nominating such Persons whom we approve," a Philadelphian who called himself "A Brother Chip" advised his "Brethren the Tradesmen, Mechanics. &c." in 1770, "our Freedom of voting is at an End." In other seaports, large and small, artisans and their allies made their presence felt either in the patriot movement or in electoral politics or both, despite what one Philadelphia merchant called the "Many Threats, Reflections, Sarcasms, and Burlesques" aimed against them.

The artisans' political fortunes varied from place to place. Ironically, in Boston, where laboring people defied British authority in the streets as nowhere else in America, mechanics made the least impact as a distinct interest, in part because the British military occupation from 1768 to 1776 muted social divisions among the patriots even after the redcoats departed. In New York City, by contrast, artisans won a substantial number of local offices and controlled the extralegal committees, although they were unable, until the very eve of the Revolution, to wrest political control from the merchants and lawyers. The New York Mechanics' Committee, which in 1774 superseded the local Sons of Liberty as the head of the local resistance movement, ceased to be the predominant voice in city affairs only when the British occupied Manhattan in 1776. (The occupation may have been a major reason why New Yorkers failed to produce a state constitution anywhere near as democratic as Pennsylvania's.) Similar artisan groups spearheaded radical activity in Baltimore and Charleston (before the British occupied the latter in 1780).

The city democracy truly flourished in Philadelphia, where radical artisans joined forces with the lowest classes of mechanics and unskilled laborers. The year 1770 was the turning point. Craftsmen, infuriated by the attempts of some local merchants to evade the patriots' nonimportation agreements against British goods, formed the first mechanics' committees. In that year's assembly elections, a radical local anti-British slate (including a tailor, one Joseph Parker) triumphed at the polls. Two years later, the Mechanics' Committee demanded publication of assembly debates and the opening of public galleries in the legislatures, as well as a variety of economic reforms, including abolition of the provincial excise taxes on liquor. Then, between 1773 and 1776, radical artisans steadily replaced moderates on the city's Committee of Inspection and Observation, which oversaw local resistance efforts. By the time Congress signed the Declaration of Independence in the Pennsylvania State House (since renamed Independence Hall), artisans occupied almost half the committee's seats.

Confronted by a Quaker-controlled state assembly that refused to vote for independence from Britain, the Inspection and Observation Committee held its own open-air town meeting in May 1776, with more than four thousand persons in attendance. The committee called for the convening of a patriot Provincial Conference to draft a new state constitution—"the Coup de Grace to the King's authority in this province," wrote one young militia captain. And at this point, the mechanics' constituency became closely allied with another important political stratum: radical democratic professionals and writers, many of modest wealth and little previous political influence. This group included Timothy Matlack, a debt-ridden hardware retailer, schismatic Quaker, champion cockfighter, militia battalion commander, and excellent penman (who probably handwrote the officially engrossed version of the Declaration of Independence signed by Congress); the deist Thomas Young, a self-educated physician to the poor and (said John Adams) "eternal fisher in troubled waters"; Benjamin Rush, the College of New Jersey (now Princeton) graduate and evangelical Presbyterian, who likewise served Philadelphia's poor (and, as a delegate to the Second

Continental Congress, signed the Declaration of Independence); and James Cannon, a Scots-trained professor of mathematics at the College of Philadelphia. Above all, they included the most gifted democratic writer in the English-speaking world, Thomas Paine.

Although he had emigrated from England only two years earlier, Paine (a former corset maker, sailor, shopkeeper, and excise official) had already won renown as the most uncompromising and effective advocate for American independence, on the basis of his immensely popular pamphlet, Common Sense, published in January 1776. With his limpid logic and acidulous sarcasm (calling William the Conqueror "[a] French bastard landing with an armed banditti"), Paine took the polemical style of earlier political pamphleteers, stripped it of its pretense, and rendered it accessible to those readers and unlettered listeners who gathered in the plebeian taverns and debating clubs that he himself habituated. In the span of a single sly statement—"Male and female are the distinctions of nature, good and bad the distinctions of heaven, but how a race of men came into the world so exalted above the rest, and distinguished like some new species, is worth inquiring into"—Paine could kindle ordinary Americans' accumulated sense of personal insult at monarchical society into revulsion and revolution. His democratic ideas were no less disturbing to many leading patriots than they were to Loyalists. Believing in the basic harmony of reasonable individuals—and thus society if left to its own devices—Paine considered aristocratic government, established by a parasitic caste of the pedigreed and privileged, as the chief author of human misery.

> Society is produced by our wants, and government by our wickedness; the former promotes our happiness positively by uniting our affections, the latter negatively by restraining our vices. The one encourages intercourse, the other creates distinctions. . . . Society is in every state a blessing, but government, even in its best state, is but a necessary evil.

For Paine, government was rife with opportunities for the privileged few to oppress the many. Accordingly, Common Sense offered some egalitarian fundamentals for benign republican rule: unicameral state legislatures elected by a broad franchise; a national legislature; frequent elections; and a written constitution securing individual rights, including rights to property and religious freedom. In Massachusetts, a scandalized John Adams replied to what he would later call Paine's "yellow fever" by writing a brief defense of mixed government, Thoughts on Government. A Philadelphia patriot worried that Paine's proposals would stir "the multitude in a perpetual ferment like the ocean in a storm." But in mid-1776, Paine and his radical friends held the initiative in Pennsylvania.

The radicals' position in that critical year was bolstered, and further radicalized, by the presence of the thirty-one companies of the Philadelphia militia, headed by their Committee of Privates. Led by mechanics and tradesmen of modest means, the committee provided its rank and file, known as "Associators," with something of a political education, not unlike what the English agitators in Oliver Cromwell's New Model Army had attempted in the 1640s and 1650s. (The militiamen did not hesitate to speak up, through the committee, on matters ranging from unrestricted manhood suffrage to "equal consultation" about the design of uniforms.) Several radical leaders had close ties to the militia: James Cannon was secretary of the Committee of Privates, while Thomas Young and Timothy Matlack were militia officers. This gave the Associators a direct connection to the constitution-making process. And in a memorial to the Continental Congress, issued nine days before the open-air meeting on the obdurate assembly, the committee members vented their antagonism to the British and the patriot elite as well, declaring their "sense of being oppressed by the very men whose liberties and estates they are called out to defend."

With assembly conservatives in disgrace, the moderate assembly majority leaderless, and the Continental Congress on record calling for new state governments where none "sufficient to the exigencies of their affairs" existed, the Philadelphia radicals stepped into the breach. (Paine served as their adviser.) Closely controlling the nominations and elections to both the proposed Provincial Conference and its constitutional convention, they packed the groups with sympathetic delegates, including a disproportional number of country democrats from the discontented western parts of Pennsylvania. The drafters met, with Benjamin Franklin as their president, and the final product was that remarkable new state constitution. Some of the provisions, such as the unicameral legislature, extended institutions already in place; others, including the broadened suffrage and the more equal representation plan, were brand new. An even more radical provision, outlawing "an enormous proportion of property invested in a few individuals," narrowly failed to win approval. The greatest controversy occurred in the Provincial Conference, where the rural democrats, aided by the more pious of their Philadelphia counterparts, won a requirement that all delegates to the constitutional convention affirm the divinity of Jesus Christ and the divine inspiration of the Bible—a measure hotly contested by delegates James Cannon and Thomas Young, who called it "bigoted."

Time would prove unkind to the Pennsylvania Constitution of 1776, and to the coalition that created it. It attracted criticism as soon as it was approved, even from radicals like Benjamin Rush. (Among the constitution's numerous defects, Rush argued, was the unicameral legislature, which he thought would be more vulnerable to corruption from above than a two-tiered body, where democrats could concentrate their power in the lower house.) Alarmed moderate and conservative notables from around the state, seeing democracy boiling over, quickly regrouped as the Republican faction, and they capitalized on some overbearing miscalculations by the radicals. Unlike the Berkshire democrats of Massachusetts, the Pennsylvania radicals failed to seek approval of the new constitution through a popular referendum, fearing that, though they had united the country and the city, they were more advanced in their democratic views than the people at large. The decision ensured their constitution went into effect, but at the cost of alienating a considerable portion of the moderate citizenry. The new legislature also enacted a series of test laws between 1777 and 1779 that demanded oaths of allegiance to the revolutionary government, and were deeply offensive to Quakers. By 1789, the anticonstitution forces built a base of public support that included some of the better-off mechanic elements. Finally, in September 1790, the Republicans won ratification of a new state constitution that eradicated most of the democratic provisions of its predecessor (although not the liberal suffrage), installed a bicameral legislature, and created a governorship with sweeping appointive powers.

The story was nearly the reverse in New York. Subject to British occupation after 1776, New York's artisan democrats never seized power as the Philadelphians did, but they forcefully resumed their political activities as soon as the British evacuated in 1783. Late in that year, they elected a radical Whig ticket to the state assembly by a 4 to 1 margin. Thereafter, they organized the Committee of Mechanics, which pressed for the exclusion of ex-Tories from politics, formed an umbrella group for master craftsmen called the General Society of Mechanics and Tradesmen, nominated and elected several craftsmen to the state assembly, and agitated for democratic reforms, including popular election of the mayor. In 1786, numerous mechanics joined with professionals and merchants as members of the fraternal Society of Saint Tammany or Columbian Order, led by their "Grand Sachem," an upholsterer named William Mooney. The businessman and philanthropist John Pintard, a Tammany officer, described the society as "a political institution . . . whose democratic principles will serve in some measure to correct the aristocracy of our city."

In their successes as well as failures, the city democrats' experiences of the Revolution pointed out some of their connections and differences with country democrats. Both groups vaunted themselves as productive, independent citizens—"honest Laborious husbandmen and machanicks," in the words of a New Hampshire petition in 1783. Both groups were wary of political operations dominated by, in their eyes, well-connected but nonproducing gentry and merchants, on the principle (as one Connecticut shoemaker put it) that "Might generally overcomes Right." Both groups saw government's chief proper function as the promotion of equal access to opportunity and personal independence.

But there were differences that played out at many levels. Country democrats, especially in places where they were underrepresented in state legislatures, were more isolated than their urban counterparts from the operations of government and from the dynamics of economic power—so much so that even after the Revolution, the basic legitimacy of the state and (after 1789) federal governments would be less assured in some troubled rural areas than it was in the cities. Like the North Carolina Regulators in the 1760s or the participants in the New England Regulation twenty years later, country men, in their insularity and frustration, were quicker to turn violent when they found more regular channels blocked or unresponsive. Until the late 1790s, they would show far less reluctance than city democrats to oppose and violate federal laws, sometimes aggressively. Moreover, city democrats, still for the most part seaport dwellers, were men of commerce—"American Commerce; unfettered by the influence of tyrants," ran one later celebratory toast—interested in getting their fair share of oceanic and coastal trade and gaining access to their own banking facilities, as well as encouraging internal commercial routes. Government aid to such projects did not disturb them, so long as the projects were for the general welfare and did not favor monied insiders. Many country democrats, by contrast, were distant from extensive commercial contacts and tended to distrust public projects as inherently biased. There were, to be sure, some country democrats who wanted to develop closer links to eastern markets and (especially in boom times) acquire as much bank credit as they could. But any downturn in the business cycle could easily stoke their hostility against the instruments of economic improvement and the well-connected men who ran them.

The two democracies also differed in cultural tone. Religion, including evangelical religion, played an important role in the lives of many city democrats; indeed, by the end of the eighteenth century, the seaport cities were the largest centers of Methodist and Baptist worship in the country. Paine's Common Sense, although the product of a quintessentially skeptical urban intelligence, was thick with biblical allusions and millennial language, instantly recognizable to its city and country readers alike. Some of the leading Philadelphia city democrats, including Benjamin Rush and Christopher Marshall, were devout believers. Yet the cities also displayed great spiritual variety, ranging from the more rationalist forms of Protestant worship such as Universalism to non-Christian freethinking deist sects, and also including Jews, Roman Catholics, and nonbelievers, the last group the largest of all. Ethnically and linguistically as well, the cities were more diverse than the rural settlements, which forced city democrats to pay close attention to integrating different constituencies, and also attracted fresh waves of ambitious and talented political émigrés from overseas, especially from England and Ireland. Although rural settlements, especially in the North, were coming increasingly within the orbit of Enlightenment culture and high political debate (through the diffusion of newspapers, almanacs, magazines, and, via early town lending libraries, books), the country democracy had nothing to compare with the philosophical societies, colleges, and debating clubs, high and low, of its urban counterpart. If the unpolished country democrats harbored prejudices against what one of them called, suspiciously, "men of learning," the city democracy's faith in reason bred a certain naive and, in retrospect, self-defeating intellectual arrogance, evident in the Philadelphia radicals' political overreaching. That overreaching, and the arguments over Christian religious tests in the Pennsylvania Provincial Congress in 1776, also showed that religion could divide democratic partisans.

The alliance of country and city that forged the Pennsylvania Constitution of 1776 proved these tensions could at least temporarily be contained. But the eventual breakdown of that alliance, and the more common distancing between country movements and city ones in other states, showed how difficult that containment could be. Those difficulties and divisions would recur in the years immediately after independence, when political turmoil led to the creation of a new national government.

THE REVOLUTION AND "PROPER *DEMOCRACY*"

How successful, overall, was the democratic impulse that arose during the Revolution? Narrowly defined, the results, as inscribed in the state constitutions, can appear modest. As of 1790, fewer than half of the original thirteen states provided an approximation to white manhood suffrage by replacing freehold qualifications with minimal taxpaying requirements. (Massachusetts actually stiffened property requirements in its 1780 constitution.) None, except Pennsylvania, broke completely with the ancient ideal of mixed and balanced government whereby distinct branches of the state were supposed to correspond to ranks in society. To the extent they did shift, at least in theory, it was often toward sharpening the distinction between persons and property, linking the upper houses of the new legislatures to the representation of propertied interests—on the presumption, stated most starkly in Massachusetts, that "men possessed of property are entitled to a greater share in political authority than those who are destitute of it." Revolutionary state-builders hedged in the democratic element by establishing bicameral legislatures (except in Pennsylvania and Georgia); by approving property requirements, sometimes quite severe, for officeholding; by retaining powerful appointive state and local offices not elected by the people; and by continuing malapportionment of the legislatures to favor the wealthier and more settled districts.

The very fact, though, that the patriots won American independence deprived an entrenched monarchical interest of wealth and power. Although not confined to royal officials or rich and well-born colonists, the Loyalists, who would now be replaced by rebels, included some of the country's most powerful families. The reversal was particularly wrenching in New York, where the Revolution devastated the colonial ruling class of Loyalist mercantile and seigneurial families centered in Manhattan and the Hudson Valley, and where power shifted to relative newcomers, led by Governor George Clinton, who drew their power from upstate middling farmers. Similar sharp transitions occurred in New Jersey and North Carolina, but every new state felt the shift to a greater or lesser degree. Exclusion from the franchise, by provincial congresses and state legislatures, of identified resident Tories and all who refused to swear oaths of allegiance to American independence further tied political loyalties to political rights.

Democratic interests and ideas also made considerable headway within the patriot movement, quite apart from the singular developments in Pennsylvania. In Maryland, armed uprisings by militiamen precipitated a significant reduction in property requirements for voting and won an expansive Declaration of Rights as part of the new state's constitution (one of seven such declarations adopted around the country). New York, New Jersey, New Hampshire, North Carolina, and South Carolina also significantly liberalized their suffrage laws. (Massachusetts and Maryland, as well as New York, nearly adopted a minimal taxpaying requirement.) Religious tests that excluded all but Protestants from the franchise, common throughout the colonies, were dropped everywhere except in South Carolina. In North Carolina, Georgia, and (in some counties) New Jersey, as well as Pennsylvania, voting by written ballots became the norm, and the New York convention proposed trying the system since some had claimed it "would tend more to preserve the liberty and equal freedom of the people."

Other important changes accompanied suffrage reforms. Outside the Chesapeake region, lawmakers undertook serious efforts to reduce malapportionment in their legislatures. North Carolina's constitution provided equal representation for every county in both houses of the legislature; New York, New Jersey, and South Carolina stipulated periodic changes in representation to help ensure continued equity and proportionality. Constituents became bolder in instructing and petitioning their representatives, a right explicitly endorsed by four of the seven state declarations of rights. Although many important state offices stayed appointive, the new constitutions took the power of appointment out of the hands of the governors and gave it to the legislatures, or to some combination of the executive and legislative branches—a mark of the Revolution's bedrock antimonarchialism.

Officeholding democratized markedly. "[S]ince the war," one disgusted Massachusetts conservative remarked in 1786, "blustering ignorant men, who started into notice during the troubles and confusion of that critical period, have been attempting to push themselves into office." In the lower legislative houses, a much-expanded number of representatives in the mid-1780s included far greater proportions of ordinary farmers, artisans, and other men of middling wealth and station than had sat in the colonial assemblies—even in the states that retained property-holding requirements for lawmakers. In the upper houses in most states, places were found for ambitious men of unassuming background and modest attainments, such as the upwardly mobile Scots immigrant farmer Alexander Webster of New York's rural Washington County, or John Birdsong of Chatham, North Carolina—a man so obscure that his name does not survive on any tax list or census recording. Everywhere, electioneering and undisguised competition for legislative office intensified. Thanks to state constitutional provisions for annual legislative elections, secured in every state except South Carolina, the glacier-like pace of office turnover prevalent in the provincial assemblies became a break-neck scramble, with half or more of the representatives in any given legislature changing in any given year.

The Revolution's democratic impact was not confined to voting qualifications, representation arrangements, and election results. Nothing like the articulate democratic outburst that gripped America in 1776 had occurred anywhere in the world since the days of the Levellers and Diggers. Speaking with special warmth for "the poorer sort, who are perhaps nine tenths of the useful part of mankind," democratic partisans demanded any and every sort of political innovation in order to secure what one called "Proper *Democracy* . . . where the people have all the power in themselves." There were calls to abolish the posts of governor and lieutenant governor, along with the legislative upper houses (where, a Pennsylvanian declared, "a small number of grandees . . . thirst for power at the expense of the people"), and there were calls for rotation in office, simplified legal codes, and popular ratification of specific laws, as well as for annual elections and a widened suffrage. The din was so loud, conventional republicans observed, that the patriot leadership found itself fighting on two fronts, against *"popular licentiousness, anarchy, and confusion"* as well as against the British monarchy.

The explosion forever changed the context of American politics and culture. Revolutionary committees of correspondence, Sons of Liberty, mechanics' electoral tickets, county conventions, as well as the patriot militia and Continental Army—all had had the effect of announcing the end of the old deference and sporadic mob violence of the "people out-of-doors" and the beginning of a new abiding presence of ordinary Americans in public and political life. No matter how troublesome it might be, that presence had to be recognized and taken into account, as the shrewder patriot leaders understood. Failing to do so (Jefferson's friend Edmund Pendleton acknowledged) was "disagreeable to the temper of the times." With politics thrust to the forefront of Americans' minds, the Revolution's democratic strivings fundamentally altered how they perceived themselves and each other.

Consider the formal portraiture of the age. Shortly before the Revolution, John Singleton Copley, the most accomplished painter in New England, and a Loyalist, could depart from his upper-class patrons and execute a plain but respectful portrait of a highly successful Boston silversmith and devoted patriot. Paul

Revere looks out with a pensive expression, his shirt neck open, the tools of his trade by his side—a portrait of the artisan as a thoughtful man of substance. A bit later, in the work of a younger, less expert artist, the patriot Charles Willson Peale (a volunteer in George Washington's army, veteran of Valley Forge, and officer in the radical Philadelphia militia), the democratic sensibility deepened greatly. In his famous depiction of the Battle of Princeton, Peale presented a victorious but less-than-godlike, bottom-heavy General Washington, one waistcoat button missing, standing against a backdrop that in one version pointedly included a marching line of ordinary American soldiers and their redcoat prisoners.

After independence, Peale also painted one of the chief Philadelphia radicals, Timothy Matlack, who went on to become Pennsylvania's secretary of state and keeper of its great seal. The picture shows Matlack in his full political glory, a self-made new man of power dressed in flashy buff-blue trousers with matching waistcoat, surrounded by statute books and revolutionary charters. More than a decade later, the factional struggles in Pennsylvania had cost Matlack his secretaryship, but he had won a patronage job as the state's master of the rolls, and Peale's son Rembrandt painted him again, a reflective public servant and patriot who lived by his pen. Ordinary people not only were present; they had begun, as the conservative Gouverneur Morris said about the New York mob, "to think and reason"—and to help run political affairs. What painters expressed on canvas, gentry political leaders understood as a public sensibility that could not be ignored.

Even amid the acute internal crises that followed independence, the new revolutionary governments managed to heed and incorporate popular discontent, although in rough and incomplete ways. The sharpest conflicts surrounded the so-called New England Regulation, a string of rural uprisings best known for the Massachusetts rebellion led by an ex-army captain from Berkshire County, Daniel Shays, in 1786. Following the adoption of the new state constitution, the Massachusetts legislature, in order to repay its Revolutionary War debt, adopted stringent financial policies, which prompted distressed country towns to hold popular conventions demanding debtor relief. When these demands fell on deaf ears, Shays and his compatriots in other parts of the state took up arms and disrupted local courts, only to be crushed by a privately funded militia organized by Governor James Bowdoin.

The Shays affair dramatized not only the rawness and limitations of American democracy in the aftermath of independence, but also its possibilities. Under sharp duress, and unable to organize a timely, effective, and legitimate political opposition, the Shaysites loaded their muskets, scaring gentlemen of property and standing all across the new republic. Yet the affair did not end with the dispersal and indictments of Shays's bedraggled recruits. Sympathetic with the rebels' plight (if not their tactics), and horrified by the ham-handed repression, Massachusetts voters turned out in extraordinary numbers in the statewide elections the following spring, removed Bowdoin and his most adamant allies from office, and elected a government that reached an accommodation with the rebels (including a pardon of Captain Shays). In all, one democratic Massachusetts farmer recalled years later, "everything appeared like the clear and pleasant sunshine after a most tremendous storm . . . a striking demonstration of the advantages of a free elective government."

DEMOCRACY AND THE FEDERAL CONSTITUTION

Not every American greeted the outcome in Massachusetts, or the turbulent politics elsewhere during the 1780s, with such sanguinity—and these more pessimistic reactions helped lead directly to the Philadelphia Constitutional Convention in 1787. In addition to the Shays scare, political developments at the state level shocked patriot leaders who had hoped the Revolution would bring calm and enlightened government. With the democratization of the state legislatures, licentiousness seemed to be running rampant. Narrow-minded men, suspicious of government power and fiercely protective of their local interests—lacking what James Madison called "liberality or light"—started pressing for punitive legislation against former Loyalists, as well as for stay laws and other forms of debtor relief that would soon destroy the new governments' finances. Worse, the national government, under the loosely knit Articles of Confederation, was so feeble that it had become nearly impossible to conduct a foreign policy, secure the nation's defense, and complete commercial treaties, let alone settle the leftover debts from the Revolution.

When, in 1787, with the Shays Rebellion fresh in their minds, fifty-five delegates assembled in Philadelphia to discard the Articles summarily in favor of a new federal plan, fears of a tyrannical *demos* were pervasive. Above all else, the delegates wished to create a new, more perfect union that would promote an enlightened class of rulers who would think continentally instead of in straitened, self-interested terms. Delegates spoke openly of the need to restrain what one Virginian called "the turbulence and follies of democracy," and what a New York delegate had called "popular phrenzy." Yet the majority of the convention, as of the country, also believed that sovereignty belonged, ultimately, to the citizenry. Once the delegates convened in secret session, the temper of the times seeped into the room.

The delegates' antidemocratic assumptions were voiced most cogently three weeks into their deliberations, when the brilliant young nationalist from New York, Alexander Hamilton, broke his silence and proposed some guiding principles. "All communities," he said, "divide themselves into the few and the many. The first are the rich and well-born, the other the mass of the people." Because the latter, Hamilton claimed, were "turbulent and changing" and "seldom judge or determine right," it was vital to give the former—the rich—"a distinct permanent share in the government." Hamilton then proposed creating a federal political hierarchy that would come as close as possible to the British state, with an executive elected for life and an upper legislative chamber elected to serve on good behavior.

A few of the delegates, including Gouverneur Morris, thought Hamilton's speech the most profound and best argued of the entire convention. Yet after listening respectfully to his advice, the delegates basically ignored it. Instead, the Framers' final document reflected James Madison's idea that the creation of an extended republic with large electoral districts would favor the selection of "men who possess the most attractive merit," while inhibiting the formation of an "unjust and interested majority" out to subvert the rights of others, especially property rights. Instead of aligning the government directly with the rich and wellborn, the convention favored strong institutional filters on the powers of the ordinary citizenry. The executive would not be elected directly by the voters but in the Electoral College, by electors chosen by the states. Neither would the Senate, the powerful upper house of the national Congress, be elected directly, unless the states so dictated, which none of them would. A national judiciary, headed by the Supreme Court, would be appointed by the indirectly chosen executive with the advice and consent of the indirectly selected Senate. The only national office for which the Constitution stipulated popular elections was for members of the House of Representatives, to be chosen by the same electorate that voted for "the most numerous branch" in each of the state legislatures.

Power would indeed shift to the advantage of the enlightened few over the impassioned many. But still, there were concessions: it would do so without establishing a formally class-based government, abrogating popular sovereignty, or forsaking the Revolutionary contributions of ordinary Americans. "A dependence on the people is, no doubt, the primary control on the government," Madison would write in defending the Constitution in *Federalist*. The design for the Senate, a hotly contested issue, was an excellent case in point. As the writer who called himself "A Democratic Federalist" conceded, the proposal for the Senate had an appearance of aristocracy that was alarming. But in fact, the new body was formally just as representative and democratic as the House "without one distinction in favor of the birth, rank, wealth or power of the senators or their fathers." Depending on what the states decided, there were no fixed property qualifications for electing a senator, and none at all for serving as one. Senators were not supposed to represent a social class, estate, or interest; rather, they represented their respective states, gave small states a check on the larger states' advantages in the House, and provided an important mediating force between encroachments by the Executive and "the precipitation and inadvertence of the people"—all without encroaching on "the real principles of liberty." So it went throughout the new federal plan. If designed to restrain and guide democracy, the Constitution hardly repudiated it, no matter how much some of the Framers might have wanted to do so. Instead, the delegates constructed a stable and energetic but properly classless national government.

Occasionally, one delegate or another sounded a more Hamiltonian note. A particularly tense exchange occurred in response to the proposed linkage of the suffrage eligibility for the House of Representatives to those for elections to the state assemblies. Gouverneur Morris, proclaiming himself unafraid of being labeled an aristocrat, charged that this franchise would be much too broad, and called instead for a freehold property qualification to vote for all federal officers. Give the votes to people with little or no property, Morris said, restating the traditional conservative wisdom, "and they will sell them to the rich who will be able to buy them." James Madison basically agreed, noting that, although Morris's plan might be imprudent, "the freeholders of the country would be the safest depositories of republican liberty."

The most eloquent rebuttal came from Benjamin Franklin—now eighty-one and so weakened in body, though not in mind, that he sometimes had to be carried to the convention's meetings in a sedan chair. "It is of great consequence that we should not depress the virtue and public spirit of our common people," Franklin began, noting how much of both qualities the people had displayed during the Revolutionary War. That spirit, he contended, was a direct result of "the different manner in which the common people were treated in America and Great Britain." To insist on a freehold suffrage requirement would risk opening the door to further restrictions in the future. At all events, Franklin insisted, the elected had no right to narrow the privileges of the electors. Morris's proposal was overwhelmingly defeated. To advance further the popular legitimacy of their work, the delegates then decided to submit the Constitution for approval not to the state legislatures (whose interests might conflict with those of the proposed national government) but to specially elected state ratifying conventions.

A more divisive conflict at the Philadelphia convention, carefully submerged in the final document, concerned slavery. At the Revolution's commencement, slavery existed in all thirteen of the colonies, but a combination of moral revulsion and economic marginality had led to its decline in the North. By 1787, Massachusetts, Pennsylvania, Connecticut, and Rhode Island had undertaken formal emancipation, and the institution was crumbling in New Hampshire. Delegates to the Philadelphia convention included some of the most stalwart antislavery men in the country (among them Franklin, a slaveholder himself until 1781), who had treated southern demands on slavery-related issues with an ironic contempt. Yet delegates from the southern states, above all South Carolina and Georgia, made it clear that they would not approve of the more perfect union unless it gave some positive protections to slavery.

The result was a series of compromises that, during coming decades, would loom large. The final draft avoided mentioning slavery explicitly. (It would, James Madison said, be "wrong to admit in the Constitution the idea that there could be property in men.") But the delegates effectively barred the federal government from taking any action against slavery in the states, counted slaves as three-fifths of full citizens for the purposes of representation in the House of Representatives and the Electoral College (as well as for direct taxation), and included a provision guaranteeing slaveholders return of their runaway slaves. In a bitterly debated measure, they also barred congressional interference with the transatlantic slave trade for twenty years. Some in the lower South thought the concessions too wispy, but voices of compromise prevailed. "In short," Charles Cotesworth Pinckney told the South Carolina convention called to debate the Constitution's ratification, "considering all circumstances, we have made the best terms for the security of this species of property it was in our power to make. We would have made them better if we could; but, on the whole, I do not think them bad."

There was little room to accommodate Americans who, in the various state ratification conventions, denounced what they regarded as the Constitution's deeply antidemocratic features. Some of the milder critics, including Thomas Jefferson (who was away in Paris as the American minister to France), fixated on the original document's lack of a declaration or bill of rights—a complaint overcome when, at the most sharply divided ratification conventions, Madison and others gave informal assurances that the Constitution would be amended to provide such protections. (Although dubious about the worth of such "parchment barriers" to tyranny, Madison single-handedly codified and then pushed hard for rapid approval of the first ten amendments, the Bill of Rights, which the states would finally ratify at the end of 1791.) Other, sterner critics ripped into what they considered the Constitution's aristocratic, centralizing bias. "[I]t appears that the government will fall into the hands of the few and the great," declared Melancton Smith in New York. "This will be a government of oppression." More colorfully, the Massachusetts war veteran and farmer Amos Singletary charged that under the new Constitution, "they will swallow up all us little folks, like the great *Leviathan* . . . just as the whale swallowed up *Jonah*."

Slavery was also an issue at the state conventions. While southerners railed against the Constitution's provision permitting Congress to halt the international slave trade after 1808, some northerners objected to the clause counting three-fifths of the slave population as a basis for federal representation—a measure (Melancton Smith again) that would "give certain privileges to those people who were so wicked as to keep slaves." These criticisms failed to halt the ratification of the new federal plan by state conventions that, by design of the state legislatures, were elected with a purposely broad set of franchise qualifications—the broadest in the history of the infant republic. Objections to the rule of a supposedly enlightened, disinterested elite would continue, though, to inform democratic undertakings for decades to come.

The most immediate consequences of the debates over the Constitution for democratic politics were the divisions they caused between country and city democrats. Pro-Constitutionalists and Anti-Federalists alike recognized that opposition to the new federal plan would be greatest in rural areas distant from seaboard towns and cities. "I dread the cold and sour temper of the back counties," the conservative Framer Gouverneur Morris told George Washington. Rural anti-Federalism was, however, a complicated phenomenon. Prominent gentry critics such as the Virginia slaveholders George Mason and Richard Henry Lee objected mainly to what they considered the Constitution's overcentralized structure and to the lack of a written bill of rights. Drawn from the same ranks of cultivated, cosmopolitan notables as the delegates to the Philadelphia convention—Mason had been a delegate, one of three who stayed to the end but refused to sign the final document—these gentry Anti-Federalists asserted that the nation's leaders should be drawn from a gentlemanly elite, and they shared the disquiet about democracy that drove some of the Framers. But in line with thinking dating back to British Whig oppositionist writings of the 1720s, they also worried that no group of men could be trusted with too much power. In Mason's words, the new federal design would "commence in a moderate Aristocracy" and probably wind up as either a monarchy or an "oppressive Aristocracy."

A much harsher anti-aristocratic animus emanated from the yeomanry. Unconvinced that any group of uniquely virtuous natural leaders existed, these men beheld the Federalists' claims to disinterested patriotism as camouflage for their pursuit of wealth and domination. The "lawyers, and men of learning, and moneyed men, that talk so finely, and gloss over matters so smoothly," the farmer Singletary charged, would "get into Congress themselves" and place "all the power and all the money into their own hands." Writing under the pseudonym "Aristocrotis," the backcountry Pennsylvanian William Petrekin mocked the wellborn and "the full blooded gentry" who believed they monopolized the "necessary qualifications of authority; such as the dictatorial air, the magisterial voice, the imperious tone, the haughty countenance" that were necessary to run the government "upon true despotic principles."

These country democrats were not simply challenging natural aristocracy's claims to disinterestedness; they were asserting their own interests. By virtue of their numbers and their control of productive land, they argued, they themselves ought to dominate government. Rejecting completely the theory of virtual representation, they insisted that representatives ought to be direct agents of their constituents, and resemble them closely. And there was a moral dimension to the backcountry argument, which cast the yeomanry, neither rich men nor poor men, as the best rulers. Melancton Smith told the New York ratifying convention that "those in middling circumstances . . . are inclined by habit, and the company with whom they associate, to set bounds to their passions and appetites . . . hence the substantial yeomanry of the country are more temperate, of better morals, and less ambition, than the great," who resembled "a hereditary aristocracy." Smith concluded that "a representative body, composed principally of the respectable yeomanry is the best possible security to liberty." Backcountry evangelical preachers and laymen, hundreds of whom served as delegates to the state ratifying conventions, also objected to the Constitution's centralizing thrust, much as they did efforts to centralize ecclesiastical authority, as a threat to "the glorious liberty of the children of God." Some, especially Methodists, also complained about the Constitution's accommodations to slavery.

By contrast, the artisans and mechanics in all the seaboard

cities enthusiastically supported the new Constitution. With their livelihoods tied to foreign trade, local artisan suppliers as well as mechanics faced competition at the war's end from British imports. They saw the new federal plan, with its promise of a coherent national commercial policy, including a tariff, as a blow for American economic nationalism and a direct benefit to themselves. At the height of the ratification debates, masters and journeymen in all of the major ports mounted their largest public demonstrations since the end of the Revolution, marching craft by craft and holding aloft emblems of their trades and patriotic pro-federal banners. There were, to be sure, some urban naysayers, such as Philadelphia's "Montezuma," who, much like the backcountry democrats, denounced the Constitution's friends as "the Aristocratic Party of the United States," out to create a new *monarchical, aristocratical democracy.*" But dissenters were in the minority among the city democrats in 1787–88. The alliance between the city democracy and the mercantile elite played a crucial part in securing adoption of the new federal Constitution.

The differences between the country and city democrats would persist long after the Constitution debates, causing difficulties for Americans with egalitarian beliefs and loyalties at every level of political society. Yet the differences sometimes diminished. Rural estrangement from the new federal plan, and the state political elites that backed it, remained strong, and occasionally turned violent, after 1788. Shortly after Pennsylvania's state convention ratified the Constitution, anti-Federalist yeomen rioted in Carlisle, in scenes that reminded some fearful Federalists of the Shaysite uprisings. In rural districts throughout the state, resistance to farm foreclosures and tax collection dating back over years turned increasingly desperate and ferocious. In western Virginia and North Carolina, secession movements arose, uneasily uniting planters, backwoodsmen, and land speculators, to win independence from, respectively, their states' Tidewater and central-valley political elites. (Their efforts would achieve admission to the Union for Kentucky in 1792 and for Tennessee four years later.)

Policies initiated by the new federal government after 1789, under President George Washington, further inflamed the situation, prompting showdowns that involved, among thousands of others, the aging North Carolina mystic and former Regulator Hermon Husband. But by then, objections to Washington administration policies had inflamed city democrats as well. In the early 1790s, as prosperity stalled and tariff protection wore thin, urban democrats complained that import merchants seemed to prize their commercial connections to Britain above republican solidarity, and that haughty, well-connected financial interests were manipulating the government to enrich themselves at the expense of the common citizenry. Although respect for the Constitution did not decline, the seaport alliance of merchants and mechanics that had backed the Constitution's ratification disintegrated. The elements emerged for a re-creation of the kind of democratic insurgency combining city and countryside that had once succeeded in Pennsylvania, but now on a national instead of merely a statewide basis. What remained unclear was who might organize such an insurgency—and whether, under the terms of the new national Constitution, it could even establish its political legitimacy.

FRANKLIN'S DEATH

In April 1790, Benjamin Franklin died at age eighty-four. He had spent most of his time since 1776 in Paris, arranging for vital trade treaties and government loans for the Revolutionary War effort, while he enjoyed the city's cosmopolitan pleasures and basked in his reputation as the premier American *philosophe*. After negotiating the conclusive Treaty of Paris in 1783, he stood second only to George Washington as America's foremost hero.

Recalled home to Philadelphia in 1785, Franklin turned to a number of philanthropic, educational, and reform endeavors. In 1787, he advised a group of local journeymen printers when they struck their employers over wage cuts. The same year, he helped reorganize a disbanded abolition society founded by the Quaker humanitarian Anthony Benezet. Also in 1787, Franklin agreed to serve as a delegate to the Federal Constitutional Convention. Although he had misgivings about specifics in the new national plan, he refrained from airing them in public, remarking that the new government would not turn into a despotism unless "the people shall become so corrupted as to need despotic Government." His last public act, two months before he died, was to sponsor a petition to the new Congress advocating the gradual abolition of slavery.

Strange things began happening to Franklin's reputation during these final years. He had always elicited distrust in the elevated ranks of Philadelphia society, as a shrewd, humble man made good, a wealthy outsider who had challenged the power of the province's old proprietary party, the demiurge behind the democratic constitution of 1776. Now, after his sojourn in Paris and his participation in unsettling reform projects back home, his social cachet in select circles sharply declined. A friend, Deborah Norris Logan, later recalled "the remark of a fool, though a fashionable party-man at the time, that it was by no means 'fashionable' to visit Dr. Franklin." And after his death, when Franklin's name became linked posthumously to a new upsurge of democratic politics, his memory became deeply suspect among the well-to-do and politically conservative. Some friends of the new Washington administration began ridiculing the departed statesman—the son of a Boston candlemaker—as an upstart soap-boiler, a "fawning mob orator," and "a whoremaster, a hypocrite and an infidel."

The American Revolution had proved more egalitarian in its outcome than many of its leaders had hoped or expected it would be in 1776. At the state and local levels, portions of the *demos* once largely excluded from the exercise of power were now among the people's governors. Efforts to rein in the egalitarian impulse had faltered. When those efforts finally succeeded, with the ratification of a new federal constitution in 1788, the

Framers had felt compelled to bend to what James Wilson called "the genius of the people."

A tiny group of state and national leaders, hoping to enlarge the influence of a disinterested natural aristocracy, had invented a national government that would not permit those natural aristocrats to speak only with each other. Yet the structures of American politics, at every level, were still highly uncertain. The federal convention had established the basic framework for a classless republic, but no more than that. Questions abounded, not least over the fate of the democratic presence that the Revolution had created. How would elections to the new government be conducted? Would what James Madison once called the "arts of Electioneering which poison the very fountain of Liberty" clog the Constitution's carefully designed filtration of talent? Would efforts to restrict those baneful arts intrude on the public's liberty? Of what, exactly, did that liberty consist?

Democracy had happened in America between 1776 and 1787. But as the mounting attacks on Franklin's memory thereafter suggested, democracy's achievements were fragile, its institutions only barely formed, and its future far from guaranteed.

2

THE REPUBLICAN INTEREST AND THE SELF-CREATED DEMOCRACY

The Framers of the federal Constitution tried to balance the imperatives of popular sovereignty against the fear of excessive democracy. They could not, even with the addition of the Bill of Rights. Within five years of the Constitution's ratification, new forms of democratic politics emerged, alarming many of the nation's leaders and perplexing others. Thomas Jefferson would eventually become the head and chief beneficiary of this democratic resurgence. But its most striking early manifestations came from well outside Jefferson's world of gentry politics.

In April 1793, a few weeks into George Washington's second term as president, a group calling itself the German Republican Society announced its formation in Philadelphia. Led by a printer and state representative, Henry Kammerer, a physician, Michael Leib, and an ex-army officer and former congressman, Peter Muhlenberg, the members acknowledged their common ethnic background but addressed the republic at large, as American citizens, on issues of national importance. Declaring that "there is a disposition in the human mind to tyrannize when cloathed with power," the new society expressed its disenchantment with federal policies and promised to watch elected officials with an eagle eye. Several weeks later, also in Philadelphia, a larger group, the Democratic Society of Pennsylvania, with no particular ethnic connection, organized itself on the same principles. Its leaders included Benjamin Franklin's favored grandson, the editor of the democratic *Aurora General Advertiser*, Benjamin Franklin Bache.

By the end of 1794, more than thirty of these so-called Democratic-Republican societies (each had a distinctive name, but most included either the word *Democratic* or *Republican*) arose from upper Vermont to South Carolina, and as far west as Kentucky. They mounted elaborate dinners and Fourth of July celebrations; they extolled the French Revolution (in progress since the year of Washington's inauguration), erected tricolored liberty poles, and listened to orations on mental liberty and freedom of the press. They debated current political affairs, published addresses and resolutions criticizing the Washington administration, and agitated for social reforms. They corresponded with each other. Popular democratic politics reappeared everywhere—and quickly came under suspicion as illegitimate and possibly subversive, unfit for a postrevolutionary republic. Each society, one disgusted Virginian wrote, was an "odious conclave of tumult."

The Democratic-Republican societies appeared alongside a growing opposition, inside the government, to the Washington administration. Divisions surfaced in the nation's first capital, New York City, as soon as the First Congress convened in March 1789. Representatives from backcountry districts railed against what they deemed the administration's pompous and monarchical public manner—what one Pennsylvanian called "all the faulty finery brilliant scenes and expensive Trappings of Royal Government." Beginning in 1790, Treasury Secretary Alexander Hamilton's accomplished and audacious reports on the public credit, funding the national debt, and establishing a national bank stirred sharp debate inside President Washington's cabinet and the Congress. Over the next two years, the first semblance of a formal political opposition, led by Secretary of State Thomas Jefferson and Congressman James Madison, spread across the countryside through networks of dissident editors and notables. In 1793, as American opinion began to divide sharply over the French Revolution and American foreign policy, the opposition, known as the Republican interest, stepped up its efforts to halt what it perceived as the government's accelerating Anglophilic, antirepublican drift.

The rise of the Democratic-Republican societies, just when international tensions began to worsen, presented an opportunity and a challenge to Jefferson, Madison, and their allies. On the key national issues, ranging from Hamilton's financial program to foreign affairs, the societies and the mostly patrician Jeffersonian opposition agreed. The societies made no pretense about their support for the Republican interest, and they greatly amplified public criticism of the administration and its supporters. Their activities could be a valuable reinforcement, out-of-doors, to the opposition's efforts inside the cabinet and in Congress. The problem, though, was that the societies were also a self-consciously anomalous force, without any obvious place within the frame of the new Constitution, working independently of the lines of interest and influence where the opposition leaders operated. The societies intended not simply to support certain positions and political leaders, but to become the vehicles for a continuing independent expression of the popular will. With an ebullient grandiosity befitting the age, they hoped to destroy systems of social and political deference that had survived the Revolution. They wanted to create new networks of intelligence and enlightenment that would help emancipate all humanity.

To their opponents in the administration, who appropriated the name Federalists, the societies exemplified unbridled democracy at its worst, and posed a clear and present danger to the republic. The societies' friends in the Republican opposition were not always so sure what to make of them—an uncertainty that turned into acute uneasiness when some of the rural societies appeared to cross over from protests to active disloyalty. Finally, under the withering assaults of the Federalists, the Republican interest and the societies came to understand that they could not do without each other. A democratic widening of American politics ensued, not as great as the society men originally envisaged, but greater than anything Jefferson, Madison, and their fellow gentry oppositionists could have imagined in 1789.

AGAINST MONOCRACY: JEFFERSON, MADISON, AND THE VIRGINIA IDEAL

Jefferson and Madison were born eight years apart and raised roughly thirty miles from each other in neighboring counties of the Virginia Piedmont. Scions of leading planter families, both were well educated (Jefferson at William and Mary and with the great law teacher George Wythe at Williamsburg, Madison at Princeton); both were imbued with the rationalist values of the Enlightenment; and both were drawn to politics despite their indifferent public personae. They would enjoy a long and productive friendship and collaboration.

Yet Jefferson and Madison were also very different men, and their differences were particularly evident at the new federal government's founding. Jefferson, the charming, rangy, elusive polymath, displayed the greater intellectual ambit of the two, and a penchant in private for flights of political fantasy. Madison, half a foot shorter, nervous, and achingly shy, had the more systematic mind, one capable, as Jefferson's was not, of building grand and nuanced practical designs out of his political principles. A tireless committeeman and preeminent member of the Second Continental Congress from 1779 until 1783, Madison had acquired from the Revolution a broad view of American government that vaunted the nation's well-being over sectional or local interests. With that view, he became the chief theorist of the Federal Constitution, favoring a large republic with a strong central government and an energetic executive. Jefferson, who in 1779 began the first of two disastrous terms as wartime governor of Virginia, believed in American nationalism, but also had a greater fear of government's coercive abuses. Hence his wariness, which he conveyed to Madison from his minister's post in Paris in 1788, of approving the Constitution without a bill of rights—the "principal defect," he wrote, in the Framers' work.

Their differences were philosophical as well as temperamental. Madison, with more than a trace of Calvinist pessimism, was drawn to inventing reasoned political institutions in order to quiet what he saw as mankind's innate passion for destructive conflict. Jefferson, in his more haphazard yet sanguine way, preferred proposing plans to liberate individual reason, and enhance what he saw as mankind's potential for harmony and order. Far more instinctively than Madison, Jefferson viewed political turbulence as beneficial: "It prevents the degeneracy of government," he wrote, "and nourishes a general attention to the public affairs." Those disagreements began to recede, however, in 1790, after Secretary of the Treasury Hamilton announced the first portion of his ambitious financial program and Congressman Madison attacked it.

Madison and Hamilton had been friends and colleagues since they first met in the Continental Congress in 1782—and were closer in their politics, it seemed, than were Madison and Jefferson (who had never laid eyes on Hamilton until he joined Washington's cabinet). Madison and Hamilton's shared nationalism and their mounting frustration at the ascendancy of the state governments under the Articles of Confederation outweighed their other political considerations in the mid to late 1780s. Both men attended the Annapolis Conference, a failed effort to alter the Articles, in 1786. Both were, in different ways, outstanding advocates of a strong central government during the federal convention at Philadelphia. Above all, over the winter of 1787–88, using the joint pseudonym "Publius," they composed the most powerful of *The Federalist* papers to defend the convention's work, eloquently expressing their distrust of majorities, their fear of faction, and their belief that robust central government could be an antidote to selfish human frailty and divisiveness. "Hearken not to the unnatural voice which tells you that the people of America . . . can no longer live together as members of the same family," declared Madison in *Federalist 14*.

Yet when Hamilton, secretary of the Treasury, sought to improve upon the Framers' work, his friendship with Madison abruptly ended. Hamilton, the ingenious, West Indies–born New York lawyer and former army officer, was convinced that the Constitution could not guarantee greatness—or even survival—for the new republic. History taught him that no matter how they were governed, agrarian societies like America's produced little more than what was needed to sustain their people in modest comfort. Contrary to the then-fashionable classical and contemporary poets' portrayal of idyllic pastoral life so dear to Jefferson's heart, Hamilton was convinced that such conditions were morally enervating and politically dangerous. Uninspired to improve their circumstances, individuals would lapse into habits of public indifference and brutish self-regard. Lacking a substantial material surplus on which to draw, the government would have a difficult time raising a credible military force to ward off hostile nations. "[O]ne of two evils must ensue," Hamilton wrote in *Federalist 30*, "either the people must be subjected to continual plunder, as a substitute for a more eligible mode of supplying the public wants, or the government must sink into a fatal atrophy, and, in a short course of time, perish."

Alternatively, an America that mobilized its boundless material resources through public and private credit would, in Hamilton's view, protect both commerce and the nation, and encourage an intensified, urbane sociability. "Industry is increased," he wrote to Robert Morris in 1781, about the benefits of public debt and a national bank, "commodities are multiplied, agriculture and manufacturers flourish, and herein consist the true wealth and prosperity of a state." In order to secure this, Hamilton looked instinctively to Great Britain, both as a model and as an irreplaceable commercial ally. The immense increase since 1750 of Britain's funded debt—the system of mortgaging government revenues by selling public securities in order to finance recurrent wars—had been accompanied by an extraordinary growth of the British economy. By imitating that system with a privately directed national bank, foreign impost revenues, and internal excise taxes, Americans could establish their own government securities as a stable currency while giving their merchants access to the large pools of capital required to develop the country. Because those monies would be used chiefly for economic improvement and presumably not for wars, the consequent expansion of national wealth would help to fund the debt. Finally, Hamilton argued that the United States would have to sustain cordial relations with the British government, lest the nation lose the enormous public revenues as well as private profits received from its commerce with Britain. Without those revenues, he was certain, America could not honor its national obligations.

Hamilton released his plans to Congress in stages, beginning in January 1790 with his report on public credit, followed almost a year later by a report on establishing a national bank (accompanied with a request for an excise tax on whiskey), followed a year after that by a report on manufacturing. In order to restore public confidence in American finances, Hamilton's opening report called, first, for the repayment at face value of all national securities from the Revolutionary and Confederation periods to the current holders of those securities and, second, for the federal government to assume all state debts left over from the Revolution. The latter proposal came with the understanding that each state would be compensated for its donation once the total debt was retired. As Hamilton saw it, the plan offered a simple solution to the tangled problems of uniting and repaying the state and national public creditors, as well as the means to offer generous federal relief to indebted states. Not coincidentally, the plan would also create a large federal debt whose funding, supported by imposts and excise taxes, would be the key to achieving Hamilton's vision of American prosperity and power—"the price of liberty," he wrote.

To Madison, the debt funding and assumption schemes reeked of oppressive favoritism. By paying only the current holders of national securities—monied speculators who had purchased the securities at cut-rate prices in the 1780s—Hamilton would completely ignore the claims of the original holders—ordinary citizens of limited means who had accepted or bought their securities in good faith but who had been forced by the uncertain postwar economic climate to sell their paper at a fraction of its face value. "[T]here must be something wrong, radically & morally & politically wrong," Madison observed, "in a system which transfers the reward from those who paid the most valuable of all considerations, to those who scarcely paid any consideration at all." Federal assumption of state debts under Hamilton's program, meanwhile, would benefit those states, above all Massachusetts and South Carolina, that were still heavily in arrears far more than it would those (including Virginia and all the other southern states) that had largely retired their debt.

Jefferson would level similar charges against Hamilton's larger financial program, but initially he was more cautious than Madison and remained publicly noncommittal. His long journey home from his posting in France and his indecision about joining Washington's cabinet as secretary of state delayed his arrival in New York until late March 1790—more than a month after Congress had already defeated Madison's effort to block Hamilton's plan to compensate the current holders of government paper. Once he had settled in, Jefferson helped arrange what he described as a compromise meeting, in which Madison agreed to permit approval of a revised version of Hamilton's assumption proposal in exchange for establishing the federal government's permanent capital at a site well to the south of New York, on the Potomac River bordering Maryland and Virginia.

Jefferson later told President Washington, a bit defensively, that in 1790 he had no clear idea of what Hamilton's financial system entailed and that the quick-tongued New Yorker had duped him. Whatever the truth in that, Jefferson certainly was alarmed at the depth of the disagreements in Congress and hoped to find some middle ground. (If Hamilton and his foes were not reconciled, he wrote to his fellow Virginian, James Monroe, the arguments over the debt would cause "our credit . . . [to] burst and vanish," and the nation would disintegrate.) Only in January 1791, after Hamilton unveiled his bank proposal and Congress approved it, did Jefferson take the full measure of Hamilton's plans and assume a firmer adversarial stance. In private (and on strict constructionist constitutional grounds that Madison had already explained in the House), Jefferson futilely tried to persuade Washington to veto the bank bill. Thereafter, until the end of 1793, Jefferson would help lead the attack on Hamilton and Hamilton's proposals, but he would do so behind closed doors and in personal letters, lest he appear a disloyal cabinet member or the leader of a faction—anathema in a political atmosphere that despised parties as corrupt fomenters of division and enemies to the government itself. It fell to Madison, the younger and shyer man, to serve as chief public spokesman for the embryonic opposition, on the floor of the House and, writing anonymously, in the fledgling, outnumbered opposition press.

The early congressional clashes over Hamilton's policies had a strong sectional character, pitting the North against the South. Nearly two-thirds of the House votes in favor of Madison's failed discrimination proposal came from Virginia; when the assumption plan finally passed the House, more than half the southern congressmen stubbornly cast negative votes, despite the prearranged compromise about moving the capital to the Potomac. The House tally approving the bank bill was even more dramatic: northern representatives nearly unanimously backed the bill but the southerners voted heavily against it. Slavery, the most obvious difference between the sections, cannot explain the emerging partisan divide. Northerners, some of whom were still squabbling about emancipation in their own states, did not perceive an anti-slavery agenda behind Hamilton's proposals. On slavery issues, Virginians in the First Congress commonly voted with the North. Narrower local self-interest played a larger role, especially with respect to Hamilton's assumption plan, which appeared unfavorable to every southern state except South Carolina. But there were also more profound social and ideological issues at stake for Jefferson, Madison, and their southern allies.

Hamilton's unembarrassed Anglophilia offended some southerners, especially Virginia planters hit hard by British military depredations during the Revolution and still uncompensated for their losses, including losses of slaves. More important, Hamilton's economics, founded on his reported claim that "a public debt is a public blessing," confirmed his treachery in the minds of southern planters and farmers. On the eve of the Revolution, Virginians, many of whom had unwisely refused to retrench in the face of weakening tobacco markets, owed more money to British creditors than the inhabitants of any other colony, and nearly as much as all of the other colonists combined. It was a miserable situation, not simply because it offended what were supposed to be gentlemanly norms about insolvency, but because it left the indebted planters lashed in a terrible dependence to distant British merchants.

The more forward-looking planters acknowledged that they would have to mend their ways if they were to keep from repeating the cycle of debt dependency. But no amount of agricultural self-improvement could undo what Jefferson and others considered the corrosive and degrading effects of Hamilton's debt-based finance system. That system, they contended, blatantly favored certain classes of Americans, generally northerners (speculators in government stock, residents of states with large debts), to the exclusion, and at the expense, of everyone else. Speaking in the House against the proposed bank, James Jackson of Georgia called it an unconstitutional monopoly, "calculated to benefit a small part of the United States, the mercantile interest only; the farmers, the yeomanry will derive no advantage from it." Instead of increasing the store of national wealth available to all, Hamilton's plans would replace the old imperial debt system with a pernicious new one, run by well-connected men who produced nothing yet who lived handsomely off the proceeds gained from other men's products.

Jefferson and others could also not help detecting royalist designs in Hamilton's economic policies. In restrospect, that suspicion was unfair. Hamilton's admiration for British government and political economy no more made him a crypto-monarchist than his opponents' later enthusiasm for the French Revolution made them incipient Jacobin terrorists. Moreover, as some of Hamilton's northern friends tartly pointed out, it ill behooved Americans, including Jefferson and Madison, who lived off the unrequited labor of human chattel to call any other group of Americans exploiters. Yet having lived for most of their lives under monarchy, it was understandable that royalism became the chief point of reference for Hamilton's foes, who appreciated certain American social and political principles that the Treasury secretary detested. Those principles—which the opposition would soon pit against a somewhat more measured anti-Hamilton epithet, *monocracy*—formed the elements of what would become a distinct Virginia political ideal.

Jefferson was especially prone to wrap his political judgments, including those about Hamilton, inside praise of rural virtues, while condemning large cities. "Those who labor in the earth," he wrote famously in 1783, "are the chosen people of God, if ever he had a chosen people." In drawing this distinction, he did not mean to dismiss the cultural and intellectual amenities of urban life (which, during his extended residences in New York, Philadelphia, and, especially, Paris, he enjoyed to the hilt). Nor did he despise urban commerce, including the transoceanic commerce that helped enrich American farmers. Rather, he was registering a Virginian's suspicions of urban speculators who contributed nothing to the production and distribution of goods, as well as of what he called "the mobs of great cities"—the hordes of hangers-on and impoverished persons who, because they were reliant on the goodwill of employers and patrons, could never be trusted to arrive at virtuous, independent political judgments. To protect the republic from being corrupted by these dependent men, Jefferson looked to expanding the influence of America's free majority of self-reliant planters and yeomen (he never really distinguished between the two)—honest, moderately prosperous, and productive toilers whose reason, supposedly, was not clouded by servility to others. Encouraging these men would ward off what he called in a letter to Madison in 1785 the enormous inequality in property that produced "much misery to the bulk of mankind"—inequality that Hamilton's plans would ratify and exacerbate.

Madison echoed his friend's somewhat static pastoral republicanism from time to time. "'Tis not the country that peoples either the Bridewells or the Bedlams," he wrote in 1792. "These mansions of wretchedness are tenanted from the distresses and vices of overgrown cities." But Madison added his own nationalist vision of effective, harmonious government, as he had propounded it in *Federalist 10* and 55. In the 1780s, that vision had alarmed many prominent Virginians as too centralizing; but in the 1790s, Madison showed that his nationalism was at odds in several ways with his ex-friend Hamilton's. In doing so, Madison achieved a degree of reconciliation with portions of the gentry that had opposed the Constitution, and solidified a new coalition of former Federalists and anti-Federalists from 1787 to 1788 against Hamilton's plans.

Breaking with Hamilton involved no intellectual inconsistency on Madison's part (although Hamilton would bitterly claim it did). Contrary to Madison's vision of the new constitutional order, Hamilton's fiscal plans would, he believed, ally the federal government to a particular class of speculators, create (through the national bank) a means to dispense bounties to political favorites and bribes to opponents, and introduce what Madison called the "corrupt influence" of "substituting the motive of private interest in place of public duty." More generally, Madison observed, the funding system would enlarge "the inequality of property, by an immoderate, and especially an unmerited, accumulation of riches." The delicate balance of social forces so vital to Madisonian popular sovereignty would be destroyed—and with it, Madison's design for an enlightened republic.

Over the course of the 1790s, Jefferson and Madison would help turn their objections to Hamilton's project into a coherent alternative vision of America, influenced by Virginia aspirations and prejudices but capable of appealing to other groups, including the reemerging urban democrats of Philadelphia, New York, and other cities. In 1791, however, Jefferson, Madison, and their allies in Congress were struggling, not very successfully, to keep Hamilton's proposals from sweeping aside all opposition. Despite the advantages in congressional representation given to the southern states under the three-fifths clause of the Constitution, Hamilton appeared able, at will, to push his bills through the House as well as the Senate. And Hamilton had the trust of his old commanding officer, a Virginian far more imposing than Thomas Jefferson—President Washington, who, in politics, surmounted all local connections and came as close as any American ever would to an elected Patriot King. "Congress may go home," the country democrat Senator William Maclay wrote. "Mr. Hamilton is all powerful and fails in nothing which he attempts."

Opposing Hamilton inside the government without appearing to defy Washington was a major problem confronting the Virginians. A related, larger difficulty was to find political tools that could rally and unify voters and officeholders from around the country without seeming to disrupt the spirit of national harmony. Grappling with both problems forced Jefferson, Madison, and their disgruntled allies in the political elite to stretch their ideas about democracy.

FIRST STIRRINGS OF REPUBLICAN ORGANIZATION

At the end of February 1791, three days after President Washington signed the bill establishing Hamilton's bank, Jefferson contacted Madison's old Princeton classmate, the journalist and poet Philip Freneau, and offered him a lowly translator's clerkship in the State Department at an annual salary of $250—a pretext for persuading Freneau to come to Philadelphia and edit a new, nationally distributed opposition newspaper. The project was perilous, financially and politically, and all parties concerned had to move gingerly, but to Freneau, the prospect of leading the attack on Alexander Hamilton was too tantalizing to pass up.

After two short, unsuccessful postcollege stints as a school-teacher, Freneau, an adventuresome young man with literary ambitions, had sailed on a privateer during the Revolution, fallen captive to the enemy, and suffered terribly aboard one of the Royal Navy's notorious prison ships. His memories of that suffering forever smoldered in his writing. Politically close to Thomas Paine—whom Jefferson also, briefly, considered trying to lure into the administration in 1791—Freneau established his reputation in Philadelphia after the war as both poet and polemicist, then moved to New York City, where, as editor of the *Daily Advertiser*, he gained additional notice in 1790 with vituperative attacks on Hamilton's debt-funding and banking proposals. Recommended not just by Madison but by another prominent Princeton graduate and Virginian, Henry ("Light Horse Harry") Lee, Freneau seemed the ideal choice to counter John Fenno, the editor of the quasi-official administration newspaper, the *Gazette of the United States*—the purveyor, in Jefferson's excited view, of "doctrines of monarchy, aristocracy, and the exclusion of the influence of the people." After dickering for five months about business arrangements, Freneau accepted both the clerkship and the editorial post. At the end of October 1791, he put through the press the first issue of his twice-weekly *National Gazette*.

By establishing a national newspaper, the leaders of the emerging Republican opposition displayed their growing coherence and self-confidence as a political force, but they also displayed a limited conception of democracy and dissent. Freneau would bring to the Republicans the slashing, egalitarian style of the Revolutionary-era city democracy. At a time when newspapers were just beginning to reach the more remote corners of the country, the *National Gazette* promised to stimulate sympathetic opinion as no existing newspaper could. Yet in Freneau, Jefferson and Madison had also found someone whose instincts and loyalty they thought they could trust—an ink-stained democrat, yes, but also one who could work well with the opposition's gentry leadership. ("With Mr. Freneau I have been long and intimately acquainted," Madison reassured another Republican.) More generally, the *National Gazette* would be instrumental in helping those leaders (particularly Madison, who would write several important articles for the paper in 1792) to connect with their notable friends and subscribers around the country, and who would in turn influence their own friends and neighbors. If, as Jefferson put it, Freneau's paper was to serve as an anti-administration "whig-vehicle of intelligence" with a democratic edge, it was a vehicle that traveled from the top down, closely watched by men who thought of themselves as the country's natural leaders.

This style of organizing through the ministrations of a political elite dominated Republican national efforts through the elections of 1792. When Jefferson and Madison embarked in the late spring of 1791 on what would become a famous "botanizing tour" of New York and New England, rumors flew about how they were actually establishing closer political contacts with friendly local powers, especially Robert R. Livingston and Aaron Burr in New York City. The rumors had merit; but whatever occurred, the tour bespoke what were still the Republicans' limited views of what constituted a legitimate opposition. Inside and outside Congress, political dissent would mainly involve the cooperation of a few leading gentlemen who would handle their affairs discreetly, more like diplomats than like grubby politicians. Newspapers and pamphlets written by trustworthy allies would shape public opinion. And nothing would be said or done that might be construed as unfriendly to President Washington.

Ideas about building permanent electoral machinery that might fuse the national leadership with the voters were nearly as alien to the Republican leaders as they were to Federalists. James Madison, writing in the *National Gazette*, asked his readers to face the fact that something he called "parties" had come to exist in American politics, and that there were not several of these parties (as he had said there might be in *Federalist 10*) but only two. Yet Madison made it clear that only one of those two parties, his own,—the "friends to republican policy . . . in opposition to a spirit of usurpation and monarchy"—was the legitimate legatee of the Revolution and the Constitution. Once that legitimate party prevailed, Madison and his allies believed, the "monocratic" crisis would end, parties would be rendered unnecessary, and the high-minded decisions of enlightened natural leaders would, at last, guide the nation.

The structure of politics at the state level further discouraged partisan electioneering. In virtually all of the southern states, neither the governor, congressional representatives, state legislators, nor presidential electors were selected by a statewide vote. Elections had a localist character, centered around individual candidates, that made them almost impervious to national organizing. In New England, where statewide elections were much more common, a haphazard multiplicity of election tickets, with some candidates appearing on several lists for the same election, made it almost impossible to build coherent political organizations. Only in New York and Pennsylvania were electoral procedures more favorable to would-be Republican and Federalist organizers. Yet, even in those states, major candidates eschewed party labels.

Intrigue, deception, and bungling in high places, befitting a late-eighteenth-century *opera buffa*, overshadowed popular organizing—such as it was—on the national political stage. One little scandal began innocently enough in April 1791, when Madison gave Jefferson a copy of Thomas Paine's latest work from London, the first part of Paine's defense of the French Revolution, *Rights of Man*. (Madison had borrowed the copy belonging to John Beckley, the clerk of the House of Representatives and an admirer of Paine.) After reading the book with delight, Jefferson, following Beckley's instructions, forwarded it to the printer in charge of preparing an American edition, but he unwisely included a note praising the book as an antidote to certain "political heresies which have sprung up among us"—an unmistakable reference to some recently published political writings by Vice President Adams. Not thinking to ask Jefferson's permission, the printer included the note as a preface, and all hell broke loose. Hamilton severed relations with Jefferson for good. The embarrassed Jefferson wrote a hurried explanation to Washington and later apologized to Adams. Under the pseudonym "Publicola," Adams's twenty-four-year-old son, John Quincy, leapt to his father's defense in the newspapers. For years thereafter, the elder Adams would have little to do with Jefferson, who, despite their political differences, had been a long-standing friend, collaborator, and correspondent.

A few months later, Hamilton strayed into an even wilder and juicier scandal of his own that would take much longer to come to light. One summer day, Maria Reynolds, outwardly a respectable lady in much distress, introduced herself out of the blue to the Treasury secretary, told him her husband had abandoned her, and requested funds to enable her to stay with friends in New York. Much affected by the woman's story, Hamilton, a married man, gave her some money—and then commenced an affair with her that continued for over a year. In time Mrs. Reynolds, working in collusion with her all-too-present husband, James, ensnared Hamilton into paying hush money. The liaison continued, until the husband and an accomplice, awaiting trial on charges of fraud stemming from a different matter, began spreading rumors that they had proof, written in Hamilton's hand, of financial misconduct at the very highest levels of the Treasury Department. Three concerned congressmen (including Senator James Monroe), accompanied by clerk of the House John Beckley, confronted Hamilton in private with notes he had written Mrs. Reynolds; Hamilton told his visitors the whole story. Satisfied that no public monies had been involved, the congressmen decided to drop the matter. For the time being, nothing seemed amiss, at least publicly—but Beckley, angry at Hamilton's attacks on Jefferson, held on to the Hamilton-Reynolds letters, in case they might some day prove politically useful. It would take a few years, but that day would come.

The scandals and the skulduggery marked the persistence of an older form of elite politics, revolving around personal character, honor, and gentlemanly reputation. Another episode unfolded during the vice presidential contest in 1792. Early in the year,

Republican leaders, not wanting to challenge President Washington, concocted a plan to run the popular governor of New York, George Clinton, against Vice President John Adams, and thereby register the electorate's displeasure with the administration. In the spring, Clinton was narrowly reelected governor over John Jay—but only because of flagrant voter fraud by some of his upstate supporters. Jefferson, alarmed at the possible fallout from the fraud revelations, counseled Clinton to resign from office. New York's hyperambitious young U.S. Senator Aaron Burr confused matters further when he allowed friends in New York and Pennsylvania to circulate his name as a possible alternative challenger for the vice presidency. Madison and Monroe wanted nothing to do with Burr; fortuitously, Hamilton, who also loathed Burr, bid his fellow New York Federalists to go easy on Clinton, while he threw his wholehearted support (complete with unsolicited campaign advice) to John Adams. The Republicans wound up sticking with Clinton, who kept his New York job and ran a respectable second to Adams in the Electoral College, carrying nearly all of the South, including Virginia. Burr, meanwhile, blamed the Virginians for thwarting his candidacy and began quietly nursing his disappointments.

After 1792, Republican leaders, driven as much by confusion and fear as by principle, began enlarging their views about political organization. Although candidates aligned with the Republican interest ran well enough in the congressional races to gain a majority in the House, the majority was small, and the Federalists still controlled both the presidency and (by a wide margin) the Senate. The results posed a difficult puzzle: if the Republicans truly represented, as Madison claimed in an essay for the *National Gazette*, the interests and the ideals of "the mass of people in every part of the union, in every state, and of every occupation," why did every opposition candidate not win every election by a landslide?

The problem involved two distinct but related matters: Why was voter turnout, especially in national elections, so low—often less than one in four eligible voters, considerably less than in local and state elections? And why did the active voters elect congressional representatives who, once in office, gravitated disproportionately to the Federalists? The influential John Taylor of Caroline (known by the Virginia county where he resided, and speaking on behalf of his fellow Virginians in Congress) blamed a conniving "paper interest" consisting of roughly five thousand of Hamilton's friends, who had gained "an irresistible *influence* over the Legislature" and over the electorate through propaganda and the granting of personal favors. Under the circumstances, it was easy to understand why the electorate had grown lethargic while what Taylor called "the artificial interest" controlled the federal government.

One possible corrective, proposed by Taylor in 1794 and followed up years later by Jefferson, was to embolden state legislatures to assume a more active role in governing the nation. Because the state legislatures elected U.S. senators, their collective influence over the direction of the federal government could well prove decisive. But Republican leaders also decided they would have to redouble their efforts to educate and mobilize the virtuous but misinformed citizens. Establishing Freneau's *National Gazette* had been an important step; so, later, had been Taylor's call to elect representatives who shared a "similarity of interests" with their constituents. But the *Gazette* was doomed to fold in 1793, the victim of a yellow fever epidemic that swept through Philadelphia. And before the *Gazette's* demise, the national returns in 1792 showed that the gentry Republicans needed to innovate further if they were to overthrow the "paper interest." They would end up taking instruction from men with more democratic instincts than their own, organized in the Democratic-Republican societies.

"THE CAUSE OF *EQUAL LIBERTY* EVERY WHERE"

The Democratic-Republican societies were conceived in response to domestic political problems and beholden to the examples of 1776. But they also looked to the revolution in Paris for examples and solidarity—and in the societies' early months, it seemed that foreign affairs would dominate everything else. In April 1793, right after the German Republicans had organized in Philadelphia, a British packet arrived in New York with the first news of the execution of Louis XVI and France's declaration of war on Britain and Holland. Two days later, the new French minister to the United States, "Citizen" Edmond Charles Genet, arrived in Charleston to a rousing reception, then set off on his problematic mission: to whip up American support for the regicide republic. The Washington administration, which had quickly proclaimed the nation's neutrality, requested Genet's recall to France a mere four months later. During the summer, the headstrong, bombastic envoy thoroughly alienated even his best American friends in high places, including the pro-French Secretary of State Thomas Jefferson. The political fallout hastened Jefferson's decision to retire from the cabinet late in 1793, and Jefferson warned his ally James Madison that Genet's American friends would *sink the republican interest.*

Those friends included, most conspicuously, the new Democratic-Republican societies, who saw Genet as a besieged apostle of revolutionary defiance. A few weeks after his arrival, a committee from the German Republican Society waited on Genet in Philadelphia and urged "the perpetual union and freedom of our respective republics." Genet was the man who came up with the suggestion that the larger Philadelphia group look to the future and name itself the Democratic Society instead of the Sons of Liberty. Certain societies in the Carolinas and Kentucky, with Genet's encouragement, aided French plans for insurrections against Spanish-held Louisiana and Florida, and for securing rights to navigate the Mississippi River. Longer than most pro-French Americans, the societies stood by Genet against what one club called "the most indecent calumnies" directed against him.

Some administration supporters seized on the connections and battered both the Republican opposition and the societies as (in the Massachusetts conservative Fisher Ames's words) "the impure off-spring of Genet." But the Genet affair obscured how principled dissent over the Washington administration's policies, at home and abroad, had triggered the societies' rise—dissent far more important than the exhortations of Citizen Genet. There was no need, the societies insisted, to look across the Atlantic to see liberty besieged by tyranny: "the peaceful Temple of Liberty is threatened in this Western hemisphere," the Philadelphia society declared. Disgust at Hamilton's financial programs had been growing for three years, among city and country democrats alike. The alliance between Federalists and urban mechanics over the Constitution had broken down over popular fears that Hamilton's paper system was designed to enrich a few speculators and merchants at the expense of the many. Similar anxieties gripped rural areas that had never been enamored of the new federal plan.

In local fights as well, there was mounting alienation over perceived Federalist favoritism toward the wealthy and well connected. One telling battle unfolded in New York City, where master mechanics had to wage a long battle against Federalist state legislators to gain a charter for their General Society of Mechanics and Tradesmen. "Those who assume the airs of 'the well born,'" wrote one self-styled "Friend to Equal Rights," "should be made to know that the *mechanics* of the city have *equal rights* to the merchants, and that they are as important a set of men as any in the community." Another city democrat asked why monied interests like banks could easily win official incorporation while more democratic ones could not. The New Yorkers finally won their charter in 1792, but the damage was done.

The societies' outrage at Hamiltonian finance and Federalist elitism would always be at the core of their protests against the Washington administration. Their complaints repeated those of Jefferson, Madison, and the Virginia opposition, but in a very different key. Hamilton's innovations augured an accumulation of power in the hands of the federal government that the society men thought would pervert commerce and introduce, the Democratic Society of New York proclaimed, "the corrupt principles and abandoned polity of foreign climes." Mainly, Hamilton's program promised to set one class above all others: the insider monied men and speculators who manipulated government to gain special favors and advantages at the direct expense of ordinary citizens—and who then expected ordinary citizens to regard them as their superiors. "Our councils want the integrity or spirit of republicans," one western Pennsylvania society asserted, because of "the pernicious influence of stockholders or their subordinates." An eighteenth-century sense of class injustices and insult pervaded the societies' meetings. "Less respect to the consuming speculator, who wallows in luxury, than to the productive mechanic, who struggles with indigence," ran one New York society toast. Jefferson and his gentry allies saw the struggle before them in terms of urban corruption and rural virtue. The societies saw themselves embattled by arrogant parasites who demanded they defer.

The administration's foreign policy, and the way it was promulgated, brought popular malaise to a head and sealed the link of domestic concerns to international politics. By refusing to side with revolutionary France against Britain and Holland, President Washington (with Secretary Hamilton's concurrence and over Secretary Jefferson's strenuous objections) in effect declared that the Franco-American mutual defense treaty of 1778, so vital to winning American independence, had died along with Louis XVI. The administration saw no favorite in the cataclysmic conflict between beleaguered republicanism and rampant monarchy, its critics claimed. And the president had proclaimed the nation's neutrality without consulting the Senate, the first such independent executive action on a major foreign policy matter. Not only had America deserted an old friend (now a republican friend) at war against the rotten old regime; it had done so, some charged, by an act of presidential usurpation on behalf, the Democratic Society of Pennsylvania said, of "the aristocratical faction among us."

The protests and related activities of the city-based societies, especially Philadelphia's Democratic Society, attracted the greatest initial public attention. With more than three hundred members (making it the largest urban society of all), and meeting in the nation's temporary capital (which had been relocated from New York in 1791), the Philadelphia group resembled the city's democratic movement from the Revolution. Thomas Paine, ever on the international front lines of political upheaval, was himself in Paris, where, as an elected member of the revolutionary National Assembly he voted against the king's execution on humanitarian grounds and wound up, rather ironically, spending most of 1794 in a Jacobin prison, expecting to be executed. But many of Paine's political associates and admirers from Philadelphia's radical intelligentsia were prominent members of the Democratic Society, including the watchmaker-turned-astronomer David Rittenhouse, Dr. Benjamin Rush of both the Continental Congress and the Pennsylvania Provincial Congress of 1776, and Benjamin Franklin Bache, whose Philadelphia *Aurora General Advertiser* had become the leading anti-administration newspaper. Apart from some conspicuous self-made men of wealth (including the banker Stephen Girard), as well as professionals and minor public officials among its officers, the majority of the members were ordinary artisans, including journeymen as well as master craftsmen. The rank and file may have included some of the lower class of laborers of the kind who had filled the militia companies in 1776, but primarily they were from the aspiring yet humble middling sort, the self-designated "productive" classes. The same membership pattern appears to have prevailed in the other seaport societies. The rural clubs, likewise, brought together a leadership of prominent landed locals with lowlier farmers, land renters, and artisans.

The Philadelphia society and the rest of the seaport groups linked America's fate to that of the new French republic and adapted the approved French rhetorical styles of revolutionary correctness. On May 1, 1794, about eight hundred members and supporters of the Philadelphia group, addressing each other as "Citizen," gathered at a grand festivity to celebrate, in part, the armies and government of France. A few weeks earlier, New York's Democratic Society had honored the momentous French military victory against the British at Toulon (taking the time to toast Thomas Paine and his *Rights of Man*). Early in 1795, the Boston society, replying to some Federalist name-calling, announced that "if to advocate the right of Free Enquiry and Opinion, and to wish success to the cause of *equal Liberty* every where, compose the character of *Jacobins*, we avow ourselves JACOBINS."

Such passionate pronouncements fooled those who would be fooled by them. Rather than start a new American revolution and execute George Washington, the revived city democrats wanted to secure the Revolution they had believed was already won, against resurgent aristocracy and even monarchy. If, at times, the urban Democratic-Republicans could sound gullible and sometimes callous in their enthusiasm for *la révolution*, they themselves were no terrorists or Robespierreists. The city societies repeatedly affirmed their loyalty to orderly government and the federal Constitution. Their own constitutions and bylaws were models of democratic decorum, providing for annual elections of officers by secret ballot, open participation by the membership, and regular monthly meetings. Just after they declared themselves "Jacobins," the Boston Democratic-Republicans qualified themselves: if the term meant violent opposition to the constituted authorities of the United States, or efforts to suppress free inquiry and expression, then "we detest the appellation."

The groups' primary task was to provide a continuing forum to prevent American liberty's downfall, and to express that dissent in the name of the people. Lacking, under the Constitution, any institutional popular safeguard, between elections, against the perceived aristocratic revival, each society assumed that role for itself, combining the functions of a public observation committee, a tool for political education, and a fraternal order. Allied with independent radical editors—Bache and his successor, William Duane, as well as Eleazer Oswald in Philadelphia, Thomas Greenleaf in New York—they released ever-more pointed, occasionally vicious commentary on political events and administration actions, with language steeped in the apocalyptic furor of the time. It was, the society leaders freely admitted, a civic role unspecified in the Constitution—but only aristocrats and monarchists, they insisted, would claim that the Constitution's internal checks and balances were sufficient guarantees against tyranny. "Let us keep in mind," the Pennsylvania society declared, "that supineness with regard to public concerns is the direct road to slavery, while vigilance and jealousy are the safeguards of Liberty."

The societies interpreted "public concerns" broadly and pursued humanitarian as well as political causes. Much of their activity involved creating a new public space for discussion of controversial political topics, and the dissemination of circulars and memorials, as well as remonstrances to the president and Congress. Like the Republican opposition, the societies were convinced that the Federalists secured their rule in part through a combination of purposeful misinformation and public ignorance. They aimed to build from the bottom up—just as the gentry Republicans did from the top down—new networks of political intelligence that would challenge the prevailing Federalist point of view. This required full freedom of assembly and the press. "It is the unalienable right of a free and independent people to assemble together in a peacable manner," one North Carolina society resolved, in a typical pronouncement, "to discuss with firmness and freedom all subjects of public concern, and to publish their sentiments to their fellow citizens."

Freedom of expression was, of course, the basis for further reforms. Some societies demanded fairer representation in state legislatures, in part, a South Carolina club observed, because impartial distribution of seats would prove "a means of disseminating political knowledge among the inhabitants." Other society men called for reductions in legal fees, the abolition of imprisonment for debt, and reform of criminal codes to eliminate capital punishment for minor offenses. The most imposing efforts involved establishing public libraries and library companies and demanding legislative aid to free public schooling to break down class privileges and cultivate an enlightened free citizenry. "The progress of education—," one society proclaimed at a Fourth of July celebration. "May it cause a speedy abolition of every species of dangerous distinction, and render every American a patriot from principle." Memorials and resolutions from Democratic-Republican groups proved instrumental in getting two states, New York and Delaware, to establish rudimentary public-school funding laws.

In attacking ignorance, the societies' efforts at public enlightenment, including their parades and festivities, were part of a larger assault on deference. Popular habits of subordination to, and even reverence of, what one society called "aristocratical finesse" were essential to sustaining the Federalists' rule, the democrats argued. Too many ordinary citizens, even in republican America, still felt awe, resignation, and even shame in the presence of their alleged superiors—men with better educations, finer speech and more elegant clothing, smoother hands and smoother manners than theirs. This sense of inferiority was demoralizing, and it bred apathy and worse. "As ignorance is the irreconcilable enemy of Liberty it is also the immediate parent of guilt," the New York society declared. "[I]t poisons every pure fountain of morals in a state, and generates the greater proportion of crimes, that infest and disturb the peace of society." Demoralization and criminality, in turn, justified and reinforced the basic elitist presumption that the lower orders were savages who needed oversight by their benign, gentlemanly superiors.

Overthrowing the Federalists' aristocracy required erasing that sense of embarrassment and inferiority. The escalating fervor in the denunciations of the societies indicated that the societies' refusal to defer was upsetting their foes deeply, as they had intended. And the rapid growth of the societies around the country in 1793 and 1794, even in the face of fierce attacks, suggested that popular submission might finally be breaking down. "In fine," the New York society observed, "the splendid frippery, the pompous sophistry, with which the bands of slavery have been tinselled over, are now found like a species of rotten wood."

At their most visionary, the societies foresaw the triumph of what Tunis Wortman, of the New York Democratic Society, called "social virtue." With an enthusiasm that was becoming common among Enlightenment writers, high and low, the members celebrated men's capacities to enlarge the sphere of happiness once aristocracy had fallen. Their cause, as they saw it, was the democratic cause of 1776, but it was also the cause of humankind—a cause they believed, with dead seriousness, that fate had entrusted to them and their fellow democrats in the Old World. Their final goal was nothing less than the universal victory of egalitarian government. "When once that happy aera dawns upon the world," Wortman wrote,

> luxury, wealth, and sumptuous dissipation will give place to the charms of public spirit, and to the solid delights of a general and expanded philosophy: no distinctions will be known but those which are derived from a happy combination of virtue with talents. . . . The arts of civilized life will then be esteemed and cherished: Agriculture and manufactures will flourish; commerce, unrestrained by treaties and unshackled by partial provisions, will become as extensive as the wants and intercourse of nations. Philosophy, the sciences, and the liberal arts will advance in a continued and accelerated progression. Sanguinary punishments will then be forgotten and unknown. Persecution and superstition, vice, prejudice, and cruelty will take their eternal departure from the earth.

Out of free inquiry and political equality would come a euphoric new order of the ages.

In directing the attentions and exertions of the citizenry toward these various missions, great and small, the societies declared it essential that they operate, as the Philadelphia group put it, "regardless of party spirit or political connection"—statements which have helped persuade some historians that the societies were public pressure groups and not incipient political parties. In fact, the lines between the societies and the Republican interest were extremely blurry, especially in the larger seaboard cities. Intimate contacts existed between prominent Republicans—including, from Pennsylvania, Albert Gallatin and Jefferson's fellow political plotter John Beckley—and local figures with knowledge of the societies' activities (among them the president of the New York society, Gallatin's father-in-law James Nicholson). Societies would sometimes pay tribute to individual Republicans—and, on at least one occasion in Philadelphia, the entire Republican congressional delegation. Some Democratic-Republicans, like the Philadelphians Henry Kammerer and Peter Muhlenberg, had served as elected government officials even before the societies began. According to the *Aurora*, in 1795 all of Philadelphia and New York City's congressional representatives were society members, as were two Philadelphia representatives to the Pennsylvania state assembly. Beginning in 1794, members of the New York City society quietly enlisted to canvass their neighborhoods and solicit votes for Republican candidates.

Republican leaders, meanwhile, without trusting the Democratic-Republican societies enough to embrace them publicly, certainly noticed their political activities and sometimes worked with them, informally and behind the scenes. Madison, who along with Beckley always kept close tabs on local politics, was impressed by the New York and Philadelphia societies' festivities and protests, and with their sub-rosa efforts around election times. "It is said," he wrote warmly to Jefferson late in 1794, concerning a close congressional race in New York City, "that if Edwd. Livingston, as is generally believed, has outvoted Watts, . . . he is indebted for it to the invigorated exertions of the Democratic Society of that place, of which he is himself a member." The techniques of the city democrats to gain and consolidate support were particularly effective. As early as 1794, James Monroe helped initiate through his New York friends a pro-Republican town meeting in Manhattan on foreign affairs, attended chiefly by mechanics. The assembled appointed a committee that prepared resolutions (later endorsed by the city's

Democratic Society). A week later, a reconvened town meeting of "on moderate estimate 2000 citizens" approved the committee's resolutions; and a week after that, the Democratic Society sponsored a large pro-Republican, pro-French parade and celebration.

Yet if the Republicans and the societies had similar politics and common members, and if they sometimes worked hand in glove, they were not identical; nor were the societies creatures of the Republican interest. Every society member may have been a Republican, but not every Republican was a society member, or even completely happy with the societies' existence. As their actions during the Genet affair had shown, the clubs could be unruly and take positions that were politically untenable. Their status, as unelected bodies who claimed to speak directly for the people, was disquieting to some Republicans. "[T]he middling class of people about the country . . . generally reprobate Democratic Societies," a self-described plebeian and "old whig of 1775" wrote in a leading New York Republican newspaper. The Republicans would never relinquish to the societies the management of nominations and campaigns. The societies, for their part, had strong partisan interests and ties but operated as independent organizations, believing they were directly expressing the popular will through their activities—assuming a voice of their own that provoked Federalist outrage.

The administration's friends possessed their own lines of political influence to counter the Democratic-Republican clubs. The Society of the Cincinnati, the ex-army officers' group founded in 1783, was widely perceived as a political auxiliary of the Washington administration. During the storm over Citizen Genet, Federalist forces (organized in part by Alexander Hamilton) exploited their close contacts with pro-British merchants and other notables around the country in order to mount local protest meetings and circulate anti-Genet petitions. It was one thing, though, for gentlemen to band together with no official political motives or to encourage their fellow leading citizens, in an ad hoc way, to express their views on public matters. It was quite another, in the Federalists' eyes, for ordinary citizens to organize overtly political clubs, complete with their own constitutions and officers and regular private meetings. The Democratic-Republicans' repudiation of that principle struck Federalists as popular usurpation. The groups were "unlawful," the prominent Federalist Oliver Wolcott Jr. insisted, "as they are formed for the avowed purpose of a general influence and control upon the measures of government."

Reasoned, elitist constitutional objections like Wolcott's were overwhelmed by the apparent determination of other antisociety critics to prove that they were precisely the supercilious snobs the Democratic-Republican groups accused them of being. William Cobbett, the young, émigré conservative English editor, disparaged the Democratic Society of Pennsylvania as a bunch of "butchers, tinkers, broken hucksters, and trans-Atlantic traitors." One "Acquiline Nimble Chops, Democrat," contributed a mock epic poem, *Democracy*, lambasting society supporters as demagogues who had stirred up the thoughtless multitude of artisans, "the greasy caps." The city democrats reveled in such insults, happy to have provoked their enemies into showing just how hateful they really were.

Outwardly, and somewhat deceptively, the Democratic-Republicans appeared to have effaced the old distinctions between the city and country democracies. The rural societies, along with their urban counterparts, disapproved of Federalist policies, foreign and domestic, and openly criticized pro-administration congressional candidates; they proclaimed the equal rights of man (including their own right to associate); and from time to time, they praised the French Revolution. But the differences between city and country democrats, visible during the Revolution, quietly persisted. The rural societies' public statements lacked the elaborate Enlightenment defenses of mental freedom that were common in the city groups' addresses. Although formally secular, the country democrats occasionally revealed their deep religious attachments. (One Pennsylvania group, the backcountry Republican Society at the Mouth of Yough, took it upon itself "to introduce the Bible and other religious books into their schools.") The rural meetings were also much less regular than the city groups' monthly gatherings, and when they did meet, it was as often to agitate over purely local concerns—protection from Indians, opening the Mississippi to American commerce—as it was to discuss the neutrality proclamation or other national issues.

Above all, the rural societies were less prone to acknowledge (let alone extol) the soundness of the U.S. Constitution and the legitimacy of federal rule, and more prone to turn to direct resistance, including violence, to government authority. "[A] Democracy by representation is the best mode of Government, which the wisdom of man hath devised," was as far as the Democratic Society of Kentucky would go in endorsing the new federal system. "[P]atriotism, like every other thing, has its bounds," one circular from west of the Alleghenies remarked; loyalties "to government cease to be natural, when they cease to be mutual." In Pennsylvania, the Republican Society at the Mouth of Yough paid lip service to the authority of the state of Pennsylvania and the United States, but also tried to claim exclusive authority over four counties.

The differences between the seaboard cities and rural districts to the west accompanied another separate set of sectional divisions, between northern and southern democrats over slavery. The northern societies included several outspoken antislavery men, among them James Nicholson and Alexander McKim, the presidents, respectively, of the Democratic Society of the City of New York and the Republican Society of Baltimore. In a defense of the societies, Duane of the Philadelphia *Aurora* charged that President Washington had never truly been a supporter of America's revolutionary ideals, as "twenty years after the establishment of the Republic" he was still "possessed of FIVE HUNDRED of the HUMAN SPECIES IN SLAVERY." Conservative propagandists attempted, in word and in picture, to portray the societies as friendly to blacks as well as hostile to slavery, noting at one point that their French ally Genet was a member of the antislavery Société des Amis des Noirs in Paris. But antislavery views were decidedly inconspicuous among Democratic-Republican planters and farmers in Virginia and states southward. Some of the more mainstream heroes of the societies, above all Jefferson, were as vulnerable, if not more, to criticism over slavery as Washington was, and some society leaders—Alexander Smith in Virginia, John C. Breckinridge in Kentucky, among others—were strongly pro-slavery. As a consequence, Duane notwithstanding, even the northern societies refrained from saying much about slavery, preferring to focus on the common Federalist foe (which itself included slaveholders in its ranks and was hardly an antislavery force). The more consequential split within the society movement was between the seaboard and rural societies, as would become obvious by the end of 1794.

THE FEDERALIST COUNTERATTACK

The Whiskey Rebellion of 1794, centered in western Pennsylvania, came to exemplify the refractory post-Revolutionary country democracy, and it caused the Democratic-Republican societies their first major emergency. In 1791, in a vote that sharply divided eastern urban mercantile districts from the backcountry, Congress approved an excise tax on distilled liquor as part of Secretary Hamilton's fiscal program. Westerners objected on many counts: the tax was inequitable, it was aimed at rural men distant from power; and it revived a particularly obnoxious Old World means of gathering revenue. Whiskey was a barter medium as well as an item for sale in cash-poor regions; taxing it would interfere with the most mundane exchanges between ordinary farmers. As soon as the law went into effect, angry backcountry men tarred and feathered would-be federal tax collectors, and, here and there, they destroyed the houses and barns of neighbors who cooperated with the government. In August 1792, four western Pennsylvania counties organized committees of correspondence, which pledged to use every legal measure "that may *obstruct operation of the* [excise] *Law*, until we are able to obtain its total repeal."

Hamilton reasonably called the Pennsylvanians' pledge self-

contradictory, and counseled using military force to enforce collection. In September 1792, the Washington administration
issued a warning against noncompliance. After two years of a jit-
tery impasse, however, in which noncompliance became the rule
among distillers from Pennsylvania down through Kentucky,
President Washington decided to make an example of the Pennsylvanians. In the summer of 1794, a federal marshal rode west
with writs ordering sixty nontaxpaying distillers into court in
Philadelphia. In response, an armed mob, after beating back federal troops, destroyed the home of the region's federal excise
inspector and began planning to seize the federal garrison in
Pittsburgh. The Whiskey Rebellion had begun.

The eastern urban Democratic-Republicans sympathized with
the backcountry rebels' cause, but not at all with their tactics.
The New York society called upon all the other groups to petition
Congress for repeal of the excise, yet also condemned "the too
hasty and violent resistance of our brethren in the west of Pennsylvania." In Philadelphia, Bache's *Aurora* denounced both the
Washington administration's hard line and the westerners' resort
to violence. In western Pennsylvania, however, there were problematic ties between the rebels and the local societies. In Washington County, a group of dissidents founded what they called
the Society of United Freemen (better known as the Mingo
Creek Society), assumed local electioneering and judicial functions, and operated as an extralegal court of equity for its members. As the tax rebellion spread, the Mingo Creek group seemed
to be (as one local put it) "the cradle of the insurrection." And
although it appears that the group was not formally a Democratic-Republican club, at least seven members of the neighboring Democratic-Republican Society of the County of Washington
(including its president, James Marshall) later admitted to being
deeply involved in the uprising. In the furor that followed, distinctions between one club and another became irrelevant to the
forces of order.

Cooler heads persuaded the rebels to abandon their plan
against Pittsburgh, but the continuing resistance finally con-

vinced Washington to assemble an army of approximately thirteen thousand state militiamen and volunteers—a combined force roughly as large as the entire Continental Army that defeated the British in the Revolution. With a minimum of violence, the troops restored order. Among the first of the rebels apprehended was old Hermon Husband, now seventy-three and still preaching about the imminence of the New Jerusalem. Albert Gallatin, the leading opposition congressman from western Pennsylvania, called Husband a madman because of his biblical sermons on political reform. In fact, Husband took a moderate position in the whiskey excise affair, counseling the rebels to abjure violence—but he was arrested nevertheless and held in a Philadelphia jail until May 1795, when the charges against him were dropped. (His health ruined, Husband died soon after, traveling the road back to his Pennsylvania farm.) The most radical of the rebels escaped farther inland; westerners promised to obey the law; and the Washington administration turned more conciliatory. The president eventually pardoned the two rebels found guilty of treason.

The political repercussions of the rebellion were nevertheless severe, especially for the Democratic-Republican societies. Even more disturbed by the Pennsylvanians' uprising than by the Washington administration's response, the urban societies (and a few rural ones, in Vermont, New York, and North Carolina) amplified their repudiation of the insurgents. Not only had the rebels violated regular democratic principles; they had given the Federalists both the means to smear all democrats as traitors and the pretext to suppress the Democratic societies. And this was precisely what the Federalists had in mind. "[T]hey may now, I believe, be crushed," Washington's secretary of state Edmund Randolph told the president, barely containing his delight.

In late September 1794, President Washington issued his proclamation that called up the state militias and blamed the disorder on "combinations against the Constitution and laws of the United States" in western Pennsylvania. Two months later, after the Republicans scored some key electoral victories in Federalist congressional districts, Washington, at Hamilton's urging, devoted a large portion of his annual message to Congress to attacking "certain self-created societies" that had "assumed the tone of condemnation." No one doubted that he was referring to the Democratic-Republican clubs. The president's fears were sincere enough. From long experience, he had never trusted the loyalty of the backcountry yeomen. He was perfectly convinced, as he wrote privately, that the societies' agenda was "to sow among the people the seeds of jealousy and distrust of the government by destroying all confidence in the administration of it." Because all the societies, not just those in rebellion, were extra-constitutional, Washington believed, they were a clear threat to public order and republican principles. Left unchecked, they would "shake the government to its foundation."

Given Washington's enormous prestige, his condemnations were heavy blows. They did not, however, knock out the societies. Quite the opposite: Washington's blanket condemnation shifted the onus of overreaction away from the clubs and toward the administration. At least six new Democratic-Republican societies sprang up in smaller towns and rural areas, from New York to South Carolina, during the weeks after Washington's attack. Privately, even political moderates such as the Virginian Garritt Minor averred that the president's constitutional opinions were "improper, erroneous, and subversive of our liberties." Far from cowed, several of the groups blasted back at the claim that they were illegitimate because they were self-created. The class bitterness that permeated the societies exploded, as ordinary citizens faced presidential excoriation for speaking their minds and bringing pressure to bear on government—things any gentleman felt perfectly free to do. "The government is *responsible* to its sovereign the people for the faithful exercise of its entrusted powers," the president of the New York Democratic Society hotly affirmed, "and *any part of the people* have the right to express their opinions on the government." The Philadelphia and New York societies expanded their agendas after Washington's address, the former stepping up its campaign for public school funding, the latter issuing detailed circulars on civil liberties and Americans' rights to free enquiry and association. In Manhattan, pro-administration members of the Tammany Society failed to get the membership formally to endorse Washington's message, whereupon they resigned from the society en masse, leaving Tammany a full-fledged ally of the Republican opposition.

The societies also escaped official censure by the House of Representatives, after a three-day debate that illuminates the uncertain state of American democracy in the mid-1790s. Following Washington's attack, the Senate, dominated by friends of the administration, approved a report that praised the suppression of the Whiskey Rebellion and replicated Washington's formula, singling out "certain self-created societies" that had been "founded in political error." In the House, where opposition forces held a slim majority, administration men went ahead with a censure motion, describing the societies as lethal sores on the body politic. Fisher Ames, in a fiery speech, claimed the societies had "arrogantly pretended sometimes to be the people, and sometimes the guardians, the champions of the people" with "more zeal for a popular Government, and . . . more respect for Republican principles, than the real Representatives are admitted to entertain."

The Republican leadership saw where this was headed. "The game," wrote Representative James Madison (Jefferson had retired the previous year, which left Madison as the chief of the anti-administration forces), "was to connect the Democratic Societies with the odium of insurrection, to connect the Republicans in Congress with those Societies," and to place President Washington "in opposition to both." Wary of attacking Washington directly or endorsing the societies, the House opposition objected to the censure motion on the narrow grounds that there was insufficient evidence linking the societies to the Pennsylvania outrages, and that any such evidence should be assessed by the courts, not by Congress. One Republican congressman, Gabriel Christie of Maryland, did praise the Republican Society of Baltimore by name, as "a band of patriots, not the fair-weather patriots of the present day, but the patriots of seventy five," who, when apprised of the Whiskey Rebellion, "offered their personal services to go and help to crush this commotion in the bud." Madison and a few others also raised serious questions about Washington's denunciation of the societies. Too energetic an effort to correct abuses of the rights of popular expression, Madison told the House, would threaten liberty and freedom of speech and of the press. The beleaguered societies, he insisted, presented no threat—but a congressional censure *would* present such a threat. "It is in vain to say that this indiscriminate censure is no punishment . . . ," Madison declared. "If we advert to the nature of Republican Government, we shall find that the censorial power is in the people over the Government, and not in the Government over the people." Infractions of law by ordinary citizens were punishable through the courts, but "not censurable through the Legislative body."

Madison did little to clarify, let alone defend, the role of extra-constitutional associations as part of the regular business of American politics. As of 1794, the Republican interest remained hazy about the proper mechanisms for democratic politics. But Madison and the Republicans succeeded in removing any mention of the societies from the House's condemnation of the Whiskey Rebellion. Their success emboldened society members and supporters to assert more boldly the groups' legitimacy. "After having set up a government, citizens ought not to resign it into the hands of agents—" the pro-society *Independent Chronicle* of Boston had observed months earlier, "whither does this tend but toward despotism?" In a Paineite vein, the German Republican Society of Philadelphia declared that "associations of some sort are necessary . . . to keep up the equipoise, between the people and the government." Thus encouraged, the remaining societies took up, in 1795, their last great effort: fighting against the Jay Treaty.

As soon as President Washington had announced his appointment in April 1794 of John Jay, chief justice of the Supreme Court, as special envoy to Great Britain—to settle disputes left over from the Revolution, exacerbated by recent British interference with American shipping to France and the French West Indies—the Democratic-Republican clubs protested. Not only (the societies argued) did the appointment of a judicial officer to an executive post violate the constitutional theory of separated powers—Jay himself was so flagrantly pro-British and anti-French, the Pennsylvania Democratic Society charged, that it would be "a sacrifice of the interests and the peace of the United States to commit a negociation to him." These criticisms would seem gentle fourteen months later, when the secret terms of the treaty—signed the previous November and taken up by the Senate, meeting in closed session, in early June 1795—leaked out to the opposition press.

The Democratic-Republicans insisted that the treaty was both pro-British and antidemocratic. That the Senate decided to debate the treaty in secrecy was bad enough. Worse, the treaty's terms amounted to virtually complete capitulation. Jay had failed to secure various items he had been instructed to obtain, including full confirmation of America's neutral shipping rights, the end of the impressments of American sailors into the Royal Navy, and compensation for American slaveholders for slaves seized by the British during the war. Only on the issue of British evacuation of its military posts in the western United States did Jay deliver. The treaty's supporters, above all Alexander Hamilton and his ally Rufus King of Massachusetts, defended the pact as a reaffirmation of American sovereignty that strengthened the nation's commercial relations with its most important trading partner. On the basis of those arguments, the Senate approved the treaty by a 20 to 10 margin, and in mid-August 1795, President Washington signed it. But at every step along the way, public disapproval, stoked by Republican sympathizers, mounted. There were calls to impeach Jay, whose effigy, along with copies of the hated treaty, was burned in several towns and cities. In New York, according to Hamilton, "the leaders of the clubs were seen haranging in every corner of the city, to stir up the citizens." When Hamilton and his friends tried to take over a huge antitreaty public meeting, and Hamilton declared that the people had full confidence in the wisdom of the president, opposition- ists drove them away with coarse catcalls. (Allegedly, one angry Republican threw a rock that hit Hamilton in the head; in the heated arguments that followed, Hamilton challenged Demo- cratic Society leader James Nicholson to a duel, later averted.) Some critics even demanded Washington's removal from office.

The Democratic-Republican societies pitched in with their own protests, but in a telling sectional pattern. In the northern seaport cities, the treaty's paltry concessions on neutral trading rights, along with the methods by which it was debated and approved, was cause for the utmost alarm—and for praising the resistant congressional Republicans. The southern societies, urban and rural, objected even more loudly, with the additional complaint (absent up North) that, in the words of one South Car- olina society, Britain's refusal to compensate "the value of the Negroes and other property carried away" was reason enough to scuttle the agreement.

In sharp contrast, the northern rural and backcountry groups said almost nothing. Many, perhaps most, of these groups, partic- ularly in western Pennsylvania, had fallen by the wayside after the Whiskey Rebellion. But for those that survived, from Ver- mont through rural New York State, the eventual recovery of the western posts, the granting of commercial concessions to Ameri- cans trading with Lower and Upper Canada, and the fear of war should the treaty be rejected greatly softened any hostility. In all, the country democracy split over the Jay Treaty, as the southern- ers (galvanized by the slavery issue) joined forces with the city democracy in opposition, while northern country democrats backed off.

Washington's signing of the Jay Treaty would have appeared to settle the issue, but the Republican interest, its numbers enlarged in the newly elected Fourth Congress, made a last-ditch effort to block the appropriations necessary to implement it. A minor constitutional crisis arose when President Washington dragged his feet in sending the official treaty papers to the

House. Pro-treaty forces then organized their own petition campaign, which drowned out the opposition efforts. Finally, the House vote on treaty appropriations ended in a 49–49 tie that would have to be decided by the Speaker of the House, Frederick Muhlenberg. Ordinarily, Muhlenberg, a convert to the opposition and brother of Peter Muhlenberg, who had helped found the very first Democratic-Republican society, could have been counted on to kill the appropriations. But pro-treaty men exerted enormous pressure on him, including (according to family tradition) a threat from his son's prospective father-in-law, a stalwart Federalist, that "[i]f you do not give us your vote, your son shall not have my Polly." Muhlenberg hesitated, then voted in favor of the appropriations, handing the Washington administration a crucial victory.

Once again, the combined efforts of the executive and the Senate had thwarted the congressional opposition and the Democratic-Republican societies. The first target of the opposition's frustration was Frederick Muhlenberg. Five days after casting his tie-breaking vote, Muhlenberg was accosted by his own brother-in-law, Bernard Schaefer, an all-too-rabid Republican, who called him a rank deserter and stabbed him. Poor Muhlenberg more or less recovered physically, but he was dead politically, failing to stand in 1796 for his House seat. Yet by the time he left the Congress, the greatest victim of the debates over the Jay Treaty was neither himself nor any of the congressional Republicans, but the Democratic-Republican societies.

THE FALL AND LEGACY OF THE SELF-CREATED SOCIETIES

Five months after President Washington signed the Jay Treaty, a conservative Connecticut newspaper mordantly rejoiced that the Pennsylvania Democratic Society had dissolved: "the various germs which have sprouted from that root of anarchy, will wither and die." The prediction was generally true. The Democratic

Society of New York lasted for another three years, while reports of sporadic activities by other local groups (including the formation of new ones) appeared as late as 1800. But the losing fight against the Jay Treaty was the last gasp of the Democratic-Republican societies as a force in American politics. Eight months after the Philadelphia group disbanded, the semiofficial administration newspaper, the *Gazette of the United States*, happily noted that "the Demo societies are dead," and the opposition and the surviving societies did not attempt to deny it.

There had been a great deal of determined activity, but in strictly political terms, the groups had failed. All of their major protest campaigns had been fruitless. Neither they nor their congressional friends could make much of a dent against an energetic executive—the great Revolutionary War hero—backed by a strong majority in the Senate. Sectional strains among the self-declared democrats, particularly those between the seaboard societies and the rural societies, showed with costly results during the Whiskey Rebellion and the fight over the Jay Treaty. Although the societies did escape congressional censure, the Republicans' arguments on their behalf still fell short of vindicating their right to exist.

Yet conventional standards are seldom the best for judging the effects of fledgling political movements. By reviving and updating the country and the city democracies in the idiom of post-Revolutionary politics, the Democratic-Republican societies had expanded the debates about politics and democracy in America. They had challenged assumptions about deference to political leadership that prevailed among many Republican leaders as well as among the Federalists. The intellectual and emotional core of the societies' case was wonderfully presented early in 1794 by an Irish-born Vermont editor, Matthew Lyon, an army veteran who would go on to a legendary career as an irrepressible Republican politician and manufacturing entrepreneur:

> These . . . Democratic societies . . . are laughed at and
> ridiculed by men who consider the science of govern-

ment to belong naturally only to a few families, and argue, that their families ought to be obeyed & supported in princely grandure; that the common people ought to give half their earnings to these few, for keeping them under, and awing the poor commonality from destroying one another, which their savage nature would lead to, were it not for the benignity and good sense of the few superiors Heaven has been pleased to plant among them.

A privileged few had taken it upon themselves to serve as the nation's leaders; these men used their privileges to sustain themselves in grandeur at the expense of "the poor commonality"; and they subdued the rest of the people with pretension, ridicule, and false noblesse as well as with political force. By puncturing that pretension and defying the ridicule and noblesse, the societies showed that the science of government fell well within the comprehension of ordinary citizens. And they called the only proper republican system, one which respected and unleashed that comprehension, "democracy." A New York City society member wrote that "the words Republican and Democratic are synonymous." A Massachusetts writer proclaimed that "he that is not a Democrat is an aristocrat or a monocrat."

To conservative and even moderate upholders of Washington and Hamilton, such claims sounded heretical or even traitorous, as if some of the people had forgotten their proper passive and obedient place between elections. In New York, the pro-administration members of the Tammany Society, before their walkout, hastily passed a resolution in January 1795 insisting that public political associations, though "excellent as revolutionary means, when a government is to be overthrown," created "phrenzy" that had no place in the free and happy United States. To Hamilton's friend Nathaniel Chipman, the societies and their "dictators" threatened political order and responsible representation with "all precipitation, all the heat and ungovernable passions of a simple democracy."

The Republican interest understood the societies' motivations far better than the administration did, and considered President Washington's cold attempt to crush them as, in Madison's words, "perhaps the greatest error of his political life." Still, by mid-decade, opposition leaders were unsure what role, if any, the rude democracy might play in their own political efforts and in the life of the nation. The Democratic-Republican societies left behind a changed political landscape, but their brief history had failed to resolve some crucial questions. How could a popular majority redress its grievances under the prevailing theories of separated and divided powers and of federal checks and balances? Was a majority in the House of Representatives sufficient to carry that electoral majority's wishes, or might new institutions be necessary? The Democratic-Republicans' solution to the last problem—forming political organizations outside the government—had come to naught. And in 1796—the year of the nation's first contested presidential election—American democracy, city and country, seemed more than ever on the defensive, whereas Federalist-style deference seemed regnant and vindicated.

Those circumstances would change utterly over the next four years, as the political crisis of the fragile new order worsened, nearly to the verge of civil war. They changed chiefly because too many Federalists learned too little about what a growing number of citizens now believed were their essential democratic prerogatives. But they also changed because opposition organizers—mainly in the middle Atlantic states, and in service to the Republican slaveholders of Virginia—learned some lessons from the "self-created" democracy and joined forces with what was left of it. Thus expanded, the Republican opposition would fight to validate the proposition framed by James Madison during the House debate over the societies—that in a republic, "the censorial power is in the people over the Government, and not in the Government over the people."

3

THE MAKING OF
JEFFERSONIAN
DEMOCRACY

On the last day of 1793, as the Democratic-Republican societies were trying to recover from their entanglement with Citizen Genet, Secretary of State Thomas Jefferson resigned his post, retired from politics, and returned to his epicurean estate-in-eternal progress, Monticello. Sick of the polemical fray (which he had never enjoyed), Jefferson retreated to his books, gadgets, French wines, and slaves, expecting to clear up some heavy financial debts, shake a nagging case of rheumatism, and finish his house, all in splendid ignorance—"the softest pillow" he called it, quoting Montaigne—of politics. At age fifty, a widower for eleven years, Jefferson had spent most of his adult life at the center of great public events, and he had already earned historical immortality as the author of America's Declaration of Independence. Now hopeful that the citizenry would confound the political heresies of Alexander Hamilton, he handed the reins of opposition over to James Madison and Madison's congressional allies, and slipped away to his and Madison's native rural Virginia—relieved, he said, that "the length of my tether is now fixed for life from Monticello to Richmond."

After an uneventful winter, perturbing news and irritating Federalist criticism began to reach him through the mails and the Virginia newspapers. In April, word arrived of John Jay's impending mission to Britain—an announcement made only slightly less offensive to Jefferson by reports of Hamilton's mortification at not getting the assignment. Over the late summer and autumn, Jefferson came to share Madison's view that Hamilton was shamefully seizing on the Whiskey Rebellion to advance his personal political fortunes and disgrace the Republican interest. President Washington's denunciation of the Democratic-Republican societies was, he wrote to Madison, "one of the extraordinary acts of boldness of which we have seen so many from the faction of Monocrats." At Hamilton's instigation, the Revolution's greatest man had "permitted himself to be the organ of . . . an attack on the freedom of discussion, the freedom of writing, printing, and publishing."

In 1795, when the controversy over the Jay Treaty escalated, Jefferson, although avowedly still on the sidelines, could not help weighing in with old friends. He approved of the popular protests against the treaty, including a public meeting in his own Piedmont county of Albemarle. After those protests failed, he wrote an indignant letter to his Florentine associate from Revolutionary days, Philip Mazzei, which would eventually come back to haunt him. An "Anglican, monarchical, and aristocratical party," he told Mazzei, had seized the federal government, along with certain unnamed apostates, "men who were Samsons in the field and Solomons in the council, but who have had their heads shorn by the harlot England"—a slanderous reference, Jefferson's enemies would later charge, to the incorruptible Washington.

At the close of the summer of 1796, Washington publicly confirmed what had long been suspected: he would not seek another term. He thus turned the upcoming election into the first contested race for the presidency. Opposition leaders, consulting loosely as a congressional caucus of the Republican interest, decided that Jefferson would be their strongest candidate against the president's heir presumptive, Vice President John Adams.

The remnants of the Democratic-Republican societies decided the same thing. "It requires no talent at divination to decide who will be candidates for the chair," the Philadelphia *Aurora General Advertiser* declared in mid-September, a week before Washington's announcement:

> THOMAS JEFFERSON & JOHN ADAMS will be the men, & whether we shall have at the head of our executive a steadfast friend to the Rights of the People, or an advocate for hereditary power and distinctions, the people of the United States are soon to decide.

Jefferson, gripped by a mixture of restiveness and fatalism, acquiesced in his own candidacy, and came within three Electoral College votes of defeating Adams after a bruising campaign. And so, under the existing constitutional rules, Jefferson was named the nation's new vice president. In February 1797, he departed Monticello to take up his duties in Philadelphia, leaving his debts unresolved and the new walls to his house unbuilt.

The elections of 1796 sent a confusing message. Despite Washington's anointing of Adams, the Republican interest ran strong in the South, controlling Virginia, the largest and most powerful state, and winning a large majority in the Georgia legislature. Republican tickets also carried Philadelphia (previously a Federalist stronghold) and ran better than expected in New York City. Pennsylvania broke narrowly for Jefferson, and had Adams not picked up two isolated electoral votes in Virginia and North Carolina, he would have lost the election.

The Pennsylvania race was especially important for the Republicans, who merged their election machinery with what was left of the most imposing of the failed Democratic-Republican societies, and turned the politics of protest over the Jay Treaty into a presidential campaign. With the resourceful Republican operative, House clerk John Beckley, overseeing matters, veterans of the Democratic Society of Pennsylvania—most auspiciously Benjamin Bache, Michael Leib (who had been elected to the state assembly in 1794), and a Philadelphia hatter and friend of Beckley's, Major John Smith—geared up a sophisticated statewide campaign. Handbills with the names of the Republican electors appeared in every district. A campaign staff produced fifty thousand Republican ballots (written out by hand, as the election laws demanded) and delivered them to local partisans a week before the election. Major Smith and others crisscrossed the state, holding public meetings and arousing the voters wherever they found them gathered. Torrents of campaign broadsides poured from the presses of Philadelphia, many of them appealing directly to the artisans and small tradesmen who had been the Democratic Society's membership base, urging them to decide "whether the Republican JEFFERSON, or the Royalist ADAMS, shall be President of the United States." The statewide results were more than encouraging: a 25 percent turnout of eligible voters and a narrow Republican majority, strong enough to give Jefferson fourteen of Pennsylvania's fifteen electoral votes. But the results in Philadelphia, where the former society leaders had concentrated their efforts, were staggering: more than two in five eligible Philadelphians showed up at the polls and handed the Republican slate more than 60 percent of the vote—a landslide in what been a solidly Federalist city.

The top-down opposition politics of the Jeffersonians had linked up with the bottom-up politics of the Democratic-Republican societies. The Republicans remained very much in charge, with the humbly born, hard-nosed Beckley serving as their overseer and go-between. Still, Beckley, Leib, Bache, Smith, and their friends—political professionals of indifferent backgrounds—brought a more democratic style and substance into what was fast becoming an enlarged Republican coalition that stretched into the middle Atlantic states. (Similar efforts in New York City raised hopes that it too might soon move to the Republican column.) The Federalists, meanwhile, had new problems to contend with. Accusations about a plot supposedly hatched by Alexander Hamilton to maneuver Thomas Pinckney of South Carolina into the presidency instead of John Adams—

high-level intrigue of a more customary sort—dominated the last-minute electoral jockeying and further clouded the results. Nationwide, though, the Federalists were the winners, retaining the presidency and gaining what in time became a solid majority in the House of Representatives to go along with their majority in the Senate. They also won substantial legislative majorities in New York and Massachusetts.

Early in 1797, some observers interpreted the closeness of the presidential election as a portent of an amiable Adams administration, reinforced by what the incoming president called his "ancient friendship" with Jefferson. Hamilton was, for the moment, out of the picture—he had retired to his New York City law practice in 1795. Jefferson, who saw Adams as the only sure barrier against Hamilton among the Federalists, was relieved at the outcome, and graciously professed that neither his second-place finish nor the prospect of serving under Adams had injured his pride. ("I am his junior in life," he told Madison, "was his junior in Congress, his junior in the diplomatic line, his junior lately in our civil government.") The vice presidency might even be preferable given the conflicts that surely lay ahead. "This is certainly not a moment to covet the helm," Jefferson wrote Edward Rutledge late in December. Jefferson did have pestering doubts about what he thought of as Adams's English bias in government, made worse when Adams decided to retain every member of Washington's cabinet, including Treasury Secretary Oliver Wolcott Jr., Secretary of State Timothy Pickering, and Secretary of War James McHenry—all close political friends and followers of Hamilton's. Nevertheless Jefferson remained confident that the great mass of the citizenry was Republican, and hopeful that Adams could be persuaded to oversee the government "on it's true principles."

All the upbeat auguries proved utterly wrong. The nation was entering a new and more dangerous phase of its political crisis; 1796 would prove the Federalists' last great political hurrah; and consolidated forms of democratic protest and politics would emerge under Jefferson's and Madison's leadership. The breakdown of comity, and the Republicans' eventual success, was in large measure due to Hamilton's headstrong persistence, Adams's sometimes muddled patriotic stubbornness, and Jefferson's great good fortune. More broadly, it was caused by the Federalists' incapacity to square their politics with the democratic ideas unleashed in the 1790s.

JOHN ADAMS AND THE REIGN OF WITCHES

The striver John Adams was as unlikely an aristocrat as any leading official in the early federal executive branch, despite what his opponents charged. Raised twelve miles south of Boston, the son of a pious middling farmer who made shoes part-time, Adams had hoped to become a farmer himself. His father, however, wanted him to become a minister, paid for the proper preparatory schooling, and sent him to Harvard. There, Adams became a tireless bookworm, but his interests ran to the law, not religion, and three years after graduating from college, he was admitted to the Suffolk County bar. A patriot from the very beginning of the imperial crisis, he was selected as one of Massachusetts's delegates to the First Continental Congress in 1774. Thereafter, he served his state and his country with impressive diligence in a variety of important civilian posts at home and abroad (including, from 1785 to 1788, a stint as the first American minister to Great Britain).

Garrulous, pudgy, short, and prone to anxious, self-absorbed outbursts, Adams climbed to the top chiefly because he exercised his lawyerly skills with undivided assiduity and ambition. He admitted that he was "but an ordinary man" and "not like the Lion." Yet Adams, apart from fulfilling his public duties, also wrote several formal treatises on political theory, which (although inferior to Madison's writings in originality, Jefferson's in style, and Hamilton's in both) amounted to the only extended effort by any Founding Father to formulate a comprehensive science of politics.

Adams's political philosophy is difficult to pin down. For the most part, he stated conventional republican themes in conventional terms—the need to control passion through selfless virtue, for example, and to keep political power from becoming concentrated in any individual or in any branch of the government. Like Madison and other Framers, he did not flinch at what he saw as society's natural hierarchies and at the special influence exercised by what he called America's aristocracy—an aristocracy, he duly noted, founded not simply on birth and marriage, but on education, wealth, and merit as well (and that therefore included him). With his rage for political equilibrium, however, Adams never quite grasped that under the Constitution, a new theory of popular sovereignty had replaced the traditional ideal of balancing the different social orders. After 1788, Madison, who understood the new regime perfectly, could see that the few instead of the many had become the chief threat to the American republican experiment. Adams moved in the opposite direction, pronouncing in his ponderous *Discourses on Davila* in 1790 that the genius of America lay in its mixed government, which checked *"the legislation of confusion"* by upholding decency, honesty, and order against an unstable democracy. After American independence, Adams's social views took a sharper elitist turn, away from the idea that merit was randomly distributed among all classes and toward his claim, in 1787, that "gentlemen will ordinarily, nothwithstanding some exceptions to the rule, be the richer, and born of the more noted families." Yet his affection for aristocracy did not, finally, define his political allegiances. While his conservative fears, heightened by the French Revolution, made him a stalwart Federalist in the early 1790s, his fixation on balanced government and his hatred of partisanship alienated him from other Federalists after he assumed the presidency.

President Adams's difficulties began less than a month after he took office, when he learned that France's latest revolutionary government, the Directory, had refused to receive the newly appointed American minister to Paris, Charles Cotesworth Pinckney, and had declared that henceforth all American ships carrying British goods would be liable to seizure. Enraged by the Jay Treaty, the French had been attacking American merchant-men on the high seas for months. Now the two nations seemed on the brink of war, which Adams wanted to avoid. Hoping to rise above domestic political divisions and show his good faith to the French, the president tried to name his trustworthy friend from Massachusetts, the Republican Elbridge Gerry, along with James Madison, as special commissioners, charged with joining Pinck-ney in Paris and resolving the crisis. But cabinet members Wol-cott, Pickering, and McHenry insisted that only loyal Federalists be allowed to represent the United States, and forced Adams to back down. After one of the substitute Federalist nominees, Francis Dana, declined to serve for personal reasons, Gerry was eventually reinstated to the commission, joined by the moderate Virginia Federalist John Marshall. By then, however, the political haggling had created considerable bad feeling, ending the rap-prochement between Adams and Jefferson (who believed he had been frozen out of the decision-making process despite his con-tacts in France, and truly feared an impending war) and embold-ening Hamilton's friends.

Once the American commissioners arrived in Paris, the French government, marinated in corruption and flushed by the recent military successes of its young general, Napoleon Bona-parte, unintentionally gave Adams and the Federalists a huge political gift. After granting the three envoys a pro forma fifteen-minute audience, the French foreign minister, Talleyrand, handed them over to some French agents, who, during the ensu-ing days, demanded under-the-table bribes and an official Amer-ican subsidy to France as preconditions for any further talks. The negotiations got nowhere (although the Republican Gerry lin-gered in Paris, trying to string them along, to the great displeasure of his Federalist colleagues). Finally, in the spring of 1798, Adams released to Congress the diplomatic dispatches describ-ing what had occurred, referring to the would-be bribers as "X," "Y," and "Z." War fever, combined with Federalist righteousness, quickly overwhelmed all but the most staunchly Republican parts of the country. The people, it seemed, were far more friendly to Federalist rule than the old Democratic-Republican clubs had imagined, at least when the nation's honor was at stake. The diminutive, anxious Adams suddenly became, for the only time in his life, the focus of popular enthusiasm as the heroic American commander-in-chief.

Temporarily catching the delirium himself, Adams took to delivering militant speeches, and appeared in public in military regalia, a sword strapped to his side. He also gained authorization from Congress to build up the navy, establish a new cabinet-level department of the navy, and enlarge the regular army with the addition of what came to be called the Provisional Army. Adams stopped just short of asking for a formal declaration of war against France, but a "quasi-war" ensued on the high seas. Congressional Federalists, meanwhile, were eager to give the president even more than he had requested and passed four additional measures to help create what Hamilton, in a letter to Rufus King, called *"national unanimity"*—that is, to crush domestic political dissent that they believed was out to destroy the government. Long concerned about the growing numbers of immigrants to America since the Revolution—the vast majority of whom supported the Republicans—the Federalists narrowly pushed through Congress three anti-alien bills that toughened naturalization requirements, established a registry and surveillance system for foreign nationals, and empowered the president to deport summarily any alien he deemed a threat to the nation's security. Even more ominously for the Republicans, Congress passed a loosely worded sedition bill that outlawed a wide range of statements, written and unwritten, including any that could be construed as bringing either the president or the Congress (but, pointedly, not the vice president) "into contempt or disrepute"— and made them punishable by up to five years' imprisonment and five thousand dollars in fines.

Some Republican leaders, including James Monroe, thought the Federalist onslaught was suicidal, and they counseled their colleagues to lie low. Vice President Jefferson also tried to keep his friends and allies calm. "[A] little patience," he wrote to John Taylor, "and we shall see the reign of witches pass over, their spells dissolve, and the people recovering their true sight, restore their government to it's true *principles*." Jefferson was less sanguine than he sounded. He had become a pariah inside the administration, having suffered through the publication the previous year of what he thought was the private letter of 1796 to Philip Mazzei about the former Samsons and Solomons who were now monarchists. He had no doubts that the Federalists' new laws shredded the Constitution and the Bill of Rights, and that their purpose was the "suppression of the whig presses." With the Federalists firmly in control of all three branches of the federal government, and with a vastly enlarged army soon to be placed at the federal government's disposal, the possibility loomed that they could wipe out the opposition with prison terms and bayonets before the next presidential election, which still lay two years ahead. Jefferson did propose one democratic remedy, the popular election of federal juries, to restrain the Federalist juggernaut, but the proposal got nowhere. Thereafter, he and his lieutenants turned to the alternative line of defense that Taylor had discussed years earlier and had arisen at earlier moments of crisis—interposing the state governments against oppressive federal laws.

Proposing that the states could help negate the alien and sedition acts was a desperate move, undertaken during what the Republican leaders and rank and file reasonably considered a political emergency. (Even as Jefferson and Madison were writing what would become known as the Kentucky and Virginia Resolutions, local Republican newspapers and meetings were calling for Congress to repeal the new laws.) It was also, at least in Jefferson's unrevised formulations, a constitutionally dangerous step that proved politically ineffective. Jefferson secretly drafted an initial set of resolutions at Monticello sometime in the late summer or early autumn of 1798, with the idea that some friendly state legislature would adopt them as its own. In October, at the suggestion of his Virginia ally and confidante, Wilson Cary

Nicholas, he agreed to allow John Breckinridge—a former resident of Albemarle County and, more recently, president of the Lexington branch of the Kentucky Democratic Society—to arrange for the Kentucky legislature to act on the resolutions, while pledging silence about the vice president's role in the matter. On November 13, the Kentucky legislators, with little discussion and in almost unanimous votes, passed the resolutions as Breckinridge presented them, with Jefferson's most controversial claims about state rights removed, and three days later, Governor James Garrard gave his approval. One month later, after a lengthy debate, the Virginia legislature passed a milder set of resolutions that Madison had drafted. Jefferson, with the help of John Taylor, tried to revise Madison's moderate statement, but the legislature rejected his new language and approved Madison's original.

The resolutions argued that the alien and sedition acts exceeded the federal government's delegated authorities, revisiting the ground laid out by Jefferson and Madison seven years earlier during the debate over Hamilton's bank. The resolutions also returned to past precedents in which state legislatures had questioned the constitutionality of federal laws, notably an official challenge by Pennsylvania's lawmakers to the excise law in 1791 and Virginia's resolutions against Hamilton's assumption policies and the Jay Treaty. What was new—and, particularly in Jefferson's presentations, unsafe—concerned the state legislatures' powers to decide for themselves when specific federal laws were usurpations of authority. Since the Supreme Court's power of judicial review had not yet been firmly established, there was certainly room for argument about how the sovereign people could challenge the constitutionality of federal laws, and by what procedures. But Jefferson's belief, stated in his draft of the Kentucky Resolutions, that "nullification" was the rightful remedy for unconstitutional laws, and that the members of an individual state legislature could unilaterally declare such laws "void, and of no effect" within its borders, undercut the Constitution and would have neutered the federal government. Jefferson's own thinking on the matter fluctuated. But his draft resolutions had alarming implications, especially in their ambiguity about whether the Constitution was a compact of the several state governments or, in line with the Framers' thinking, a national compact formed outside the state governments.

The final texts of both the Kentucky and Virginia Resolutions avoided these pitfalls, thanks to Breckinridge's and Madison's interventions. Yet even the more temperate versions failed to gain support from the other state legislatures. Several states followed Maryland's House of Delegates in rejecting the idea that any state government could, by legislative action, even claim that a federal law was unconstitutional, and suggested that any effort to do so was treasonous. A few northern states, including Massachusetts, denied the powers claimed by Kentucky and Virginia and insisted that the Sedition Law was perfectly constitutional, as it banned not truth but "licentiousness, in speaking and writing, that is only employed in propagating falsehood and slander." Ten state legislatures with heavy Federalist majorities from around the country censured Kentucky and Virginia for usurping powers that supposedly belonged to the federal judiciary. Northern Republicans supported the resolutions' objections to the alien and sedition acts, but opposed the idea of state review of federal laws. Southern Republicans outside Virginia and Kentucky were eloquently silent about the matter, and no southern legislature heeded the call to battle.

A more potent counterattack came from city and country democratic editors once the Federalists, fiercely but also clumsily, began putting the Sedition Law into effect. Jefferson had correctly predicted that Bache's *Aurora* would be one of the Federalists' primary targets. Bache was indicted for seditious libel under the common law, weeks before the Sedition Law indictments began, but died in early September 1798, a victim of the latest outbreak of yellow fever in Philadelphia. Other prominent figures formerly tied to the Democratic-Republicans—including Thomas Adams, the editor of Boston's *Independent Chronicle*, and the spirited Matthew Lyon of Vermont (who, as a newly elected congressman, had enhanced his notoriety in the House by spitting in the face of a Federalist colleague who insulted him)—were also rounded up. Philip Freneau escaped indictment only because he was temporarily out of an editorship, but the Irish-born John Daly Burk, one of his successors as editor of the New York *Time-Piece* (which Freneau had founded after the *National Gazette* folded), was tried on a common-law indictment. Also on the prosecutors' lists were Freneau's close collaborator, David Frothingham of the *New York Argus*, and Lyon's loudest defender, Anthony Haswell of the *Vermont Gazette* in Bennington. Other victims included James Callender and Thomas Cooper, a pair of radical British émigrés who had become prominent in America after 1796. But the main objects of attack were well-known city and country democrats who, since mid-decade, had been outspoken Republican supporters and, in some cases, strategists and organizers.

By displaying an undeferential defiance instead of panic, the editors registered more effective protests against the new laws than did Jefferson and Madison's controversial resolutions. William Duane, Bache's successor at the *Aurora*, practically begged to be arrested in 1799, when he tried to circulate petitions calling for the repeal of the Alien Friends Law and flatly charged in the *Aurora* that the American government had become the corrupt creature of Great Britain. (Born in upstate New York in 1760, Duane had lived most of his life in Ireland until returning to America in 1796; yet while he considered himself no alien at all, he opposed the law on constitutional grounds.) Duly indicted under the very law he had protested, and freed on bail, Duane published his newspaper while his trial dragged on. Suddenly, as his editor's luck would have it, he surreptitiously obtained an advance copy of a bill, proposed by a Pennsylvania Federalist senator, James Ross, that would have replaced the Electoral College in the next presidential election with a thirteen-member committee, consisting of the chief justice of the Supreme Court, Federalist Oliver Ellsworth, plus six members from each (Federalist-dominated) house of Congress. Duane allowed the bill's unauthorized publication in the *Aurora*, thereby publicizing a Federalist plot to steal the election, and brought down the wrath of the Senate, which had him indicted under the Sedition Law. At this point, Duane decided that discretion was the better part of valor and went into hiding until Congress adjourned. He had more than made his point about the vengefulness and high-handed chicanery of his Federalist foes.

Elsewhere, as well, the Federalist repression backfired. In upstate Otsego County, New York, Jedediah Peck, a surveyor, farmer, and Baptist minister, had begun his political life as a loyal member of William Cooper's locally dominant Federalist connection, but set himself apart, oddly, as a populist, antilawyer (and antislavery) country democrat. Elected as a Federalist to the state legislature in 1798, Peck's objections to the Sedition Law led to a final break with his party and, in 1799, earned him an indictment for circulating supposedly seditious petitions. Yet instead of public censure, Peck gained instant celebrity as a political hero, thronged by supporters as he traveled down the Hudson Valley to his trial in Manhattan. Across the border in Vermont, Matthew Lyon, the first man indicted and convicted under the Sedition Law, had already made a mockery of his accusers, blasting the law and its makers from his jail cell and winning reelection to Congress by a healthy margin in 1798. Friends paid off Lyon's one-thousand-dollar fine, and he too enjoyed an elaborate victory procession, all the way from the jail in Vergennes near Lake Champlain to the House of Representatives in Philadelphia.

There were additional embarrassments for the Federalists, none more comical than the prosecution of one Luther Baldwin, a Newark, New Jersey, toper who was sent to federal prison for having told a tavern-keeper that he would not care if President Adams were to get shot "thro' his arse." In Dedham, Massachusetts, the trial of David Brown, occasioned by the raising of a Republican liberty pole, suggested that even in strongly pro-Federalist New England, there was growing restiveness at the Federalists' regime. The Federalists, while throwing a scare into the Virginia Republican gentry, had aroused the anger and the resourcefulness of the Republicans' potential political base, from

New England down through Virginia—and in doing so, helped redirect the public's fury away from France and toward the Adams administration.

In 1799 and 1800, that fury, later celebrated by Jeffersonian loyalists as "the Spirit of '98," would help crack open the fissures among the Federalists that the war frenzy had hidden. It would also contribute greatly to the national political might of the resurgent Republican opposition. Yet it would be shortsighted to interpret these events as marking the inexorable rise of a new Jeffersonian democracy. There was nothing inexorable about the political tendencies of these years, as the strange presidential election of 1800 would prove. And, despite the Republicans' growing unity of purpose, there were important hidden fissures inside their ranks as well, closely connected to issues born of democracy, race, and slavery. All but invisible in national debates, these divisions had cropped up in state constitutional struggles of the 1790s.

Over the dozen years after the Federal Constitutional Convention in Philadelphia, several states either passed legislation or made adjustments to their own constitutions on important matters ranging from emancipation to voting. In New York, antislavery efforts, led by the Republicans Erastus Root and Aaron Burr as well as by the Federalist John Jay, finally won a state gradual emancipation law in 1799 that would see the institution's end in the late 1820s. (New Jersey was more recalcitrant, and would not enact its own gradual abolition law until 1804.) Regarding suffrage, representation, and related matters, the most dramatic change came in Pennsylvania with the fall, in 1790, of the democratic constitution of 1776. Elsewhere, especially in the North, the trend was toward more incremental changes that expanded popular control of government, at both the state and the local level. In 1788, for example, New York finally authorized the use of written ballots for the election of most state officials, and made polling places more accessible by establishing the township as the basis for elections. New Jersey enacted similar reforms in the same year.

In some states, notably Pennsylvania and New York, groups perceived as among the more democratic forces in state matters also were allied with the Republican opposition—battling, as one rural democrat argued, the "prevalent idea, that representation is a representation of property and not of the people:—an idea the legitimate offspring of feudal despotism." But the link between Republicanism and democratic reform was far cloudier in the slaveholding states. In heavily Federalist South Carolina, for example, Republican reformers gained a widened suffrage and moved the capital from Charleston to Columbia to make it more accessible to backcountry representatives—but the legislature also sharply increased property requirements for state officeholders. In Maryland, Federalists and Jeffersonians allied and successfully resisted calls for suffrage reform—while the reformers, also including Federalists and Jeffersonians, began picking up ground only when they explicitly restricted the franchise to white men. In Kentucky, rival factions of Jeffersonians—one concentrated in the yeoman-dominated Green River district, the other a so-called Aristocratic planter faction—battled hard over democratic reforms. The more conservative forces prevailed in part out of fear that the reformers aimed to undermine slavery. (Among the more eloquent of the reformers was an idealistic, twenty-year-old Lexington lawyer, freshly arrived from Virginia, named Henry Clay, who, writing under the pseudonym "Scaevola," proposed a new state constitution that provided for gradual emancipation.)

The outcome of the state reform politics of the 1790s contained important hints and portents about the emerging Republican opposition, especially concerning democracy, slavery, and the links between the two. The resulting tensions—between northern and southern Republicans, as well as among southern Republicans—would persist and affect the course of democratic development for decades. They would have a more immediate impact in 1800 when a group of bondsmen living in and around Richmond, Virginia, heard antislavery messages in the gentry Republicans' and city democrats' egalitarian pronouncements and plotted a rebellion that proved a factor in the presidential election.

Little of this was evident, however, in 1799, amid the continuing Federalist repression. Sedition charges, and not slavery or the suffrage, galvanized political debates. Although they stirred only opposition with their Kentucky and Virginia Resolutions, Jefferson, Madison, and the rest of the Republican gentry remained hopeful that the crisis would pass and that responsible, truly republican leaders would reclaim the country. But the Federalists believed just as strongly that the future belonged to them.

"THE 'RALLYING POINT'"

Conservative Federalists, led semiclandestinely by Alexander Hamilton, were unfazed—indeed, they were emboldened—by public reactions to Congress's war measures. Hamilton had suffered through personal disgrace in 1797 when John Beckley leaked to the scandalmonger-journalist James Callender the long suppressed news about the Maria Reynolds affair. (Hamilton publicly confessed and salvaged his honor, but the exposé virtually destroyed any future chance of his winning high elective office.) Larger political developments, in the conservative Federalists' eyes, appeared to be moving in their favor. In addition to the alien and sedition acts, Congress had approved the first direct federal tax on dwellings, land, and slaves to pay for military preparations against France. The failed Kentucky and Virginia Resolutions provoked persistent and credible rumors that the Virginia legislature had begun stockpiling arms against an attack by the national government. In the off-year congressional elections held between April 1798 and March 1799, Federalist candidates fared extremely well, especially in the South (where criticism of the Resolutions was severe), and won a commanding 60 to 46 majority in the House to go along with its large majority in the Senate. Early in 1799, a brief uprising in the heavily German areas of Bucks and Northampton Counties in eastern Pennsylvania—led by a local cooper and Revolutionary militia captain named John Fries, and directed chiefly against federal land-tax assessors—reanimated the specters of Daniel Shays and Hermon Husband. It all seemed to confirm the Federalist view that the Republican opposition had become a reckless enemy of the United States—intent, one Virginian wrote to Hamilton, on gaining "[n]othing short of DISUNION, and the heads of JOHN ADAMS and ALEXANDER HAMILTON; & some others perhaps." Hamilton—who through pressure from his allies in the cabinet and ex-President Washington was named inspector general of the Provisional Army, second in command to Washington himself—would see to it that law and order prevailed, in part by screening the names of proposed new army officers in order to guarantee their political reliability.

President Adams was in a much gloomier mood, genuinely worried over the growing bellicosity and self-confidence of his fellow Federalists (above all Hamilton, whom he had never trusted), and how they might ruin his chances for re-election. He only grudgingly gave way over Hamilton's Provisional Army commission. He grew suspicious of the large fortunes made by military contractors and well-connected speculators, and fretted about the new taxes *"liberally laid on"* that might be more than the people could bear. He stewed, at his family home in Quincy and in Philadelphia, about the widespread fears that Hamilton intended to use the army first to crush legitimate political activities in the South and then to make himself military chieftain of the nation. More a diplomat than a warrior, the president put away his sword and, in the autumn of 1798, began earnestly following up diplomatic hints from Paris, conveyed by Elbridge Gerry and others, that the French were eager to end the quasi-war crisis.

Over the ensuing year, the breach between Adams's and Hamilton's supporters threatened the viability of the newly reenergized Federalist national coalition. In the spring state legislative elections in 1799, held before the full impact of the Sedition Law prosecutions hit the country, Federalist candidates continued to benefit from the protracted anti-French fervor and actually increased their majority in the House. Thereafter, however,

Adams's decision, originally announced in February, to reopen negotiations with France, followed by his decision to withdraw to Quincy for several months, sent Federalist leaders into a whirl of retribution and behind-the-scenes plotting against both the Republicans and Adams. Hamilton was especially active, scheming to expand the military even further, to deploy the army and quell Virginia's supposedly imminent insurrection, and even to amend the Constitution in order to break up the larger states into smaller units, thereby crippling Virginia's political power. By the opening of the new year, with the presidential election only months away, Hamilton was musing in letters to his friends about whether it made more sense for the Federalists to dump Adams and thereby risk a serious schism, or to "annihilate themselves and hazard their cause by continuing to uphold those who suspect or hate them." Adams, for his part, decided to suspend further enlistments in the Provisional Army, which emboldened congressional moderates, in the spring of 1800, to kill the new army altogether.

The Republicans united behind Vice President Jefferson—"the 'rallying point,' the head quarters, the everything" of the opposition, one Virginia Federalist wrote, and the virtually certain candidate for president. Jefferson himself, although determined to keep out of the public eye, did all that he could behind the scenes, arranging for the Kentucky and Virginia legislatures to restate their objections to the alien and sedition acts and encouraging the circulation of friendly pamphlets among individual citizens in the various states. Jefferson's political friends made even more decisive preparations for the 1800 campaign. Especially in the middle Atlantic states and the upper South, Republicans learned the organizing lessons of 1796 and began putting them into practice early in 1800. In Virginia, Maryland, and New Jersey, where there had been little in the way of a statewide Republican electoral organization, elaborate local committees and networks of correspondence quickly appeared. In Pennsylvania, where Republicans were already well organized, county committees took over the jobs of framing local Republican tickets and directing the campaign in their respective districts. In the teeth of the Sedition Law, Republicans around the country banded together to support local, unabashedly partisan newspapers. And in what proved to be the election's signal state, New York, a highly sophisticated and effective electioneering operation arose in Manhattan, overseen by the man who had run with Jefferson in 1796 and would run with him again, Aaron Burr.

Burr was as charming and politically talented as he was proud and personally ambitious. Both his grandfather, the renowned evangelist Jonathan Edwards, and his father, Aaron Sr. (who succeeded Edwards as president of the new college at Princeton), died while he was an infant. Raised by relatives, Burr graduated from Princeton with honors at age sixteen, then briefly read law at his brother-in-law Tapping Reeve's prestigious school in Litchfield, Connecticut, until the outbreak of the Revolution in 1775, when he volunteered to fight. After serving with distinction as an officer on the Continental line, he established a law practice in New York City and rose quickly in politics, winning a seat in the New York assembly in 1784, getting appointed state attorney general in 1789, and gaining election by the legislature to the U.S. Senate in 1791. An outsider to New York family politics—and thus intellectually and temperamentally drawn to the Republican opposition—Burr was not a city democrat, let alone an agrarian ideologue, but a well-schooled epicurean and political adventurer whose taste for political intrigue, brilliant women, fine wine, and even finer conversation was outstripped only by his hatred of boredom. He did, however, understand the political possibilities opened by the city democracy.

Not fully trusted by Jefferson and the other Virginia Republicans (who considered him vulgar, if politically useful), Burr was still smarting over his thwarted effort to contest John Adams for the vice presidency in 1792, as well as over the national elections four years later, in which, as Jefferson's running mate, he had finished a humiliating fourth in the Electoral College balloting. (Federalist victories in the 1796 New York legislative elections also cost him his Senate seat.) Falling back on election to the state assembly, he took an interest in antislavery and led the successful effort to pass New York's gradual emancipation law in 1799, only to lose his reelection bid at the height of the quasi-war with France. In 1800, he appears to have had his eye on winning the governor's race a year later, but before that, he worked hard to ensure a Republican victory in the hotly contested New York legislative elections in April. Because they were held months before most other states' legislative races, and because they would decide which side would receive New York's Electoral College votes, the elections were a crucial early test of the presidential field. Normally pro-Federalist New York City, Burr's base of operations, loomed as the key battleground. "[I]f the *city* election of N York is in favor of the Republican ticket, the issue will be republican," an apprehensive Jefferson (briefed by Burr) wrote to Madison in March. Burr's interests and Jefferson's were once again intertwined.

Burr performed his political tasks brilliantly, enlarging on the mass electioneering methods pioneered by city democrats in 1796. Months in advance of the April balloting, he made the rounds among his numerous contacts in Manhattan; he opened his home to provide entertainment, meals, and even sleeping quarters for party workers; and he arranged regular party organizational meetings at Abraham "Bram" Martling's Tavern on downtown Chatham Street, now Park Row, the site of the Tammany Society's gatherings. Behind the scenes, he worked closely with his ally, Matthew L. Davis (an auctioneer and Tammany stalwart) to concoct a Republican ticket of prominent names from all the state's leading Republican factions. Then he helped keep the nominees' names secret until after the divided Federalists had patched together their list of candidates, a collection of unrenowned businessmen and master artisans. Coordinating their efforts with separate committees in each of the city's seven wards as well as with a citywide general committee, Burr and his lieutenants toiled ceaselessly to distribute handbills and address as many bodies of assembled voters as they could. Hamilton's Federalist friends tried to match the Republicans' efforts, but the final tally showed an unexpected Republican victory in the city, based on huge margins in the poorer wards, and a narrow Republican victory statewide. "That business [that is, the campaign] has been conducted and brought to issue in so miraculous a manner," enthused James Nicholson, the former head of the New York Democratic Society, "that I cannot account for it but from the intervention of a Supreme Power and our friend Burr the agent."

The New York results severely demoralized the Federalist leadership. Taking the outcome as a personal and political blow, Hamilton tried, unavailingly, to talk his old colleague, Governor John Jay, into calling a special session of the lame-duck Federalist legislature to enact a new election law guaranteeing the Federalists enough of New York's electoral votes. President Adams believed Hamilton was the chief cause of all his political troubles. He took the occasion of his renomination by a secret Federalist congressional caucus in early May to force out two of Hamilton's allies in the cabinet, Secretary of State Timothy Pickering and Secretary of War James McHenry, whom he was certain, correctly, had plotted against him. The Republican congressional leaders, for their part, smelled victory and at their own sub-rosa nominating caucus, held at a Philadelphia boardinghouse, named Burr, the season's political genius, as their vice presidential candidate once again. Assured that he would receive the full support of Jefferson's men in Virginia and South Carolina, Burr assented.

The most distressing piece of news for Republicans was from Virginia and involved not the elections but what Governor James Monroe described to Jefferson in April as rumors of "a Negro insurrection" in their home state. Since the Revolution, when the British had offered freedom to rebellious slaves, the possibility of some sort of slave uprising had loomed as all too real to southern slaveholders. Here and there, after American independence, runaway slaves managed to escape recapture and establish their own maroon communities, a potential threat to local stability. Even more troubling was the revolutionary example of Saint Domingue (present-day Haiti), where slaves and free blacks overthrew and massacred much of the resident French planter elite in 1791, and then established, under the leadership of the ex-slave general Toussaint L'Ouverture, the first black-controlled country in the New World. "The scenes which are acted in St. Domingo," a nervous Monroe observed, speaking for all his fellow slaveholders, "must produce an effect on all the people of colour in this and the States south of us, more especially our slaves, and it is our duty to be on our guard to prevent any mischief resulting from it."

At the end of August, Monroe learned that the rumors had merit. A major revolt, involving hundreds of slaves in and around Richmond, had only narrowly been averted days earlier. The mastermind of the foiled plot, still at large, was a literate blacksmith named Gabriel, owned by Thomas Henry Prosser, a wealthy Richmond merchant and tobacco planter with land holdings in Henrico County, about six miles from the city. Born into slavery in 1776, Gabriel had served a blacksmith's apprenticeship as a boy, attaining sufficient physical power and skill to be hired out to other masters in Richmond. A tall young man (standing six feet, two or three inches), prized by his master and mistress (who were likely the ones who taught him to read and write), he enjoyed the unusual privileges of an urban, hired-out slave, including the relative freedom of working beside free black and white artisans. What Gabriel read and with whom he conversed then is unknown. But it is clear that he imbibed much of the egalitarian political rhetoric that made the rounds in the mechanics' shops and tavern haunts, along with news and gossip about Virginia and Richmond politics.

Gabriel's plans, as he explained them to his recruits, were audacious, clever, and, in places, purposely vague in order to prevent their betrayal. Upward of one thousand slaves, as well as a small number of free blacks and white artisans, carefully picked for their loyalty, discretion, and fighting abilities, would march on Richmond and divide into three columns. The central column, armed with weapons converted from farm tools, would seize guns that the rebels understood were stored at the state capitol, then take Governor Monroe hostage. (Knowing Monroe to be friendly to the French Revolution, Gabriel actually thought he might accede to the rebels' demands.) The other two columns would set diversionary fires in the warehouse district, capture the main bridge leading to the city, and await the arrival of rebel reinforcements, recruited from Virginia towns as distant as Charlottesville.

Despite Gabriel's precautions to keep the plan secret, two slaves told their masters on the morning of August 30, roughly twelve hours before the rising was to commence. A torrential rain that evening led the rebels to hold off for an extra day, which gave the alerted authorities enough time to react in force. Governor Monroe called out units of the state militia, while irregular bands of white patrollers hunted for Gabriel and the conspiracy's other implicated leaders. Dozens of suspects were jailed over the following weeks, of whom more than sixty were tried in connection with the conspiracy. Twenty-six slaves (including Gabriel, who eluded capture for nearly a month) were convicted and hanged. One other died in captivity, allegedly a suicide.

Although it ended disastrously for the plotters, the Richmond insurrection conspiracy came close to catching the city and state off guard—far too close to allow its intended victims to rest comfortably. And it caused problems for Governor Monroe and Vice President Jefferson. Virginia Federalists predictably tried to turn the events to their political advantage, blaming their adversaries for inciting the slaves to rebel. (The editor of the Fredericksburg *Virginia Herald* stated flatly that the Republicans' talk of "Liberty and Equality has been infused into the minds of the negroes.") Northern Federalists similarly blamed what President Adams's son Thomas Boylston Adams called the Jeffersonians' "seducing theories about equality," expressed no sympathy for the rebels, and echoed the *Boston Gazette's* smug observation that "[i]f any thing will correct & bring to repentance old hardened sinners in Jacobinism, it must be an insurrection of their slaves." Early in the investigation, Richmond officials discovered that two French émigrés had indeed aided Gabriel, a fact that, had Monroe not moved to suppress it, could have fueled even more effective Federalist propaganda. Then, in mid-September, the continuing roundups, trials, and executions of slaves began to embarrass the Virginia Republicans further, seeming to confirm the extent of the plot while also making the authorities look like the truly bloodthirsty ones.

The Republicans tried their best to contain the issue until the elections were over. Finally, in October, in part because of Jefferson's advice to avoid the further embarrassment of obeying "a principle of revenge," Monroe adopted a policy of deporting convicted rebels outside the United States, a punishment that would also give the slaves' owners the chance of receiving compensation by selling their difficult property abroad.

Gabriel and his men did not come close to destroying the institution of slavery. Their insurrection scare made little difference, if any, in deciding the outcome of the autumn elections in most states. But the foiled rebellion had badly frightened Virginia's slaveholders, and caused some, including Monroe and Jefferson, to feel certain pangs of conscience once the plot had been crushed. Republican efforts to minimize the political damage became, in turn, vitally important once the state-by-state results started piling up and showed that, despite the New York election, the Federalists were running better than had been expected. It soon became evident that the selection of electors by the South Carolina legislature, held in December, would decide the national outcome. And in South Carolina, slave insurrections were taken very seriously indeed.

A TORTUOUS REVOLUTION: THE ELECTIONS OF 1800 AND 1801

The election of 1800 would turn out to be two elections—one held by the voters and state legislatures, the other, in 1801, by the House of Representatives. In a strange series of twists and turns, a combination of popular campaigning and high-level political intrigue left the result hanging in the balance for months. Old-style elite politics and newer forms of democracy inspired both intense passions and cool, hard-nosed calculations. Political leaders and rank-and-file voters alike came to believe, with the utmost conviction, that victory for their side was essential to the nation's survival. The crisis of the new American order came to a head, exposing the fragility of the republic's political institutions.

By September 1800, relations between John Adams and Alexander Hamilton had sunk so low that Hamilton started writing, originally for private circulation, a lengthy pamphlet denouncing the president—"a man of an imagination sublimated and eccentric"—for nearly destroying the Union. Late in October, a copy of Hamilton's caustic remarks fell into William Duane's hands, and the *Aurora* reprinted the best portions. At the very highest echelons, plainly, Federalist solidarity had collapsed. "Mr. Adams ought not to be supported," Oliver Wolcott Jr. wrote, insisting that the president was "incapable of supporting any political system," and doubting whether his reelection would be "a less evil to the country than to incur any risque of the promotion of Mr. Jefferson." Yet at the state level, outside New York, the Federalists managed to hold on to what had previously been their strongest electoral redoubts.

Throughout the summer and early fall, the harsh ideological as well as personal tone of the campaign hardened partisan loyalties and turned the contest into a democratic outpouring. Republican speakers and editors endlessly excoriated their opponents over the alien and sedition acts, the Provisional Army, and their Anglo-monarchical proclivities. Some southern Republicans raised the issue of state rights, but generally Jefferson's supporters, fearing continued unease at the Kentucky and Virginia Resolutions, stressed their attachment to the Constitution and the spirit of 1776, now endangered by the Federalists' repression. The Federalists countered that the Republicans were bloodthirsty, godless Jacobins in disguise, who had roused up "discontented hotheads" and would reduce the country to a "land of *groans*, and *tears*, and *blood.*" The Federalists' abuse of Jefferson was especially severe, his alleged disloyalty to his country "proved" by his letter of 1796 to Philip Mazzei—damning evidence cited endlessly by the Federalist press.

The attacks and counterattacks churned public interest to the point where in the most hotly contested states, upwards of 70 percent of the eligible voters in some counties turned up at the polls. The enthusiasm did not, however, automatically translate into electoral votes for Jefferson. The heat of the campaign blurred the divisions among the Federalists, and that newfound unity, in combination with the antidemocratic biases of state election laws—by which state legislatures selected presidential electors in eleven of the sixteen states—held Jefferson's electoral totals to a minimum outside his southern base.

Although the Republicans put up a spirited, long-shot fight in New England (and nearly captured the Massachusetts statehouse), they did not win a single electoral vote in the region. Worse, in New Jersey, voters in Newark and a strong organization statewide gave the Republicans a small majority of the overall popular vote, but the Federalists, holding a two-to-one majority in the state assembly, gained all seven of the state's electoral votes. In Maryland, where the voters directly chose presidential electors, the Republicans scored a marginal popular victory but could only manage an even split between Jefferson and Adams in the electoral vote tally because the electors were chosen by district. In Pennsylvania, a continuing impasse over the state's election districting laws, prompted by partisan maneuvering in the Federalist-controlled upper house, made it seem likely that neither candidate would receive any of the state's votes, which would harm Jefferson far more than Adams. (Jefferson had won the state in 1796, and Republican congressional candidates would nearly sweep it in 1800. The legislature eventually awarded eight of the state's electoral votes to Jefferson and seven to Adams—better, for the Republicans, than no votes at all, but a clear inflation of Adams's total that might well have tipped the election.) "Pensva. stands little chance of a vote . . . ," Jefferson wrote to Thomas Mann Randolph at the end of November. "In that case, the issue of the election hangs on S. Carol[in]a." And the outcome in South Carolina, the most Federalist of all the southern states, wound up depending on a peculiar political split inside the Pinckney family.

Senator Charles Pinckney was second cousin to Adams's vice presidential candidate, Charles Cotesworth Pinckney. Both men had been born into the political elite of the South Carolina low country; both had been prominent delegates to the federal convention in 1787; but by the end of the 1790s, they were not on speaking terms. While "C.C.," along with his brother Thomas (Adams's failed running mate in 1796) were stalwart Federalists, Charles, elected governor as a Federalist in 1789, grew alienated from the Washington administration—initially (it appears) because he was passed over for the ministry to Britain in favor of Thomas in 1792, and more profoundly after 1795, when he took strong exception to the Jay Treaty. Casting his lot with the Republican planters of South Carolina's interior counties, Charles, a man of eminent self-regard, won a third term as governor in 1796. Two years later (although denounced by his former low-country friends as a corrupt class traitor, "Blackguard Charlie"), he was elected to the U.S. Senate. In 1800, having established his Republican bona fides, he managed Jefferson's presidential campaign in South Carolina.

Hamilton's maneuverings complicated Blackguard Charlie's tasks. His ties with Adams now completely cut, Hamilton tried to succeed where he had failed in 1796, by securing all of South Carolina's electoral votes for C.C. Pinckney and thereby elevating Pinckney to the presidency. Although the Republicans, by winning lopsided victories outside Charleston, commanded a majority in the new legislature, many of the Republican lawmakers were also devoted to Pinckney. And Republican standing in the state had momentarily plummeted in the wake of Gabriel's plot, forcing James Monroe to write reassuringly to South Carolina's panicked Republican lieutenant governor, John Drayton— remarks that calmed but could not completely quell suspicions that the Republican appeal to equality was too dangerous in a slave society. Seeing what was happening, Charles Pinckney delayed his arrival in the Senate and, he told Jefferson, took a "post with some valuable friends in Columbia," where he meant to remain "until the thing is settled." The details of his labors within the legislature—promises made, deals cooked up—are lost to us; what is clear is that Blackguard Charlie held the Republican caucus firmly in line behind both Jefferson and Burr. "The Election is just Finished," Pinckney wrote to Jefferson, "and We Have, thanks to Heaven's Goodness, carried it." He did not neglect to add that he, Charles Pinckney, and not just Heaven, deserved credit, as "it would have been almost death to our cause for me to quit Columbia."

In fact, by thwarting his cousin and Alexander Hamilton, Pinckney succeeded too well—although given the formally secret results of the state-by-state electoral balloting, he had no way of knowing that. Prior to the presidential balloting in South Carolina, both Adams and Jefferson had secured 65 electoral votes each. (All state electors cast their votes on the same day, December 3, although the results were not officially made public until February.) Thanks to the South Carolinians' discipline, Jefferson and Burr each received the state's 8 available votes, seemingly putting Jefferson over the top. But through a fluke in the voting, Jefferson had not defeated Burr, who also now had 73 votes. Most observers, including Jefferson and (probably) Burr, expected that one of the South Carolinians and one or two of the Georgia electors would cast a pro forma vote for some other Republican, thereby making Jefferson president and Burr vice president—but, none did, leaving Jefferson and Burr deadlocked. Under the Constitution, the House of Representatives would now have to decide the election, with each state delegation casting one vote. And to make the situation all the more perverse, the House members who voted would not be the Republican majority that the 1800 elections had produced, but the lame-duck Federalist majority elected in 1798 at the height of the XYZ crisis with France. Requiring the support of nine state delegations to elect the new president, the Republicans controlled only eight, and the Federalists six. The Maryland and Vermont delegations were evenly divided.

This issue would be decided in the new national capital, the District of Columbia, where the federal government had finally relocated earlier in 1800. The mood there was panicky. Around the country, rival groups of unofficial Republican and Federalist militia had reportedly begun to drill, in preparation for a possible civil war. Southerners, already shaken by the Gabriel conspiracy, traded rumors about Federalist plots to block Jefferson's election as president, while Federalists suspected that Virginians were willing to impose Jefferson on the nation at bayonet point if necessary. Albert Gallatin drafted a memorandum which insisted that any Federalist effort to usurp the election would have to be "resisted by freemen wherever they have the power of resisting." Soon, Jefferson himself would be warning of armed resistance. Adding to the atmosphere of chaos and impending doom, a mysterious fire in early November that destroyed the building housing the War Department was followed ten weeks later by an equally mysterious fire that destroyed portions of the Treasury Department. Amid the ruins and the inevitable partisan charges about who set the fires, the House settled down inside the north (or Senate) wing of the new Capitol, the only part of the building as yet completed, to decide who would be the next American president.

Aaron Burr could have instantly ended the crisis by removing his name from consideration for anything but the vice presidency. But he refused, despite making all sorts of statements of fealty to Jefferson—and by late December, when he fully realized that he had a credible chance to win the presidency, he decided to play out the string, come what may. Of course, as Burr knew well, any victory margin in his favor would come from Federalists who preferred someone they saw as a corrupt northern opportunist to the satanic Thomas Jefferson. The House, amid round-the-clock intrigue, began its voting on February 11. On the first ballot, Jefferson won the support of eight states, Burr of six, with the two divided states, Vermont and Maryland, so badly split that they cast no votes. Twenty hours and twenty-six ballots later, the results remained the same.

Ironically, it was Hamilton who, having already made John Adams's life miserable, would help decide the matter in Jefferson's favor. Jefferson, with his Gallic enthusiasms, was bad enough to Hamilton, but had more of a temporizing than a violent temperament, whereas the profligate, ambitious Burr would be infinitely worse. A plan cooked up by Federalist intransigents to continue the stalemate until Adams's term expired, and then elevate the Federalist president pro tempore of the Senate to the Executive Mansion, struck Hamilton as wrongheaded. A far wiser course, he told associates, would be to allow Jefferson's election, but only on condition that the Virginians agree to various political concessions, which would include sustaining both the existing fiscal system and the Federalists' neutral foreign policy.

One of Hamilton's correspondents, James Bayard of Delaware, broke the deadlock. Bayard was his state's lone congressman and could decide everything by switching from Burr to Jefferson. After discussions with two of Jefferson's supporters—though not with the candidate himself—Bayard was persuaded that Jefferson had made specific concessions about preserving the public credit. Bayard was also bemused by Burr's odd behavior—refusing to seek the presidency actively, while also refusing to eliminate himself as a candidate. And so Bayard helped worked out an arrangement: he would withdraw his support for Burr by voting a blank ballot, Vermont's and Maryland's Federalists would absent themselves and thereby hand their respective states to Jefferson, and South Carolina's Federalists would, like Bayard, vote a blank ballot. After the thirty-sixth ballot, with ten states voting for Jefferson, four for Burr, and two abstaining, the Virginian was declared the nation's third president, and Burr its third vice president.

Jefferson's friends were elated. Jefferson, however, who had won the presidency by the skin of his teeth, serenely kept his own counsel. With barely two weeks to go before his swearing-in as president, he withdrew to his boardinghouse. There he would make sense of his victory and then try to convey that sense to the nation the best way he knew how, in a carefully composed inaugural address.

MARCH 4, 1801

Before daybreak on inauguration day, a heartbroken and sullen John Adams departed the Executive Mansion and began the long coach ride to Quincy, his public career finished. In December, hours before the presidential electors met to confirm his defeat, Adams had received from home the devastating news of the death, at age thirty, of his second son, Charles, a troubled alcoholic whom he had renounced as a worthless rake. Fighting with grief and guilt, Adams pulled himself together and dutifully completed his last ten weeks in office, working on treaty negotiations with France and filling vacancies in the bureaucracy and the army with reliable moderate Federalists and personal friends. He signed into law the sweeping Judiciary Act of 1801, a parting shot from the lame-duck Federalist Congress, which reorganized the federal judiciary, reduced the size of the Supreme Court (depriving Jefferson of adding his own selection when the next seat came open), and created sixteen new federal judgeships to which Adams named steadfast Federalists.

Trying to put the best face on his defeat, Adams blamed Hamilton, but not just Hamilton. "No party that ever existed knew itself so little, or so vainly overrated its own influence and popularity, as ours," he later wrote to his friend Benjamin Stoddert.

> None ever understood so ill the causes of its own power, or so wantonly destroyed them. If we had been blessed with common sense, we should not have been overthrown by Philip Freneau, Duane, Callender, Cooper, and Lyon or their great patron and protector. A group of foreign liars, encouraged by a few ambitious native gen-

tlemen, have discomfited the education, the talents, the
virtues, and the property of the country. The reason is,
we have no Americans in America. The Federalists have
been no more Americans than the anties.

From the start of his administration, Adams mused bitterly, he,
the man of balance, had tried to keep the extremists at bay, but
he (and, he implied, the country) had been overmatched. "Jefferson had a party, Hamilton had a party, but the commonwealth
had none," Adams concluded.

Six hours after Adams left the city, Thomas Jefferson—dressed
in a plain suit, his graying red hair unpowdered—walked with little fanfare in a brief militia procession from his lodgings to the
Capitol, took the presidential oath of office, and delivered the
speech on which he had worked the previous fortnight. Some of
those who crowded the Senate chamber could barely hear his
thin, high-pitched voice, but Jefferson had given an advance copy
to a new and friendly local paper, the *National Intelligencer*,
edited by Samuel Harrison Smith, so that the entire city of Washington could know his words before day's end.

What Jefferson said was directly at odds with what Adams was
thinking. In the most important speech of his life, Jefferson displayed his singular ability to mold the political situation before
him with his words, turning democratic hopes and assumptions
into political facts. He began by acknowledging the rancor of the
recent election, but suggested it was nothing more than the normal to-and-fro of a people able "to think freely and to speak and
to write what they think." Now that the citizenry had voted,
"according to the rules of the Constitution," all Americans would
"of course, arrange themselves under the will of the law, and
unite in common efforts for the common good."

As political rhetoric, this was a risky but brilliant combination
of disingenuousness and indirection. Not only had the recent
election been full of high-level intrigue; it had been fought so
fiercely in part because Jefferson's supporters believed (with
good reason) that Americans could no longer think, speak, and

write freely. Jefferson insisted on the legitimacy of his selection, no matter how close it had been, by pointing to the very document, the Constitution, that the Federalists had charged he wished to undermine. There was no reason to assume, less than three weeks after the electoral fracas had ended, that Americans would unite behind his leadership as a matter of course. (It is impossible to imagine the Republicans extending such great goodwill had either of the "monocrats," Adams or Pinckney, prevailed.) But by saying it was so, Jefferson dared to think he could make it so.

Eager to promote reconciliation, Jefferson blamed the recent electoral tumults mainly on the political struggles in Europe, and on Americans' disagreements over the proper "measures of safety" to take in response. He then sounded what many took as the address's unifying keynote, that "every difference of opinion is not a difference of principle," and that, finally, however divided Americans' opinions might be, "[w]e are all republicans: we are all federalists." Reading those words as they appeared in print—as *Republicans* and *Federalists*—helped persuade numerous leading Federalists to retract their past doubts and predict that, as Hamilton wrote several weeks later, "the new President will not lend himself to dangerous innovations, but in essential points will tread in the steps of his predecessors." It may also have affirmed their belief that the assurances made to James Bayard during the last days of the election in the House were both authentic and sincere.

Yet if Jefferson planned nothing dangerous, he had no intention of sustaining his predecessors' policies, as far as he could help it. Understood fully as he wrote them, without capital letters, his remarks about republicans and federalists may only have meant that Americans shared a commitment to a republican government under the Federal Constitution—not that Republicans and Federalists were equally legitimate contenders for power. In a wonderfully tempered passage, Jefferson repudiated the Federalist claim that the national government lacked what Hamilton liked to call "energy":

I know, indeed, that some honest men fear that a republican government can not be strong, that this Government is not strong enough; but would the honest patriot,
in the full tide of successful experiment, abandon a government which has so far kept us free and firm on the
theoretic and visionary fear that this Government, the
world's best hope, may by possibility want energy to preserve itself? I trust not. I believe this, on the contrary, the
strongest Government on earth.

If Jefferson was willing to call his adversaries "honest"—elsewhere in the speech he referred to those "whose positions will
not command a view of the whole ground"—he also quietly
called them deluded.

Against the Federalists, Jefferson reiterated the democratic
principle that public honor and confidence should result "not
from birth, but from our actions." And as "the sum of good government," he described qualities that promised basic departures
from the previous administrations' policies, specifically, "a wise
and frugal government, which shall restrain men from injuring
one another, shall leave them otherwise free to regulate their own
pursuits of industry and improvement, and shall not take from
the mouth of labor the bread it has earned." Whatever concessions his supporters may have made to Bayard over the public
credit in order to get Jefferson elected, major portions of the Federalist edifice of internal taxes, a standing army, and regulation of
speech and opinion were about to fall.

Jefferson revealed his truest intentions a year and a half into
his presidency, when, after facing stiff resistance from Federalists
in Congress, he told Levi Lincoln that by establishing republican
principles, he would "sink federalism into an abyss from which
there shall be no resurrection for it." He undertook that mission
with the backing, as he told the British radical émigré and scien-
tist Joseph Priestley just after the inauguration, of "a mighty wave
of public opinion" that had arisen against the Federalists'
encroaching tyranny. The change would be dramatic. A popular

song sung in anticipatory celebration of Jefferson's election made clear what the new president himself later announced, with calm finesse, in his inaugural address:

> THE gloomy night before us flies,
> The reign of terror now is o'er;
> Its gags, inquisitors, and spies,
> Its herds of harpies are no more!
>
> Rejoice! Columbia's Sons, rejoice!
> To tyrants never bend the knee,
> But join with heart and soul and voice,
> For *Jefferson and Liberty*.

Looking back as an old man, Jefferson would speak of the election as the "revolution of 1800," remarking that it was "as real a revolution in the principles of our government as that of 76 was in its form," one "not effected indeed by the sword . . . but by the rational and peaceable instrument of reform, the suffrage of the people." His moderation, in leading this democratic revolution, consisted mainly of his recognition of Solon's ancient wisdom, that (as he put it) "no more good must be attempted than the nation can bear."

Jefferson's "revolution of 1800" did leave open some major questions about the democratization of American politics. The egalitarian fundamentals of his appeal, along with the democratic electioneering efforts undertaken by his supporters, surpassed anything seen before in national affairs. The Republicans' absorption of the techniques and the constituency of the city democracy—most notably under Beckley's direction in Philadelphia and Burr's in New York City—had created both a Republican infrastructure of newspapers, public events, and loyal operatives, and a national coalition of planters, yeoman, and urban workingmen allied against a Federalist monocracy. In four of the five states where the voters directly chose presidential electors—Virginia, Kentucky, North Carolina, and Maryland—Jefferson won a popular majority. Yet various structural factors, along with partisan maneuvering, limited the scope of Jefferson's victory and created some large historical ironies. In three of the states decided by the popular vote, the electors were chosen by district and not statewide, which deprived Jefferson of twelve electoral votes. In two other states where the legislatures chose electors, New Jersey and Pennsylvania, the Republicans also won statewide victories not reflected in the electoral voting, costing Jefferson upward of fourteen additional electoral votes. Except for southern slavery, and the inflation of the southern vote by the three-fifths clause in the Constitution, Adams, aided by the split electoral votes in pro-Jefferson states—especially the split caused by the successful obstructionist Federalists in Pennsylvania—would have won reelection. And for all of Jefferson's reliance on democratic principles and tactics, he might never have gained the presidency without the insider wire-pulling of a renegade South Carolina low-country aristocrat—along with later help from, of all people, Alexander Hamilton.

The Republicans did win a smashing victory in the congressional elections, picking up twenty-three seats in the House (enough to seize a formidable majority) and seven seats in the Senate (giving them a majority of two, the first time ever they controlled the upper chamber). Coupled with Jefferson's narrow victory, it was enough to justify claims that a seismic shift had occurred. Yet Federalism was far from dead, at least in the northern states. And the Republican coalition of city and country democrats, built in part out of the elements of the Democratic-Republican societies, was still commanded by Virginian gentry slaveholders. Traditional political arrangements, conducted by elected officials—gentlemen for the most part, well removed from the voters—still largely determined national political affairs. It remained far from clear that the patrician Republican leaders considered partisan popular politics—described by Jefferson as recently as 1789 as "the last degradation of a free and moral agent"—as anything more than an unfortunate and temporary expedient to ward off monocracy.

Jefferson and his allies had achieved an accession to national power that removed the Federalists from power in two of the three branches of the federal government. Considering the alarming state of American politics after 1796, that achievement was not small. But the tensions within the emerging Jeffersonian order, including those provoked by Gabriel Prosser's plot, were strong enough to ensure renewed and bitter battles over what, exactly, was the sum of good government.

4

JEFFERSON'S TWO
PRESIDENCIES

The first thing that Thomas Jefferson saw as president was
the dark face of John Marshall, the chief justice of the
Supreme Court, who had just sworn him into office. The
two were second cousins, related through the august Randolph
family of Virginia—and they intensely disliked each other's politics. Marshall was now the country's preeminent moderate Federalist, one of John Adams's few trustworthy political friends,
confirmed (in the waning days of Federalist rule) as his hand-
picked chief justice. He regarded Jefferson as a self-important
dreamer—"the grand lama of the mountain"—blind to the practical imperatives of national government. Jefferson thought Marshall a hypocrite and a sophist, dominated by "the plenitude of
his English principles." Yet on this day, shared political fears and
desires overrode the Virginians' mutual suspicions.

Shortly before the noontime ceremony, Marshall began writing
a letter to Adams's running mate, Charles Cotesworth Pinckney,
expressing his cautious hope that "the public prosperity and happiness may sustain no diminution under democratic guidance."
Marshall explained that, though "[t]he democrats are divided into
speculative theorists and absolute terrorists: With the latter I am

not disposed to class Mr. Jefferson." After breaking off to officiate at the inauguration, Marshall returned to his letter, still wary but encouraged. Jefferson's speech, he said, was "well judged and conciliatory" even though "strongly characteristic of the general cast of his political theory." Marshall found little to admire in that theory, but he and Jefferson had overseen a peaceful transit of power, despite the turmoil of the previous two years. "The changes of administration, which in every government and in every age have most generally been epochs of confusion, villainy and bloodshed, in this our happy country, take place without any species of distraction, or disorder," one spectator at the inauguration wrote. This cheerful result was due largely to the capacity for moderation of men like Jefferson and Marshall.

Even as they staked out moderate ground, the president and the chief justice were destined to clash before long. Some days earlier, while completing the last-minute Federalist expansion of the federal judiciary, Marshall (in his plural capacity as secretary of state) had affixed the official seals on the commissions of more than three-dozen so-called midnight judgeship appointments, including one for a Georgetown lawyer named William Marbury. Amid the distractions of Jefferson's election and inauguration, Marshall failed to have the commissions delivered. While Marshall was giving Jefferson the oath of office, the documents sat forgotten on a desk at the State Department, where President Jefferson would discover them, accidentally, two days later. Already infuriated at the Federalists' judicial maneuverings, Jefferson pondered over whether the undelivered documents were now dead letters. From this incident would issue a memorable skirmish in the continuing struggle between Republicans and Federalists—a struggle that would now turn on battles over the fledgling federal judiciary.

The larger struggle over democracy created fresh difficulties for the new Republican leadership. Having ousted their common enemy from national power, the Republicans began to divide into moderate, radical, and so-called Old Republican factions, with very different conceptions of democracy—differences that threatened Republican unity at the state and local levels as well as in Washington. "I confess I do not like tampering with established systems or forms of government," wrote Pennsylvania's preeminent moderate Republican Thomas McKean. ". . . I never desire to see any more Revolutions, and pant after tranquility, peace and sociability." Other Republicans thought McKean and those like him were Federalists in disguise. Blessed by a sudden outbreak of peace in Europe, and by a stroke of enormous good luck in the Caribbean, Jefferson, leaning to the moderates, proved remarkably successful at carving out a middle Republican course during his first administration, while holding the Republicans together and reducing the active Federalist threat. But during his second term, stresses at home and abroad grew so intense that Jefferson would leave office in 1809 frustrated and exhausted—and with the nation's survival, let alone American democracy's, far from assured.

MONOCRACY ATTACKED

Even before he finally moved into the cavernous new president's house in late March, Jefferson began implementing a two-track strategy for destroying Federalism: reconciling moderate Federalists to his own administration while extirpating the excesses of Federalist rule. Accordingly, he appointed his cabinet and chief envoys with care, trying to appear as nonconfrontational as possible. As expected, he chose his old collaborator James Madison as secretary of state, and, to intense Federalist displeasure, named the Genevan émigré Albert Gallatin as secretary of the treasury. But he balanced the group geographically and politically by appointing the moderate New Englanders Levi Lincoln, Henry Dearborn, and Gideon Granger as, respectively, attorney general, secretary of war, and postmaster general. The Federalist Rufus King was given the crucial post of minister to Great Britain, while the ex-Federalists Robert R. Livingston and Charles Pinckney (the proud "Blackguard Charlie") took up similar assignments in France and Spain. In the continuing press wars with the Federalists, Jefferson turned to the *National Intelligencer* as the quasi-official administration organ, edited by the reliably fair-minded Republican Samuel Harrison Smith. Jefferson, one Federalist opponent observed, did his best to surround himself with "mild and amiable men," in contrast to the sorts of designing ideologues who had helped make his predecessors' cabinet a torment.

With this political camouflage in place, Jefferson began to dismantle the Federalists' chief legacies. Although the Sedition Law had expired on inauguration day, ten of its victims were still in legal trouble. David Brown remained behind bars in Massachusetts, unable to pay his fine; twice he had written clemency petitions to President Adams, who ignored them. Eight days after the inauguration, Jefferson, who had always considered the law a nullity, pardoned Brown in full, along with all others still in prison for sedition when he assumed office; four days after that, he agreed to remit a sedition fine assessed against the Virginia journalist James Callender. Later, Jefferson discontinued the Sedition Law prosecution still pending against William Duane of the *Aurora* and lifted all other penalties and prosecutions. In his first annual message, delivered on December 8, he bid the incoming Republican Congress to repeal the Federalists' naturalization laws of 1798, asking, "[S]hall oppressed humanity find no asylum on this globe?" Congress duly complied.

On fiscal policy, Jefferson frontally attacked the Hamiltonian system by initiating the complete elimination of federal internal taxation, including the land tax and the hated whiskey excise. Secretary Gallatin initially balked at removing the duties, not because he approved of them but because his first priority was to cut the huge debt inherited from the Federalists. Jefferson insisted that ending the excise, an enormous political symbol as well as a public burden, be included as part of Gallatin's plans. Gallatin, and then Congress, assented in no uncertain terms: "let them all go," Gallatin said, "and not one remain on which sister taxes may be hereafter engrafted."

Patronage questions caused Jefferson greater difficulty. Faced with a federal establishment monopolized by Federalist appointees, he could hardly avoid firing some officeholders and substituting his supporters. But lacking any precedents, eager to calm partisan tensions, and appalled at the politics of spoilsmanship practiced at the state level, Jefferson at first attempted to minimize patronage replacements, except for replacing "midnight" appointees or those accused of official misconduct. He modified his policy in July, in part because of complaints from office-hungry local Republicans and, even more, because hardline Federalists rejected his olive branch. After trying to replace Adams's midnight appointee Elizur Goodrich with the aging but committed Republican Samuel Bishop as port collector in arch-Federalist New Haven, Jefferson received an angry remonstrance from a group of eighty powerful New Haven merchants, complaining that his choice was incompetent and that they, the merchants, were "a class of citizens" who deserved special favor in the matter. The president, affronted, publicly defended Bishop and asked the merchants some barbed questions of his own: "Is it *political intolerance* to claim a proportionate share in the direction of the public affairs? Can they [that is, the Federalists] not *harmonize* in society unless they have every thing in their own hands?" Jefferson claimed that his call for unity at the inauguration and later had "been quoted and misconstrued into assurances that the tenure of offices was to be undisturbed." Appointees, he reiterated, would be judged not by their birth or standing but by their achievements and actions.

Jefferson's response pleased his more partisan backers in New England and the middle Atlantic states, and infuriated the Federalists. In retrospect, it appears that the Federalists overreacted. Jefferson actually had fairly elevated ideas about staffing the upper branches of the civil service with respectable, well-educated men. Although he moved outside the clusters of wealthy families that Adams had favored, he still believed, as he would later write, that most citizens were "unqualified for the management of affairs requiring intelligence above the common level." All told, during his eight years in office, he removed 109 of the 433 federal officials with presidential appointments; of the removed, more than one-third were midnight appointments by Adams. But Jefferson came increasingly to believe that the Federalists had drawn the circle of eligible appointees much too tightly, favoring eastern urban gentlemen with business and family connections at the exclusion of rural men and westerners, humble-born citizens of accomplishment, and (as he put it) men of "every shade of opinion which is not theirs." Without endorsing partisanship for its own sake, Jefferson challenged the Federalists' standards of political preferment and staked out the limits of conciliation.

Patronage battles were linked to the momentous contest over the federal judiciary. The federal bench was thoroughly Federalist, and the Judiciary Act of 1801 had opened the way for many of Adams's late appointments and curtailed future Jeffersonian influence by reducing the size of the Supreme Court by one justice. Yet while the president favored vacating the midnight appointments, he rejected an all-out partisan attack on the independence of the judicial branch. As late as December 1801, Jefferson declared that although the judiciary, "and especially that portion of it recently erected," would "of course present itself to the contemplation of Congress," he had in mind no reforms greater than a reduction in the size of the federal court system.

The affair of the undelivered judicial commissions eventually moved Jefferson to seek sterner measures. After discovering John Marshall's forgetfulness, Jefferson quickly decided to grant appointments to twenty of the forty-two names selected by Adams, exclude the others, and add five Republican appointments of his own—an exemplary act, in his mind, of moderate leadership. The Federalists, however, would not be placated by what they considered an underhanded maneuver that exploited a technical error. In December, four of the Adams appointees excluded by Jefferson, including William Marbury, petitioned the Supreme Court for a writ that would require Secretary of State

Madison to deliver their commissions. Chief Justice Marshall granted the petitioners' preliminary motion and scheduled hearings. In private, Jefferson exploded. The Federalists, he wrote on the day Marshall ruled, "have retired into the Judiciary as a stronghold . . . and from that battery all the works of republicanism are to be beaten down and erased." He would now try to destroy the Federalists' domination of the courts, beginning with repeal of the Judiciary Act of 1801.

Led by Kentucky Senator John Breckinridge, Jefferson's old co-conspirator from the Kentucky Resolutions effort four years earlier, congressional Republicans charged their adversaries with judicial tyranny and introduced a bill to repeal the act in January 1802. The Federalists replied that the new administration was seeking to subvert the Constitution and destroy the independence of the federal courts. The Republicans prevailed narrowly in the Senate and more convincingly in the House, then took the additional step of passing a law delaying the next Supreme Court term for over a year, lest the Court invalidate the repeal before it took effect. Some indignant justices threatened to strike down the meddlesome legislation and cause a full-blown constitutional crisis. "I believe a Day of severe trial is fast approaching for the friends of the Constitution," Samuel Chase wrote, "and I fear we must be principal actors and may be sufferers therein." Chief Justice Marshall, after considering resistance, heeded the calmer heads on the Court, and the justices decided to bide their time.

The measured, temperate side of much of Jefferson's public rhetoric during his early months in office, even when he was replying to Federalist rebukes, has lulled some later writers into regarding him, wrongly, as an accommodating trimmer, and his attacks on the Federalists as half-hearted. To be sure, Jefferson never went as far as some of his supporters wished, nor as far as the more highly strung Federalists predicted. On some important matters he stopped short of his own political and constitutional principles. Above all, regarding Hamilton's bank, Jefferson did nothing, heeding Secretary Gallatin's advice that the institution, if stripped of its political favoritism, had its potential benefits, while recognizing that to destroy it outright before its charter elapsed in 1811 would throw the nation's economy into chaos. Jefferson understood that, given his lack of an electoral mandate, too sudden or too hostile an effort at reform might well backfire. "What is practicable must often control what is pure theory," he wrote Pierre du Pont de Nemours in January 1802. Within the constraints of existing political circumstances, Jefferson believed, he was doing his utmost to destroy the Federalists' unrepublican perversions—and that issues requiring compromise could be laid aside for another time. But when Federalists pushed him, he pushed back hard, even if he retained his outwardly temperate mien.

The outstanding feature of Jefferson's first two years as president was the rapidity with which the harmonious tone of inauguration day soured—as a result, chiefly, of the bitter opposition to his presidency mounted by the Federalists. Initially, over the winter and spring of 1801, many of even the most caustic Federalist writers expressed a fatalistic resignation to the Republican victory and remained hopeful that the Jeffersonians' downfall would be swift once they tried to implement their policies. By late summer, the Federalists' strategic high-mindedness had curdled, while their political unity held. Every new replacement appointment by Jefferson became the subject of intense criticism and purported exposés from the Federalist newspapers. The courts became a special focus of Federalist outrage. Having already condemned Jefferson's early decision to hold back a few of the undelivered judicial commissions, the Federalist press seized on his involvement in the outstanding Sedition Law cases, interpreted it in the direst conspiratorial light, and assailed the administration for unconstitutional tampering with the judicial process. While the press attacks unsettled some moderate Federalist leaders, most were persuaded that the Republicans had begun a Jacobinical persecution of the wealth and talent of the country. By the time the new Congress assembled in December and heard the new president's first annual message, some Federalist editors had already called for his impeachment, on the flimsy grounds that his involvement in the Duane and Callender cases amounted to a high crime against the Constitution. The subsequent congressional debate over repeal of the Judiciary Act, in which Federalist spokesmen cast Jefferson as diabolically ambitious and vengeful, further pushed the opposition toward claiming his very election had been tainted and lacked legitimacy.

Much subtler now, but nearly equal in eventual importance, were growing strains within the victorious Republican coalition. Some years later, Jefferson claimed he "had always expected that when the republicans should put down all things under their feet, they would schismatize among themselves . . . into moderate and ardent republicanism." The Republicans had barely begun to put all things under their feet when schisms cracked open.

Vice President Aaron Burr, a faction unto himself, presented personal as well as political problems. Jefferson suspected that Burr had been an intriguer during the election crisis of 1800–01, and kept his distance. Late in 1801, Burr tried unsuccessfully to capitalize on Federalist alienation and enhance his own stature by helping to stall repeal of the Judiciary Act. The feint failed, leaving Burr, according to one Federalist congressman, "a completely isolated man." But though he was down, Burr was not out.

Of greater political and ideological significance were the signs of division between Jefferson and a knot of southern agrarian slaveholder ideologues, most conspicuously the twenty-eight-year-old Virginia representative John Randolph. Pallid, beardless (due to a childhood illness), and fonder of his hunting dogs than of most men and all women, Randolph was the best orator and wittiest insulter in the Congress, and the Republicans' floor leader in the House. A fearsome defender of state rights and hater of Federalist New England, Randolph had already raised doubts about unnamed moderate supporters of Jefferson's "whose Republicanism has not been the most unequivocal." Once Jefferson began preaching and, even worse, practicing conciliation, Randolph grew bitter, as did a number of his important southern agrarian Republican patrons and friends, among them the Speaker of the House, Nathaniel Macon of North Carolina.

Jefferson also faced suspicious city and country democrats, sometimes aligned with the agrarian ideologues, who pushed him to undertake more dramatic political, economic, and judicial reforms. They included some familiar veteran agitators with careers dating back to the Revolution, among them the Berkshire clergyman Thomas Allen and his Baptist itinerant ally John Leland, the Boston artisan radical Benjamin Austin, and the still-feisty sixty-five-year-old Thomas Paine (whom Jefferson officially welcomed back to America as a hero in 1802). Younger democrats of rising importance included the country Pennsylvanians Simon Snyder and Nathaniel Boileau, the radical British émigré editor John Binns, and the Kentucky Green River yeoman leader Felix Grundy. A few of the country democrats, such as John Bacon of western Massachusetts, actually managed to gain a voice in Congress. Most imposing of all, though, were the collaborative efforts of the Philadelphia city democrats William Duane (back to editing the *Aurora* and safe from prosecution) and Michael Leib, formerly of the Democratic Society of Pennsylvania, who had been elected to Congress in 1798. At the *Aurora*, Duane commanded the country's most trenchant and influential independent Republican newspaper; together, Duane and Leib had turned their Philadelphia Republican machine of the 1790s into an electoral force to be reckoned with by national as well as Pennsylvania politicians.

Like the planter ideologues, the city and country democrats spoke of the dangers that excessive official power posed to American principles, especially what the *Aurora* called "the arbitrary power assumed by the courts." Like the planters, they recycled the republican rhetoric of the Revolution against those Republicans they believed were insufficiently vigilant against crypto-monarchism—acting as, in Jefferson's words, radical "high-fliers" against the mainstream "moderates." Yet the planters and the democrats were quite distinct. Apart from Michael Leib, who struck up a working connection with John Randolph in Congress, the leading city and country democrats never displayed special solidarity with the slaveholders. The planters were generally unsympathetic to the kinds of judicial reform, including the popular election of judges and the eradication of British common-law precedents, favored by the democrats. City democrats such as Duane, Paine, and Austin were hospitable to a dynamic, expanding commerce; the planter ideologues opposed further commercialization and (at least rhetorically) detested the entrepreneurial ethos. Above all, northern city and country democrats were generally hostile to the planters' chief property interest, chattel slavery—a difference graphically portrayed early in 1802 when virtually all of the northern Republicans broke ranks and defeated a bill imposing a five-hundred-dollar fine on anyone caught "harboring, concealing, or employing" a fugitive slave, proposed by Joseph Hopper Nicholson of Maryland.

The moderate Republican faction might well be called the Madisonians. Not only was James Madison the greatest political figure among them; most were Republicans who had originally favored ratification of the U.S. Constitution only to become estranged, like Madison, by the policies of George Washington, John Adams, and, above all, Alexander Hamilton. Unlike the planter ideologues and country democrats (most of whom had Anti-Federalist backgrounds), the moderates did not abhor strong national government, but only what they considered specific abuses of power epitomized by Hamilton's funding program and the alien and sedition acts. On the state as well as the national level, they were friendlier than other Republicans were to government efforts at encouraging economic development, including the chartering of state banks and preserving a reformed Bank of the United States. They were far less committed than either the city or the country democrats were to constitutional and judicial reform. And the moderates were willing to risk alienating the other Republican factions in order to win over moderate Federalists. "[I]t would be better to displease many of our political friends," Gallatin wrote, "than to give an opportunity to the irreconcilable enemies of a free government of inducing the mass of Federal citizens to make a common cause with them."

And what of the president? Although he was basically a moderate, in private, particularly in his personal correspondence, and occasionally on public issues, Jefferson's chronic impulsiveness and his irritated distaste for his stubborn Federalist foes could shatter his measured demeanor. One can read the inaugural address and other declarations of harmony as, in part, the thin-skinned Jefferson's attempt to change the tone of politics and forestall the kinds of vicious political and personal attacks that abounded in 1800. But those attacks came anyway, and at times they threw Jefferson into such a fury that he would veer toward more militant Republicans. Years later, recalling his friend's outbursts against "monarchists" and all who tolerated them, Madison would write of how "allowances ought to be made for a habit in Mr. Jefferson as in others of great genius of expressing in strong and round terms, impressions of the moment." But Jefferson often made no such allowances for himself and his adversaries.

Publicly, Jefferson tried to remain friendly with all Republican camps, preserving harmony while remaining personally in command. He saw clearly the risk that pursuing conciliation with the Federalists too ardently might, as he told Gallatin, "absolutely revolt our tried friends." Intellectually, Jefferson was too much the experimenter and Enlightenment visionary to dismiss unorthodox democratic ideas, or their proponents, out of hand. It is difficult to imagine any other moderate Republican helping to arrange for the return to the United States of Tom Paine, infidel and calumniator of George Washington. Yet Jefferson not only arranged the trip; he arranged it at government expense and greeted Paine with a warm public address in the autumn of 1802, commending him to live long and "continue your useful labors"— a severe provocation to the Federalists, and a momentary alarm to moderate Republicans. Likewise, Jefferson refused to disengage from talented combative democrats like William Duane, despite complaints from moderate Republicans. Duane might be "over zealous," he told Madison, but he was an honest Republican who reflected the views "of a great portion of the republican body."

And so the Republican attack on monocracy advanced in 1801 and 1802, enraging the Federalist opposition but failing to convince many Republicans that the administration was acting with sufficient vigor. Once the Republican divisions appeared, the Federalists took courage. The repeal of the Judiciary Act early in 1802—achieved only by a tiny margin in the Senate—looked like it might be a turning point. "[W]e plainly discern that there is no confidence nor the smallest attachment prevails among [the President's party]," House minority leader James Bayard wrote to Hamilton in April. "The spirit which existed at the beginning of the Session is entirely dissipated. A more rapid and radical change could not have been anticipated."

A little more than two years later, Bayard would be out of office, Jefferson's Republicans would reign supreme, and Hamilton would be dead.

JEFFERSON ASCENDANT

Early in his presidency, in his more placid moods, Jefferson was apt to minimize the clash between Republicans and Federalists as the product of disputes over international diplomacy. Those disputes seemed to abate in 1801 and 1802. The rise to political supremacy of Napoleon Bonaparte, whom Jefferson despised and feared, sapped the Republican leadership's fervor for France and narrowed the differences between Jeffersonians and Federalists. ("[A] gigantic force has risen up which seems to threaten the world," Jefferson would write to an English friend two years later.) The pause in European hostilities following the signing of the Anglo-French peace treaty of Amiens in 1802 further tranquilized America's foreign relations with France and Britain. Yet the lull was deceptive, and proved only that the interests of the United States were inextricably bound up with the desires and designs of the two great Atlantic powers, regardless of the situation in

Europe. Remarkably, amid the lull, Jefferson completed the most auspicious act of his presidency, the Louisiana Purchase.

The continuing entanglements among the United States and the Old World powers were partly the result of rapid American movement and settlement westward. Prior to Jefferson's election, two new trans-Appalachian states, Kentucky and Tennessee, had been added to the Union. Following "Mad" Anthony Wayne's victory over the Shawnees, Ottowas, and other tribes at the Battle of Fallen Timbers in 1794, settlers flocked to Ohio, which was admitted as the seventeenth state in 1803. Politically, all three new states leaned toward the Jeffersonians. Commercially, their interests led them to place additional pressure on the administration to sustain Americans' rights to free navigation on the Mississippi River, as well as their rights to free deposit of goods in New Orleans as guaranteed by Thomas Pinckney's treaty with Spain signed in 1795. So long as feeble Spain, on its last legs as an imperial power, controlled New Orleans, and with it the expansive Louisiana Territory to the west and north, western American flatboats could expect no interruption in supplying eastern and international shippers with ample agricultural goods. European power politics, however, complicated by the revolutionary stirrings of the age, intervened.

In 1800, Bonaparte, envisaging a revival of the French empire in North America after nearly half a century of decline, secretly arranged with Spain for a retrocession of the Louisiana Territory, including New Orleans, to France—an arrangement to be formally announced at a later date. Also in secret, he plotted the overthrow of Toussaint L'Ouverture. Some leading northern Federalists, including John Adams—who as president appointed a consul general to Saint Domingue in 1799 and instructed him to emphasize amity as well as trade—had encouraged the insurgents. Jefferson, however, was deeply concerned, even prior to the Gabriel Prosser scare, about the effects L'Ouverture's revolution might have in the United States. Although he tolerated commerce with Saint Domingue when it seemed likely to offset French designs for a New World empire, too much trade with the rebels, he wrote to Madison, would bring "black crews, supercargoes & missionaries thence into the Southern states." To the pleasure of arch New England Federalists such as Timothy Pickering, Jefferson's embrace of egalitarianism was selective. The president even dropped hints that he was willing to aid in L'Ouverture's demise if it would help persuade France to make a lasting peace with Britain. "[N]othing would be easier," he reportedly told the French chargé Louis-André Pichon in the summer of 1801, "than to furnish your army and fleet with everything, and to reduce Toussaint to starvation."

A French takeover of Louisiana was an entirely different matter. That would turn the most belligerent European power into America's western neighbor. News of the retrocession agreement inevitably leaked out. Jefferson abruptly changed course, telling the French that, were Bonaparte to grab Louisiana, the United States would ally with Great Britain against France.

Two developments later in 1802 deepened the western crisis. In June, news arrived in Paris that a French expeditionary force under Napoleon's brother-in-law, General Charles Leclerc, had routed the Saint Domingue revolutionaries and, by trickery, taken L'Ouverture prisoner. (The black Jacobin would die of cold and starvation, in April 1803, in a dungeon-room jail in the French Jura Mountains.) Then, in mid-October, the Spanish suddenly closed New Orleans to international commerce and revoked the Americans' right to deposit their goods in the port. Spain's motives remain obscure; interfering with deposit rights was a clear violation of Pinckney's treaty. In Congress, outraged Federalists and some western Republicans, certain that France was responsible for the closure, began talking of forcibly seizing New Orleans. Jefferson made some preliminary preparations for war but decided to hold off until he had received word from Robert Livingston, his minister in Paris, who had instructions to purchase New Orleans and the Florida territories from Napoleon and end the crisis peacefully.

The Louisiana Purchase was one of the luckiest strokes in the history of American diplomacy. Livingston was an experienced politician, but no match for Napoleon's supremely cynical foreign minister Talleyrand, who, as ever, held the Americans in contempt. (That the self-assured Livingston was deaf, irritable, and unable to speak French did not help the American effort.) Early in 1803, alarmed by the closing of New Orleans, Jefferson officially recognized the retrocession of Louisiana to France and nominated James Monroe (who knew France well and was trusted by western Republicans) to bolster Livingston's mission. But Jefferson, working closely with Secretary of State Madison, also sent word across the Atlantic restating America's objections to France's planned takeover of Louisiana. And after hours at the White House the French envoy Pichon, attending one of the president's famous informal dinners, noticed that Jefferson, seasoned in drawing-room diplomacy, "redoubled his civilities and attentions to the British chargé."

Monroe arrived in France authorized to offer Bonaparte upwards of ten million dollars to purchase New Orleans and the Floridas. When he met with Livingston, he learned to his astonishment that, in the interim, Bonaparte had renounced Louisiana, and Talleyrand had inquired about the possibility of America's purchasing the whole of the Louisiana Territory, the enormous uncharted expanse that lay between the Mississippi River and the Rocky Mountains. Livingston, stupefied by Talleyrand's proposal, had restated his original offer, but when he and Monroe finally comprehended what the French were saying, they quickly concluded a treaty that went well beyond their official instructions. At a total cost of fifteen million dollars—about three cents an acre—the United States would end the French imperial threat, secure New Orleans and the Mississippi River Valley, and more than double its own land area. "We have lived long," Livingston remarked at the treaty-signing ceremony, "but this is the noblest work of our whole lives."

In reality, the Louisiana Purchase was the result of many factors and the work of many people, including the ex-slaves of Saint Domingue. Conquering the island for France and reinstating slavery proved much more difficult than capturing Toussaint

L'Ouverture, in part because of the locals' continued armed resistance and in part because an outbreak of yellow fever began killing off the French invaders by the hundreds. When Bonaparte learned in January 1803 that General Leclerc himself had died of the fever, the first consul's imperial enthusiasm faded quickly. Fed up with his American adventures, in need of fresh revenues for future military campaigns, and eager to forestall an Anglo-American alliance, he solved three problems at one stroke: the bargain-rate sale of Louisiana.

In the context of the Napoleonic struggle for world supremacy, the Louisiana Purchase was a minor episode. Yet for most American citizens, it marked a virtual second Declaration of Independence. Excited talk of peace and commerce—and not of territorial acquisition—dominated the celebrations. "We have secured our rights by pacific means: truth and reason have been more powerful than the sword," the *National Intelligencer* exulted. Jefferson saw the Purchase as vindication of his preference for diplomacy over armed conflict. "Peace is our mission," he wrote to his English friend Sir John Sinclair, "and though wrongs might drive us from it, we would prefer trying every other just principle of right and safety before we would recur to war."

The New England Federalists took the greatest notice—balefully—of the vastness of the territory suddenly acquired, feeding the partisan rancor. "We are to give money of which we have too little for land of which we already have too much," exclaimed one writer in the Boston *Columbian Centinel*—a wasteland "unpeopled with any beings except wolves and wandering Indians." The Virginians, and not the nation, would benefit by carving out innumerable new states and securing their political dynasty. Yet these fears made little impact, either in Congress (which quickly approved the Purchase treaty and related enabling legislation by large majorities) or in the country at large. Shrewder Federalists conceded that the purchase would heighten the administration's popularity, particularly among eastern commercial interests who well understood the importance of securing control of the Mississippi. "[O]n the whole," Rufus King wrote, "it seems agreed on all

sides that the measure will operate in favour of the new administration, whose authority and popularity extend in every quarter."

Actually, Jefferson's strict-constructionist scruples, and his
suspicions that the Constitution did not grant the executive
explicit power to acquire new territory, did more to delay the matter than the Federalist opposition did. But his most forceful
advisers, ranging from Treasury Secretary Gallatin to Thomas
Paine, thought that the constitutional issue was wispy, and urged
Jefferson to go ahead. "It appears to me one of those cases with
which the Constitution has nothing to do . . . ," Paine wrote.
"[T]he idea of extending the territory of the United States was
always contemplated, whenever the opportunity offered itself."
Bonaparte was restless—war with Great Britain had resumed
only two weeks after the signing of the Purchase treaty—and the
amendment process was cumbersome and time-consuming. Jefferson backed off his objections, secure in his view that the Purchase would provide sufficient land to keep the United States an
agrarian yeoman's republic for all time. But, typically, Jefferson
also expressed his general view against "broad construction," lest
any Federalist—or John Randolph—think he was abandoning
principle. In the long run, he wrote, "the good sense of our country" would correct any evils that might arise from the Purchase.

Over the coming decades, the consequences of the Purchase
would indeed disturb public opinion over constitutional issues
connected to the expansion of slavery—and help rip the country
to pieces. But in 1803 those far-off cataclysms were hard to
imagine. Instead, the chief short-term political effect of Jefferson's diplomacy was to advance the political decline of the Federalists—a decline so precipitous that some ineffectual New
England hard-liners like Timothy Pickering, who despaired of
ever seizing the national government back from the Virginia
Jacobins, spoke of seceding from the Union. "[T]here is no time
to be lost, lest [Federalism] should be overwhelmed, and become
unable to attempt its own relief," Pickering wrote to George
Cabot. "Its last refuge is New England; and immediate exertion,
perhaps, its only hope."

The expedition into Louisiana led by Jefferson's private secretary, Meriwether Lewis, and William Clark helped consolidate the Jeffersonians' fortunes. Even before he had the chance to purchase the whole territory, Jefferson had obtained a secret congressional appropriation to enable the explorers to find a path to the Pacific, study the geography of Upper Louisiana, and learn the customs of local Indian trade and diplomacy. In May 1804, with the unexplored vastness now part of the United States, Lewis and Clark's "Corps of Discovery," nearly fifty in number, embarked from the settlement of St. Louis and headed up the Missouri River. Eighteen months later, the group reached the Pacific, and in September 1806, it returned to St. Louis bearing amazing stories along with specimens of exotic flora and valuable furs. As a feat of well-planned and well-executed daring, and an exercise in Enlightenment mapmaking and taxonomy, the Lewis and Clark expedition was an extraordinary success, which solidified Americans' imaginative hold on their new domain. Politically, Lewis and Clark's triumph further wounded the opposition. "The Feds alone treat it as philosophism, and would rejoice of its failure," the president wrote to Lewis over the winter of 1804–05—but eighteen months later, the "philosophism" had plainly paid off.

Political issues predating the Purchase, above all the lingering affair of the judiciary commissions, also played out to the Republicans' short-term advantage—or, more precisely, to the Federalists' disadvantage. The battle over repeal of the Judiciary Act had led congressional Federalists over the edge. "We are standing at the brink of that revolutionary torrent which deluged in blood one of the fairest countries of Europe," Minority Leader Bayard asserted at the close of his floor speech opposing repeal. ". . . The meditated blow is mortal, and from the moment it is struck, we may bid a final adieu to the Constitution." After failing to persuade the Supreme Court to kill the repeal immediately, some of the more conservative congressional Federalists continued the fight by publishing philippics, getting friends to petition the Congress, and planning test cases to help reinstate the act. But their efforts went nowhere, even in the Federalist courts. The Federalist George

Cabot complained of "how little dependence there is, even on good men, to support our system of policy and government."

The Supreme Court's now-famous ruling in *Marbury v. Madison*, delivered by the moderate Chief Justice Marshall in February 1803, halted the Federalist counteroffensive, much to the surprise of Republican and Federalist alike. For more than a year, the case had loomed as a showdown between the judiciary and the executive—and specifically between Marshall and Jefferson. And, indeed, in a detailed but taut decision, the Court lambasted Jefferson and his administration for withholding the disputed commissions from Marbury and his colleagues, calling it "not warranted but violative of vested legal right." Without holding Jefferson personally responsible, Marshall made it clear that he thought the grand lama had squandered the people's trust. No Federalist campaign pamphlet could have presented a more cogent case against Jefferson's reelection in 1804.

But Marshall's attack also misled, for it came coupled to a cleverly convoluted ruling against Marbury. The plaintiff, Marshall asserted, certainly deserved his writ, and under the Judiciary Act of 1789, the Supreme Court had the power to grant it. However, Marshall went out of his way to declare that that power expanded the Court's jurisdiction in ways that ran afoul of Article III of the Constitution, and was therefore null and void. Marshall's long and fearsome prologue tossed the Federalists a bone and allowed their press to rejoice that the Court had determined that "Mr. Jefferson, the idol of democracy, the friend of the people, had trampled upon the charter of their liberties." But in cold political terms, the *Marbury* decision turned back the Federalists' campaign over the judiciary and averted a potentially explosive constitutional crisis pitting the Court against the executive—and it left poor Marbury without his judgeship. The Jeffersonians appreciated as much. The major Republican newspapers, Smith's *National Intelligencer* and Duane's *Aurora*, as well as the vexed Jefferson let the case pass without comment.

The *Marbury* ruling contained a keynote principle for which it has since become famous—the idea that the Court has ultimate constitutional authority to overrule acts of Congress as well as the states, commonly referred to as judicial review. Yet *Marbury* hardly established the principle of judicial review of state laws, a power the Constitution had already invested in the Supreme Court. And it was, and is, far from clear that Marshall intended the *Marbury* decision to establish the Supreme Court as the final arbiter on federal legislation. He never claimed such power outright during his remaining thirty-three years on the Court, although he would have several opportunities to do so; indeed, he was always cautious whenever discussing the Court's powers. Although expansive ideas on judicial review—amounting more exactly to judicial supremacy—gained numerous champions over the coming years, in practice the principle would lie dormant for more than two decades after Marshall's death, until advanced by a Court with a very different political outlook, and in a much more politically inflammatory case concerning the legal status of an obscure black man named Dred Scott.

Marshall's genuine achievement was to fend off efforts to politicize further the national judiciary in the immediate wake of the repeal of the 1801 Judiciary Act—and thereby contribute to a beleaguered but evolving politics of moderation. He managed to attack the Republicans and remind them of the principle of judicial review without forcing a showdown with Jefferson. But he also confuted those Federalists who had hoped to use the case to cripple Jefferson and his administration. "Let such men read this opinion and blush, if the power of blushing still remains with them," declared the pro-Marshall *Washington Federalist*. "It will remain as a monument of the wisdom, impartiality and independence of the Supreme Court, long after the name of its petty revilers shall have sunk into oblivion." Temporarily, at least, Marshall's ruling helped consolidate a middle ground between judicial supremacists and antijudicial Republican dogmatists, based on a de facto compromise: Federalists would accept the repeal act and cease their partisan maneuverings, provided Republicans curtailed their own assaults on Federalist control of the judiciary.

Federalist irreconcilables, concentrated in New England, were neither placated by Marshall's denunciation of Jefferson nor capable of compromise. Worse still, the acquisition of Louisiana and the apparent rising popularity of the president seemed to augur the Federalists' total defeat in national politics. The midterm elections of 1802 had gone badly for the Federalists, who, despite their early hopefulness about divisions among their opponents, lost ground to the Republicans in some supposedly safe districts, including the Delaware seat of House minority leader Bayard. The coming presidential election, with Jefferson running once again at the head of the Republican ticket, looked like a certain rout. The Federalists, many of whom inclined naturally to pessimism in the best of times, were most alarmed by the growing signs that unchecked democracy, what George Cabot called *"the government of the worst,"* was not collapsing under the weight of its own incompetence. For that, they chiefly blamed the unscrupulous, demagogic Virginia Republicans—above all, Timothy Pickering wrote, "[t]he cowardly wretch at their head," who "while, like a Parisian revolutionary monster, prating about humanity, would feel an infernal pleasure in the utter destruction of his opponents."

Quietly, Pickering and his cabal of Federalists continued their plotting to get New England, along with New York and New Jersey, to secede. By contemplating separation, the plotters displayed less regard for the federal union than had the backers of the Kentucky and Virginia Resolutions of 1798. By homing in on the political advantages handed Virginia and the rest of the slaveholding South by the Constitution's three-fifths clause, they at once hit the Virginians at their sorest ethical point, as the preachers of liberty and owners of slaves, and reaffirmed the underlying sectional differences in national affairs. But the Federalists, even those who considered slavery an evil, were no abolitionists. ("Without a separation," Pickering wondered, "can those States [i.e., New England, plus New York and New Jersey] ever rid themselves of negro Presidents and negro Congresses, and regain their just weight in the political balance?") The immense irony of erstwhile nationalists advocating secession was not lost on such leading Federalists and Unionists as Alexander Hamilton and Rufus King, and the secession conspiracy faded for lack of support. Instead, Pickering and company turned their attention to the ever-fractious nominal Republican, Vice President Aaron Burr.

By 1804, Burr, thoroughly distrusted by Jefferson and Jefferson's friends in Congress, no longer seemed as indispensable as he had four years earlier to secure the Republicans' crucial electoral base in New York. Jefferson had long relied on the aging New York governor George Clinton for advice about policy and patronage, and in February 1804, the Republican congressional caucus duly dumped Burr and named Clinton as its nominee for vice president. Immediately, Burr set his sights on winning the New York governorship, a prospect that intrigued some Federalist hard-liners. "Were New York detached (as under [Burr's] administration it would be), from the Virginia influence, the whole Union should be benefited," an excited Timothy Pickering wrote in early March. "Jefferson would then be forced to observe some caution and forbearance in his measures." But in 1804, as in 1801, Burrite Federalists faced the stern opposition of Alexander Hamilton, who despised Vice President Burr even more than he did President Jefferson.

For years, despite public displays of mutual cordiality, Hamilton had hated and pursued Burr with a passion that, if not necessarily "pathologic" as one biographer has concluded, certainly bordered on the obsessive. To Hamilton, Burr was an undistinguished and mendacious self-promoter, a man of "an irregular ambition" and "prodigal cupidity." Hamilton's opposition made little difference to the New York governor's race, which Burr lost by a landslide, thanks in part to slanderous attacks on the candidate by George Clinton. But Burr blamed Hamilton anyway, making much ado over a particular alleged slight, and the stage was set for an "interview" with pistols at Weehawken, New Jersey, just across the Hudson from Manhattan, on the morning of July 11. The next day, Hamilton, a bullet lodged near his spine, died in agony. Burr, indicted for murder by courts in both New York and New Jersey, fled to South Carolina, ever thereafter an object of vilification. From New York, Secretary Gallatin wrote to Jefferson after Hamilton's funeral that "much artificial feeling, or semblance of feeling," worked up by the anti-Burr and Federalist interests, had mingled with the public's sincere shock and grief at what occurred. Gallatin failed to mention a riper irony: that in encouraging an alliance with Burr, certain Federalists had set in motion events that led to the killing of Hamilton, the greatest Federalist mind of all.

Following the momentous duel, the presidential election of 1804 came as something of an anticlimax. However, in sharp contrast to the contest four years earlier, it ended in one of the most lopsided outcomes in all of American history. The Federalists, overcome by their loss of the presidency four years earlier, held no nominating caucus; instead, Federalist leaders and electors privately conferred with each other and, insisting they would only choose the best man after the electoral votes had been cast, settled on Charles Cotesworth Pinckney of South Carolina and Rufus King, now of New York, as their nominees. In effect, the party ran no campaign, except for their electoral slates in the states. Pinckney and King did not lack experience, talent, or high reputation. But the Republicans, having built up their state-level organizations, stifled their internal differences, profited from peace, prosperity, and Jefferson's popularity, and rendered Pinckney and King forgotten also-rans—or, more properly, never-rans. The Republicans lost only two states and won 162 electoral votes to 14 for their adversaries. Even in the Federalist citadel of Massachusetts, the Republicans not only carried the presidential tally but increased their vote for state and local offices, completing, as John Quincy Adams told his father, a revolution in the commonwealth's politics. "The new century opened itself by committing us on a boisterous ocean," Jefferson rejoiced, taking special pleasure in the Massachusetts result. "But all this is now subsiding, peace is smoothing our paths at home and abroad, and if we are not wanting in the practice of justice and moderation, our tranquility and property may be preserved, until increasing numbers shall leave us nothing to fear from without."

Nothing to fear from without—but from within? Political developments were further solidifying the Republican ascendancy over the Federalists, but also contained some disturbing divisions and paradoxes, with greater ramifications than the Burrite schism for the Jeffersonians. Growing tensions between city and country democrats, on the one hand, and Republican moderates, on the other, intensified divisions within the party. Sectional differences presaged far fiercer national conflicts to come. And these divisions arose directly from complicated struggles, concentrated in state politics, to define a democratic polity.

FEDERALISTS, CLODHOPPERS, AND TERTIUM QUIDS: DEMOCRACY IN THE STATES

In 1806, Jefferson's favorite American architect, Benjamin Latrobe, ventured some thoughts on politics, writing that "[a]fter the adoption of the Federal Constitution, the extension of the right of suffrage in the States to a majority of all the adult male citizens, planted a germ which [has] gradually evolved and has spread actual and practical democracy and political equality over the whole union." Latrobe exaggerated. The Jeffersonian ascendancy, by repudiating the Federalists' hidebound elitism, greatly encouraged democratic ferment. After 1800, formal petitions and newspaper articles flooded state capitals demanding widened suffrage and fairer representation for rapidly growing cities and backwoods settlements. Overall, however, democratic reformers, urban and rural, won only a few solid victories. In some places, especially in the slaveholding South, even the successful reforms in the decade after 1800 achieved less than met the eye. And although Republicans were usually at the forefront of change, pressure for democratization divided moderate and radical Republicans against each other.

One set of pressures for democratic reform came from the organization of new territorial and state governments west of the Alleghenies. As fresh settlers swelled the Old Northwest population, constitutional and political organization became an issue of primary importance. Settlers in the northern territories objected primarily to the fifty-acre freehold qualification for voting in the western territories, a restriction inherited from the Northwest Ordinance of 1787. Newly established western newspapers, North and South, railed against all vestiges of aristocracy, quoting from the work of various British and American democratic reformers. In Ohio, radical Republican democrats defended the rights of "laboring men" and farmers, and demanded a constitution "that will set the natural rights of the meanest African and the most abject beggar upon an equal footing with those citizens of the greatest wealth and equipage." Other democrats were less egalitarian, notably on racial issues, but still insisted that the landholding upper class—"a kind of Noblesse," one Jeffersonian called it—should relinquish any claims to formal political supremacy. Although they did not win all they wanted, the democrats created a new state government, and after that a Republican-dominated party system, far more egalitarian than their Federalist adversaries had desired.

Practical considerations also advanced western democracy. Above all, the legal complications of surveying western land and granting freehold titles often were too cumbersome to accommodate any propertied voting requirement. In Kentucky, freehold suffrage, established in 1776 while the area was still part of Virginia, was useless given the state's Byzantine land laws and constant litigation over land titles. Hence, the state's relatively conservative state constitution of 1792 conceded universal free manhood suffrage, with no property or tax-paying requirement. In Ohio, delays in granting freehold land titles so restricted the territorial electorate that in 1798, even before statehood, the federal government enfranchised owners of town lots that were worth as much as fifty-acre freeholds. By 1815, Kentucky was the only western state that matched Vermont's complete elimination of property requirements for voting, but Ohio's constitution of 1803 established virtual adult male suffrage by imposing a minimal tax-paying requirement (while also restricting the vote to whites, as

Kentucky had done in its revised constitution of 1799). Tennessee sustained a freehold requirement that would last until 1834, but provided as an alternative a trivial six-month residency requirement that was tantamount to granting adult manhood suffrage. Kentucky, with its wide-open suffrage for white men, was the site of the most dramatic western reform clash of the Jeffersonian years. Picking up where they had left off after the disappointing constitutional struggle of 1799, Kentucky's country democrats, still strongest in the state's rapidly growing yeoman Green River district, turned back to legislative matters, and to a radical version of Jeffersonian-style judicial reform. Led by a resourceful political newcomer full of home-spun eloquence, the twenty-two-year-old lawyer Felix Grundy, the reformers undertook replacing Kentucky's centralized and (to remote settlers) inaccessible court system with circuit courts that would meet three times a year in each county for six-day terms. Demanding an "equal and impartial distribution of advantages and privileges," Grundy and his allies lambasted their opponents as an alliance of parasitic lawyers, lazy judges, and greedy land speculators who feared having local juries decide on their land titles. More moderate Republicans, including Henry Clay, replied that the proposed reforms would destroy the uniform and independent judiciary that was vital to continued economic growth. But Grundy's forces won a compromise reform in 1802 that enlarged the existing court system.

East of the Alleghenies, southern reformers won a few triumphs. Maryland reformers, supported by Baltimore's city democrats, secured an adult male suffrage law and, in time, additional concessions including popular election of the governor and the elimination of property and religious tests for public officeholders. A revision of South Carolina's constitution in 1808 partially rectified the state's gross malapportionment by giving the state's up-country counties a majority of the seats in the lower house of the legislature. A year later, the city democracy of Charleston joined with backcountry planters (including a young Yale graduate named John C. Calhoun) to secure the franchise for all white male adults who had resided in the state for two years. The Carolina up-country, where politics had been comparatively open and competitive even before the revisions, greatly increased its power in the legislature, with the promise of it increasing even further with future reapportionment now scheduled every ten years. But the reforms also left the state senate securely in the hands of the low-country grandees and did nothing to alter the state's high property requirements for officeholding. The lower-house reapportionment wound up benefiting a new class of up-country cotton planters more than it did the pineywoods yeomanry. The state's suffrage debate turned on the claim that enfranchising all adult white men would further entrench popular loyalty to the institution of slavery. In all, democratization in South Carolina ironically went hand in hand with consolidating the power of the state's expanding slaveholder elite.

Democratic reformers gained the most momentum during the first decade of the new century in the northeastern and middle states. A detailed look at events in these states shows the complexity of democratic reform as it actually proceeded during Jefferson's presidency, including the divisions reform efforts provoked among Republicans. It also reveals a pattern. Where Federalists and Federalism remained strong, the democrats' greater coherence created a viable Jeffersonian opposition and prepared the way for more successful reform efforts in later years. Where Federalists and Federalism were weakest—notably in Pennsylvania—growing pressure for democratic reform helped widen the gap between radical Republicans and moderate Republicans.

Federalist Connecticut was the most conservative northeastern state, its political institutions still governed largely on the terms of its original royalist charter of 1662. A virtual oligarchy of Federalist notables and prominent Congregational clergymen (leaders of what remained the state's formally established church) ran local affairs. Under the circumstances, state politics inspired little public interest. (In the 1790s, as few as 5 percent of Connecticut's eligible voters actually cast ballots in gubernatorial elections.) "The advancement of political science, generated by our revolution," one New York Republican paper observed, "has neither changed her constitution nor affected her *steady habits*." As the Massachusetts Federalist Fisher Ames put it, "folly"—that is, democracy—was not a fashion in Connecticut.

In these straitened circumstances, the reform leader was an idealistic renegade of the Connecticut establishment. Abraham Bishop, graduate of Yale in 1778, came from a background "respectable for order and religion," one Federalist editor observed with chagrin. In 1787, Bishop traveled to Europe and returned home nearly two years later a red-hot enthusiast for *liberté, egalité,* and *fraternité.* Over the next ten years, as one of the few outspoken critics of Federalism in the state, he became a genuine political force. Bishop denounced the Hamiltonian funding system as "the Political Baal," described Federalism as a sort of miasma that addled the brains of the voters, and ridiculed the union of church and state. When he was not taunting his opponents, Bishop was busy behind the scenes organizing editors and dissenters that one pro-Federalist newspaper grumbled about as "the democratic literate, so often, at houses of public entertainment [chiefly, taverns] who harangue the mob." Although they could not carry Connecticut for Jefferson, Bishop and his allies established the Connecticut Republicans as a distinct party organization, directed by a statewide Republican general committee that appointed county committees, which in turn oversaw town and district committees.

Just as important as the Bishop Republicans' strictly partisan efforts were their attempts to reform Connecticut politics and government. Bishop himself proposed to write a new state constitution that would totally separate church and state, provide for genuine checks and balances among the three branches of government, and widen the franchise. Federalists moved quickly and surely to crush these and other "Jacobinical" heresies by enacting a complicated and intimidating new measure, soon dubbed the "Stand Up Law," that required viva voce polling in all elections except those for governor or town representative. It would take another fifteen years before the Connecticut reformers gained the initiative. Yet the Republicans had rattled the Federalist establishment and provoked the electorate out of its political slumbers. Between 1804 and 1806 the number of voters who participated in the state's gubernatorial election would increase by 70 percent.

In Massachusetts, never a one-party state, Republican organization and pressure for democratic reform developed more successfully. The state's Federalists were just as fearful of Jeffersonian extremism as were their Connecticut counterparts—but having survived Shays' Rebellion and weathered the turmoil of the 1790s, Massachusetts conservatives shrank from the sorts of intense counterdemocratic activities undertaken by Connecticut's conservatives. Republican organizers accordingly built a political organization even more sophisticated than the Connecticut machine, headed by the party's legislative caucus, which chose the statewide central committee. County and town committees had the chief responsibility for widening popular support, circulating campaign materials, and getting Republican voters to the polls. The Massachusetts Republicans also introduced democratic procedures within the party, including countywide conventions that nominated candidates for Congress; passed resolutions on sundry public matters; and conducted, as one convention announced in 1808, "such other business as might be deemed necessary for the support of the Republican cause."

The major political battles in Massachusetts concerned the state's antiquated judiciary—not over whether to reform it but over how thoroughly it should be reformed. Between 1803 and 1805, the Federalist-controlled state legislature enacted several reforms outlined by Theodore Sedgwick, the former Speaker of the U.S. House of Representatives who had been appointed to the Massachusetts Supreme Court. Massachusetts Republicans accepted most of Sedgwick's proposals, but objected fervently to two of them: increasing judges' salaries and limiting juries' powers to interpret the law, which the reformers believed would permit the solidly Federalist state bench to continue its blatantly partisan domination. Between 1803 and 1806, the Republican legislators, although in the minority, killed every proposal to increase the salaries of the state supreme court justices. They remained equally vocal about allowing juries to interpret the law as they saw fit, sometimes reaching the point of endorsing what today would be called jury nullification. But after 1806, when the Republicans actually gained control of the legislature, the terms of debate over the judiciary and state politics lurched leftward—and the Republicans began to factionalize into moderates and democratic radicals. Country democrats, including the remainders of the old Berkshire Constitutionalist movement, demanded complete elimination of the common law, further simplification of court procedures, and the popular election of all judges. (The claim that voters lacked sufficient wisdom to choose judges, the Baptist itinerant John Leland contended, "saps the foundation of all representative government, and supports the monarchical.") Boston's city democrats, led by Benjamin Austin, also agitated on the matter. Moderate Republicans reacted with alarm and, led by the lawyer Joseph Story of Salem, moved quickly to thwart them.

The breach opened in 1806 when, with moderate Federalist support, Story chaired a special committee that insisted on maintaining the judiciary's independence and recommended, among other reforms, an increase in judicial salaries, which the legislature enacted. The radicals denounced the new law, in the apoplectic mixed metaphors of the *Pittsfield Sun*, as "nothing short of a premeditated blow at the *root of Democratic Government*, and a *Chief Corner Stone* of the great *Fabric of Aristocracy*." But the radicals lacked the legislative muscle required to repeal the law, or to get rid of Story, who, with Federalist backing, was reelected head of the lower house's judiciary committee in 1807 and 1808. With the Republican majority now sorely split, Story did not manage to complete any further moderate judicial reforms, but the radicals, too, were stymied, which created lasting divisions among Massachusetts Republicans.

The middle Atlantic states, where sophisticated party organizations had developed before 1800, presented their own peculiarities with respect to democratic politics, often closely tied to voter fraud. The one major New York reform of the period came after New York City Federalist election inspectors, in 1801, refused to allow Republican voters who had been issued temporary freehold deeds to cast their ballots. Under the city charter, dating back to colonial times, voting in local elections was restricted to freemen of the corporation or male twenty-pound freeholders. (Voting was also *viva voce*.) Most ordinary New Yorkers could not meet the financial requirements, and Federalists, in control of the corporation, refused to grant freemanships to any but their merchant friends. Consequently, in 1800, although 13 percent of the city's total population was qualified to vote in state elections, only 5 percent could vote in municipal elections. Republican operatives got around the exclusion by issuing the temporary freeholds. Incensed at their exclusion in 1801, a group of cartmen petitioned the mayor and alderman. Republicans, in and out of the city, supported them, and in 1804, the state legislature passed a law that overrode the city charter, established written ballots in city elections, and gave the vote in assembly elections to all adult male citizens who rented a tenement worth twenty-five dollars a year.

Across the Hudson River, in New Jersey, intense partisanship and lax enforcement of voting requirements bred concern among Republicans and Federalists alike. In 1802, numerous complaints arose after a Trenton election in which, critics claimed, ineligible minors, Philadelphians, slaves, married women, and others were permitted to vote. Five years later, a vigorous contest in Essex County, to determine whether Newark or Elizabeth would be the county seat, caused so many irregularities—including, allegedly, trooping scores of women, eligible and ineligible, to the polls—that the total vote in Newark alone was greater than had ever been recorded for the county as a whole. The legislature duly clarified the regulations and granted the vote to free white males who paid any state or county tax—an approximation of universal white manhood suffrage. But the new law also barred blacks and noncitizens from voting and ended the state's singular enfranchisement of propertied widows, purposefully included in the state constitution of 1776. Supporters of female disenfranchisement justified it as a response to the Essex County fiasco: the new regulations simplified matters by making it easier to determine, at a glance, who was an eligible voter. The reform struggles in Pennsylvania were the most ferocious of any in the nation. The suffrage was not at issue, as the drafters of the state constitution of 1790 took care to preserve the relatively mild taxpaying requirement stipulated in the original radical 1776 constitution. Instead, politics revolved chiefly around judicial reform, as in Kentucky and Massachusetts. But Pennsylvania was also a very special case. After 1802, when the Federalists lost in a crushing statewide defeat, the state's chief political battles pitted against each other, as nowhere else, powerful rival Jeffersonian factions of moderates, city radicals, and country radicals. These contests would eventually spill over into federal affairs and affect the brand-new national Republican coalition.

The nominal leader of the moderates, Governor Thomas McKean, had, prior to his election in 1799, served for more than twenty years as the first chief justice of Pennsylvania's Supreme Court, and had been active in drafting the 1790 constitution. More politically gifted than the aloof and arrogant McKean was his secretary and staunch ally, Alexander J. Dallas. A brilliant immigrant from the West Indies, Dallas had risen quickly in Philadelphia oppositionist politics after the Revolution—including a stint as a member of the Democratic Society of Pennsylvania—and had considerable influence and power throughout the state. Two other veterans of the political wars of the 1790s, Peter Muhlenberg and Albert Gallatin, were also leading moderates. Bitterly opposed to the Federalists' organic conceptions of hierarchical privilege and order, they nonetheless found some common ground with the Federalists about the courts. Above all, the moderates believed that through prudent economic development, ordinary men would seize upon the ample opportunities the nation had to offer and rise in the world. One prerequisite for that development was an efficient, independent judiciary, which would permit the widening of economic growth free of political connections.

To the left of the McKean-Dallas faction stood the still-vibrant Philadelphia city democracy, led by William Duane of the *Aurora* and his longtime collaborator Michael Leib. Together, Duane and Leib had built a powerful local Republican electoral machine, especially strong in the city suburbs heavily populated by laboring men. On national issues, they sided with those who wanted President Jefferson to purge the government of Federalists and overhaul the federal judiciary from top to bottom. Closer to home, they attacked the application of arcane common law by state courts, demanded the creation of arbitration courts elected by the people to decide contract and title disputes, pushed to reduce the power of trained lawyers, and sought to expand the power of the lower legislative house at the expense of the governor and the senate. The city democrats viewed McKean, Dallas, and their moderate friends as backsliders, and even traitors, to the Republican cause, and the principles of the Revolution. The contest was "no longer that of resistance to foreign rule," the *Aurora* declared, "but *which of us shall be the rulers?*"

A third group of Pennsylvania Republicans consisted of country-based insurgents who came to be known, memorably (after a derisive remark by McKean), as the Clodhopper Democrats. Their foremost figure was the future governor Simon Snyder, an exemplar of how ambitious country democrats of modest backgrounds could attain the highest state offices. Born in Lancaster, Snyder had moved to southeastern Northumberland County in 1784, a partially schooled twenty-four-year-old. By working as a journeyman tanner and as a scrivener, Snyder made enough money to purchase some land, build a mill, and open a store. His neighbors elected him justice of the peace, chose him as a delegate to the state constitutional convention in 1790, and elected him to the state legislature in 1797. After arriving in Lancaster, the state capital, Snyder befriended another freshman legislator, Nathaniel Boileau, the son of a Montgomery County farmer, who had matriculated at the College of New Jersey in

THE CRISIS OF
THE NEW ORDER

1. Thomas Jefferson, inauguration banner, 1801

2. John Singleton Copley's portrait of Paul Revere, ca. 1768

3. Charles Willson Peale's 1779 portrait of George Washington at the Battle of Princeton in 1777

4. Charles Willson Peale's portrait of Timothy Matlack, ca. 1780

5. Portrait of Timothy Matlack attributed to Rembrandt Peale, ca. 1802

7. James Madison, 1797

6. Thomas Jefferson, 1805

8. William Duane, 1802

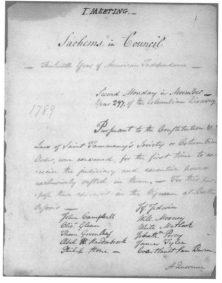

9. *Journal & Rules of the Council of Sachems of St. Tammany's Society,* New York, 1789

10. John Adams, 1799

11. Alexander Hamilton, ca. 1792

12. William Loughton Smith, ca. 1790

13. John Randolph, 1804–05

14. Tally of Electoral College votes,
February 11, 1801

15. Broadside of Thomas Jefferson's first
inaugural address, 1801

16. Abraham Bishop, ca. 1790

17. John Marshall, 1808

18. Federalist cartoon of Napoleon
stinging Jefferson into the Louisiana
Purchase, 1803

19. Federalist satire of Jefferson and
Sally Hemings, 1804

20. Federalist cartoon of Liberty nursed by Mother Mob, 1807

21. Anti-British cartoon on alleged bribery of the northwestern Indians, 1812

22. Tenkswatawa, 1823

23. Republican satire of the Hartford Convention as traitorous, 1814

24. The Battle of New Orleans, ca. 1815–20

Princeton and was then admitted to the Pennsylvania bar. Rounding out the Clodhopper leadership was the remarkable Irish-born émigré printer John Binns, whose activities across the Irish Sea as a young member of the radical London Corresponding Society landed him in prison on several occasions before he fled to America in 1802. Lured to Northumberland County by his fellow British radical exiles, Joseph Priestley and Thomas Cooper, Binns established a newspaper in 1802, the Northumberland *Republican Argus*, which, as the Clodhoppers' chief political organ, quickly became the most important rural newspaper in the state, a counterpart to the *Aurora*.

The court struggle began in 1802, and it culminated, briefly, in a statewide coalition of city and country democrats that frightened moderate Republicans and Federalists alike. Initially, Republicans of all persuasions could agree on the need to reform the judiciary and check the most blatantly partisan Federalist justices—above all, the chief judge of the western circuit, Alexander Addison, whom Governor McKean denounced as "the transmontane Golia[t]h of federalism," and whom the moderates impeached and removed from office. But Duane and the Philadelphia radicals wanted more—a clean sweep of Federalist justices from the state supreme court and a complete overhaul and simplification of the state's legal code to place it more in line with what one critic called "the plain and simple nature of a Republican government." Deriding the McKean moderates as the Tertium Quid—literally, the "third thing," standing between Federalism and genuine Republicanism—Duane, Leib, and the city democrats forged an alliance with Snyder, Boileau, and their country counterparts and founded a mass organization, complete with country committees, called the Democratic Society of the Friends of the People, an echo of the 1790s. They pressed for additional removals and managed to impeach (though not convict) three more Federalist justices. They also proposed a new state convention to overhaul the state's judiciary.

In 1805, the coalition of the Snyderites and the Philadelphia radicals, with the elderly Thomas Paine's benediction, managed to persuade the Republican legislative caucus to dump McKean as its gubernatorial candidate, in favor of Snyder. Horrified, a coalition of moderate Republicans and Federalists endorsed McKean's reelection. The ensuing campaign was one of the nastiest in Pennsylvania history, filled with Snyderite charges that McKean had systematically ignored the will of the people and McKeanite counterblasts that a victory for Snyder would plunge the state into the "pristine imbecility" of a pure democracy. Drawing his support chiefly from older, commercialized agricultural regions as well as from the major cities (other than the Duane-Leib–controlled parts of Philadelphia County), McKean eked out a five-thousand-vote majority—but, as Albert Gallatin noted, he owed "his re-election to the Federalists." Tensions arose thereafter between country and city democrats, in part because the country democrats favored various moderate Republican proposals to widen access to bank credit and promote road-, canal-, and bridge-building projects that the *Aurora* group believed favored established Philadelphia vested interests. Yet under the pressure of a sudden Federalist revival, the Clodhoppers effected a rapprochement with both the Quids and the *Aurora* democrats, succeeded in electing the Clodhopper Simon Snyder as governor in 1807, and commenced a Republican regime that would last for a decade.

The vicissitudes of Pennsylvania politics expose the shortcomings of the many interpretations that cast the politics of the Jeffersonian era as a straightforward battle between sharply demarcated partisan interests: agrarian versus commercial, or pro-capitalist versus anticapitalist, or backward-looking Federalists versus forward-looking Jeffersonians (or vice versa). For the men who lived through these politics on the ground, as well as for those who shaped them at the top, the Republican coalition, in particular, was much more complex and fractious than such interpretations allow.

What we can see, in Pennsylvania and the other states, is the emergence of a diverse new generation of democratic political leaders, ranging from the Yale apostate Abraham Bishop to self-made men such as Felix Grundy and Simon Snyder. Their vehemence against both Federalist elitism and what they deemed the tepidness of some Republicans stirred up politics in their respective states and offered portents of democratic outbursts to come. The actual achievements of these men and their followers was limited. Even where reform succeeded, the results were not always uniform or lasting. (One, little noticed at the time, was the decision by Pennsylvania, after the electoral crisis of 1800, to switch to the direct popular selection of presidential electors in time for the 1804 campaign. By 1804, a total of eight of the seventeen states provided for direct election, beginning a trend that, by 1824, would leave only six of the twenty-four states where legislatures still did the choosing.) "Democratization" chiefly marked growing differences between the somnolent slaveholding South—where, at least in South Carolina, democratization of a kind became, ironically, a bulwark for slavery—and the more agitated North—where democratization accompanied both the enactment of gradual emancipation laws in the last holdout states and the emergence of a viable Republican opposition to the Federalist political establishment. In the long run, these differences would cause the breakdown of the Union. In the short run, they highlighted the persisting divisions within American politics at the state as well as the national level, despite the formation of a successful new party and the decline of an old one— even as the newly reelected president savored his crushing triumph in the 1804 election.

THE SECOND PRESIDENCY

In contrast to the exquisite care with which he wrote his first inaugural address, President Jefferson had the chance to be loose and expansive when he came to write his second. "The first was from the nature of the case all profession & promise," he boasted to a young Virginian, John Tyler, whereas the second was "performance." The optimism was misplaced. In part because of his own political overreaching, Jefferson would leave Washington in 1809 feeling like a released prisoner. His new troubles became manifest already during the months between his reelection and his second swearing-in.

The administration's struggle against the judiciary had not ended with Marbury. Emboldened by the Pennsylvania Republicans' ouster of Judge Alexander Addison, Jefferson and his lieutenants decided to use the weapon of impeachment to attack their most obnoxious foes on the Federalist bench. Their choicest target was a deranged and allegedly alcoholic federal district judge, John Pickering of New Hampshire. Impeached by the House for drunkenness and unlawful rulings, Pickering was tried by the Senate and removed from office in March 1804 by a bare two-thirds' majority. But Pickering's was to prove only a warm-up case. On the very same day that the Senate removed him, the House passed a resolution, introduced weeks earlier by John Randolph, calling for the impeachment of a far more formidable figure, the doctrinaire yet resourceful associate justice of the Supreme Court, Samuel Chase.

Chase was, in 1804, the most powerful conservative Federalist in the federal government, and the Republicans' loathing for him ran deep. Confirmed by the Federalist-controlled Senate in 1795, he turned into a single-minded enforcer during the alien and sedition crisis. He presided belligerently over several of the most sensational sedition trials and punished those convicted to the limits the law allowed. Moderate Federalists, including President Adams, abjured his behavior, and the more radical of the Republican editors demanded his impeachment. Jefferson, in his early conciliatory phase, decided against assailing him. But Chase's bitterness and recklessness increasingly got the better of him, especially after the repeal of the Judiciary Act of 1801. In May 1803, while riding circuit in his native Maryland, he delivered, as a charge to a Baltimore grand jury, a polemic against various signs of what he called impending "mobocracy," including the administration's judicial policies and Maryland's recent adoption of universal white manhood suffrage. "The modern doctrines by our late reformers, that all men in a state of society are entitled to enjoy equal liberty and equal rights have brought this mighty mischief upon us," he raged to the jurors, his massive frame shaking, "and I fear that it will rapidly progress until peace and order, freedom and property, shall be destroyed." Jefferson immediately (and impulsively) wrote Congressman Joseph Hopper Nicholson of Maryland, broadly hinting that Chase ought to be impeached and removed from the Court, while adding that "for myself, it is better that I should not interfere."

Although Chase had plainly disgraced his position, Jefferson would have been wiser, politically and constitutionally, had he heeded his own caution and said nothing. Impeaching the incompetent Pickering, though itself of questionable constitutional correctness, was one thing; impeaching Chase, who was harshly partisan but patently fit to serve, was quite another. Chase's courtroom speech, construed by Jefferson as "seditious," hardly amounted to a self-evident high crime or misdemeanor, the sole grounds for impeachment as stipulated by the Constitution. Although the Republican press, including the *National Intelligencer*, attacked Chase repeatedly over the summer of 1803, most Republican leaders, including Congressman Nicholson, seemed unwilling to test either Chase or the Constitution—and even Jefferson in time calmed down and took no official action. Suddenly, however, in January 1804, John Randolph, the least reliable of the congressional Republicans, rose in the House and introduced his resolution. It required nearly an additional year of discussions and debate, but in the end, Randolph and his allies prevailed and the House passed eight articles of impeachment. One of the articles singled out Chase's charge to the Baltimore jury as "an intemperate and inflammatory political harangue" intended "to excite the fears and resentment of said grand jury, and the good people of Maryland" against the governments of Maryland and the United States.

The irony, for Jefferson, was that by the time he took up the Chase issue, the troublesome Randolph was on the verge of breaking with the administration over another matter entirely, the so-called Yazoo compromise, involving alleged administration corruption in a long-standing Georgia land-fraud dispute. Randolph's motives for pursuing the Chase and Yazoo matters combined ideological rectitude, personal hurts, and his sense that his influence was on the decline. Randolph and his allies were powerful enough to delay a settlement of the Yazoo case until after President Jefferson left office. The Chase impeachment, however, proceeded more swiftly, and, for the Republicans, more dangerously. There is no evidence that Jefferson, as much as he wanted Chase ousted, approved of Randolph's taking the lead in the effort. Several leading northern Republicans, in both the House and the Senate, tried to slow down the impeachment process. But in 1804, most Jeffersonians in the House of Representatives still detested Samuel Chase far more than they distrusted John Randolph. With some misgivings, they sent the articles of impeachment on to the Senate.

Chase's trial, presided over by Vice President Burr, back from his exile, and conducted with great pomp and solemnity in the Senate chamber, was a debacle. Chase, a seasoned lawyer, assembled a superb defense team, including the southern Federalists Robert Goodloe Harper and Luther Martin. In contrast to Chase's meticulous and unflappable defenders—especially Martin, a notorious drunk but a courtroom bulldog—Randolph and the House impeachment managers looked amateurish. Randolph's final summation, a rambling affair that lasted more than two hours, was described by one listener, the admittedly biased John Quincy Adams, as "without order, connection, or argument; consisting altogether of the most hackneyed commonplaces of popular declamation, mingled up with panegyrics and invectives upon persons, with a few well-expressed ideas, a few striking figures, much distortion of face and contortion of body, tears, groans, and sobs, with occasional pauses for recollection, and continual complaints of having lost his notes." The show concluded, mercifully, on March 1, 1805, three days before Jefferson's second inauguration. A majority of the senators found Chase guilty on only three of the eight impeachment articles, and just one article—the eighth, covering Chase's charge to the Baltimore jury—came within five votes of winning the two-thirds' majority required to convict and remove the accused. Six of the twenty-five Republican senators, all but one of them northerners, voted against all of the articles.*

By rejecting a constitutionally dubious impeachment drive, the Chase acquittal established practical limits on the congressional impeachment power, while it reinforced judicial independence. These were vital steps in the continuing battle over the shape of the nation's democratic institutions, and the principles they established would be respected for decades. Yet the case did stigmatize the kind of blatantly partisan behavior that Chase had assumed was his privilege. (Victorious but humbled, old Chase served out his term politely and without controversy until his death in 1811.) For Jefferson, the entire affair had proved an embarrassment, though nowhere nearly as great an embarrassment as it was for Randolph, who never fully recovered politically and who forever suspected, with good reason, that Jefferson had quietly hung him out to dry. Embittered by the outcome, Randolph and his friends, their revolt against the administration broken, would become known as Old Republicans or as Tertium Quids, neither Federalist nor Jeffersonian (but not to be confused with the Pennsylvania moderate Republicans given the same nickname by their radical foes).

The only national figure who emerged from the affair with his reputation enhanced was the outgoing vice president, Aaron Burr. When, after the clamor over his killing of Hamilton subsided, Burr had resurfaced in Washington, some northern Federalists wondered if he ought to be impeached as well, since he was still under indictment for murder in New York and New Jersey.

---

*Two of the articles, concerning Chase's alleged disregard of Virginia procedures in the sedition trial of James Callender, won not a single vote in the Senate. See AC, 8th Congress, second session, 664–9.

But neither Republicans nor southern Federalists agreed. Instead, as president of the Senate, Burr oversaw the proceedings against Chase with widely acknowledged fairness and dignity. The day after Chase's acquittal, Burr delivered a stirring valedictory speech to the Senate that reduced some listeners to tears. Soon enough, though, Burr was embroiled in his customary intrigues, which caused Jefferson's next major round of political headaches.

All the mysteries of the Burr conspiracy will probably never be revealed, but enough is known that it must be judged an authentic threat, not just to Jefferson but to the republic. This can be difficult to grasp, for in retrospect the drama easily looks like a convoluted farce, featuring a huge cast of unlikely characters. But wrapped inside the farce was a near disaster. Even before he had finished his vice presidency, Burr began plotting with the money-hungry Brigadier General James Wilkinson, who was the commanding officer of the U.S. Army and governor of the new Louisiana Territory (and, secretly, an agent for the Spanish Crown). The two conspirators' plans were mutable; new ideas kept coming to them as they boastfully tried to inveigle various American politicians, military leaders, and rich, would-be power brokers, as well as foreign diplomats, into supporting their scheme. At the very least, it seems, they expected to launch military attacks on Mexico, persuade the western states to secede, and create a new nation on the North American mainland. Only Wilkinson's defection late in 1806 halted the planned attacks.

The real threat the conspiracy posed to American democracy concerned the uncertain political allegiances of the nation's military leadership. When he took office in 1801, Jefferson, reacting to the Federalists' partisan military buildup, moved to depoliticize and reduce drastically the size of the army. (The latter effort led to the establishment of the United States Military Academy at West Point in 1802.) But the process—which curtailed opportunities for career advancement for all existing officers—took time to promulgate, leaving a disgruntled officer corps intact just as Jefferson, after the Louisiana Purchase, needed the U.S. Army more than ever to command western military posts. Then, Jefferson's unmilitary reactions to a series of British provocations on the high seas after 1805 added to the discontent among officers with state as well as national commissions. Burr tried to exploit these weaknesses as he traveled among the officer corps, feeding on the resentments against the president and promising a stirring and patriotic military adventure. Burr was convinced he owned General Wilkinson's loyalty. To his new recruits, including a Tennessee militia commander in Nashville, Andrew Jackson, whom he personally courted, he applied his full powers of charm and persuasion. "[Y]our country is full of fine Materials for an Army," he told Jackson, "and I have often said that a Brigade could be raised in West Ten[nessee] which would drive double their Number of frenchmen off the Earth." Thousands of miles to the west of Washington, the possibility of domestic military interference in internal American politics, raised by Hamilton in 1799 and 1800, loomed once again—led, this time, by Hamilton's slayer.

Finally, and fortunately, General Wilkinson's sole loyalties were to himself. Fearing that Burr's military plans had become preposterous and hoping to sustain his standing with both the American and Spanish governments, Wilkinson betrayed Burr to Jefferson. Even before Burr was apprehended and transferred to Richmond for trial on charges of treason, Jefferson, in one of his rash moments, publicly proclaimed Burr's guilt and then plunged into trying to ensure his conviction. The trial—in which Burr retained a team that included none other than Samuel Chase's defender, Luther Martin—became a political imbroglio. Federalists, including presiding Justice Marshall, used the occasion to embarrass Jefferson, going so far as to issue a subpoena to the president. (Jefferson, on straight constitutional grounds, correctly refused to reply, and from here on, his contempt for Marshall was unequivocal.) Aided by the chief justice's peculiarly narrow construction of the Constitution's treason clause, Burr won a "not proven" verdict, which Marshall recorded as "not guilty." The government tried then to have Burr sent to Ohio to face new treason charges, but Marshall granted Burr bail—which

Burr, in character, jumped. He then sailed to Europe and attempted in vain to gain an audience with Bonaparte to essay yet another intrigue.

Amid Burr's trial, and while still facing Marshall's subpoena, President Jefferson confronted a realized military threat. On June 22, 1807, HMS *Leopard*, one of a squadron of British ships stationed off the coast of Virginia, intercepted USS *Chesapeake*, on the suspicion that the American frigate was harboring four British deserters. The American commander, Commodore James Barron, rightly refused the request to search his ship—such searches were permissible on merchantmen, but not on warships—then temporized, without calling his men to their battle stations. The *Leopard* opened fire on the Americans, killing three and wounding eighteen. After the Americans struck their colors, the British boarded and seized the alleged deserters, all of whom claimed to be Americans. The *Chesapeake* then limped back to Norfolk a splintered wreck.

The *Chesapeake* incident had been long in coming. The collapse of the Peace of Amiens in 1803, followed in 1805 by the British naval victory at Trafalgar and the French army's triumph at Austerlitz, had left Britain the commander of the Atlantic, France the commander of the European continent, and the United States a neutral with no military leverage whatsoever. In the spring of 1806, a single British warship, HMS *Leander*, stationed off New York Harbor, halted as many as twenty merchantmen at a time, pending searches for deserters. In April, one of *Leander's* shots across the bow of another vessel killed an American sailor, which touched off a riot in Manhattan and furious indignation around the country. The attack on the *Chesapeake* a year later, followed by fresh British Orders in Council banning neutrals from trading with France and its colonies, poured oil on the fire. The nation was furious; Jefferson shared that fury but was more ironic: "I suppose our fate will depend on the successes or reverses of Bonaparte," Jefferson wrote some weeks after the attack. Two weeks later, he sounded angrier—"It is really mortifying that we should be forced to wish success to Bonaparte," he told John Taylor—but after initially favoring a military response, he detached himself from the war fever. Instead, he would try to mobilize the public's outrage toward a policy of peaceful compulsion.

Jefferson's philosophy of international conflict directly challenged the bellicose expediencies of raison d'état that had driven Old World diplomacy for centuries. Jefferson was no pacifist. He thought the British attacks deserved a forceful response, and rejected the idea (which many Federalists and foreigners ascribed to him) that he should pursue peace at any price. ("This opinion must be corrected when just occasion arises," he wrote in 1806, "or we shall become the plunder of all nations.") But he knew that, in part because of his own policies to reverse the Federalist debts and taxes, the country was in no position to take on Great Britain. And his Enlightenment principles led him to regard war, with its ghastly cost in lives and property, as the absolute final resort in international disputes. European powers held him in contempt for this, but that much was to be expected. Instead, with the strong backing of Secretary of State Madison (and despite the personal opposition of Treasury Secretary Gallatin) he favored commercial coercion, a form of economic warfare that had been tested and proved at least partially effective—though far less so, in retrospect, than Jefferson and others believed it had—since the agitation against the Stamp Act in 1765.

And so, in December 1807, Jefferson replied to the British with what amounted to a boycott in reverse—a proposed embargo that would prohibit all oceanic trade with foreign nations, later extended to cover land and water commerce with Canada. Given a choice of evils, war or a radical embargo, Jefferson decided to pick, as a test, what he called, in a letter to Gallatin, the "least bad." Both houses of Congress swiftly passed the embargo bill. Aghast when voluntary compliance with the measure quickly abated, Jefferson personally and relentlessly sought to enforce it, requesting supplementary laws to halt smuggling across the Canadian border and across the Atlantic. These culminated in the draconian Giles's Enforcement Bill, enacted in January 1809. Disobedience of the law, sometimes flagrant, continued, prompting Jefferson to approve mobilizing troops in upstate New York and deploying revenue ships off the Atlantic coast and on inland waters. When challenged over the embargo's severity, the president privately denounced his critics, centered in maritime New England, as disloyalists, inflamed, he wrote, by "the monarchists of the North." Yet, outside of his annual messages in 1807 and 1808, and a calm but unyielding reply to a round of anti-embargo petitions from Massachusetts, he made inadequate efforts to explain the policy to the public or to understand the public's grievances, which he believed the Federalists were exaggerating.

The embargo was certainly a roll of the dice, but it was not a witless exercise in "Quaker-gun diplomacy," as it came to be ridiculed by Federalists. By embracing neutrality, Jefferson and Madison thought they could counter the Duke of Portland's Tory ministry by influencing British as well as American public opinion. British oppositionists, especially those tied to manufacturing and American trade, could be counted on to blast the Portland ministry for advocating an oppressive imperial system disguised as a necessary exigency of war. Robbed of their best customer, Britain's sensible businessmen would, presumably, come to their senses and demand respect for American neutral rights. Jefferson also thought that, at the very least, the embargo would give the United States enough breathing room to get its own house in order. "Till they return to some sense of moral duty," Jefferson wrote of the Old World belligerents, "we keep within ourselves. This gives time. Time may produce peace in Europe. Peace in Europe removes all causes of differences till another European war, and by that time our debt may be paid, our revenues clear, and our strength increased."

Neither time nor fortune aided Jefferson's experiment. Although the British opposition came to the Americans' defense, they lacked the political muscle to budge the Portland ministry. In the United States, the embargo's effects hit quickly and hard, cutting American shipping by as much as 80 percent and causing severe hardship among craftsmen and laborers in the seaport cities and neighboring farmers. Yet the embargo, although severe, was not quite the economic disaster its harshest critics claimed it to be, in part because the prosperity of recent years gave most merchants and farmers a cushion, and in part because the federal Treasury, which ran up an extraordinary total surplus of $17 million from 1805 to 1807, could withstand a cutoff of import duties. Those hardest hit by falling commodity prices—cotton and tobacco prices plunged by 40 to 50 percent in 1808—were southern planters, who were not among the leading complainers. In the Northeast, where the coastal trade appears to have thrived, resourceful merchants found ways to circumvent the laws and get goods shipped abroad, often with the connivance of local officials, including Republicans.

The magnitude of the successful violations of the embargo, and, at times, violent resistance to it, deepened the pathos of Jefferson's situation. In New London, Connecticut, the collector of customs—a Federalist so powerful that local Jeffersonians did not wish to obstruct him—allowed dozens of ships to leave port and pick up cargoes on order before the embargo began. Massachusetts federal juries acquitted more than four out of five accused offenders brought up on charges of violating the embargo law. At least one customs house official was murdered, in coastal Maine, as a result of local resistance to the law. Smuggling was rampant across the Canadian border; newspapers and letter writers actually reported more ship activity than usual on Lake Champlain. The longer the embargo continued, the quicker public support evaporated. The quicker Jefferson lost favor, the more recalcitrant he became.

New England led an all-out personal attack on the president. Yankee coastal towns and cities condemned the "dambargo"— also known in its reverse spelling as the cursed "o grab me"— from the moment it came into effect. As Jefferson became increasingly stubborn about enforcement, his personal correspondence, which always included hate mail, filled up with assassination threats and poison-pen letters. ("I have agreed to pay four of my friends $400 to shoat you if you don't take off the embargo by the 10th of Oct 1808 which I shall pay them, if I have to work on my hands & nees for it," ran one of many.) By late 1808, the Massachusetts legislature threatened to disregard the law, while looser tongues revived talk of New England secession.

As if gathering together all of their frustrations of the past eight years, Federalist propagandists let loose, portraying Jefferson (much as they portrayed democracy itself) as at once feeble and despotic. One precocious poet, the thirteen-year-old William Cullen Bryant (whose politics later changed dramatically), composed a bit of nastiness, "The Embargo," that touched on every bit of scurrility ever aimed at President Jefferson, including the charge about Jefferson's secret love affair with his mulatto slave, Sally Hemings:

> Go, wretch, resign the president's chair
> Disclose secret measures foul or fair,
> Go, search with curious eye, for horned frogs,
> 'Mongst the wild wastes of Louisiana bogs;
>
> Go scan, philosophist, thy ****** [Sally's] charms,
> And sink supinely in her sable arms;
> But quit to abler hands the helm of state,
> Nor image ruin on the country's fate.

Jefferson's supporters, like the president himself, reacted with hurt and indignation. "We are nearly all in favor of the embargo," Governor John Langdon of New Hampshire reassured him, "and . . . would not suffer a few enemies and speculators to make their fortunes." William Plumer, a New Hampshire Federalist, left his party over the embargo, and attributed the New England uproar to "designing men" out to influence the coming elections. But if Republicans could dismiss the propaganda, they could not ignore that the embargo fight had refreshed the flagging Federalist opposition and emboldened the administration's southern Old Republican foes.

Early in 1809, as Jefferson prepared to leave office, New England's congressional Republicans broke ranks with the administration over the embargo, joined by the New York friends of Vice President Clinton and the southern clique surrounding John Randolph. Jefferson admitted in his final annual message that the "candid and liberal experiment" had failed to coerce the Old World powers, but he still believed that the British would back down and hoped Congress would extend the measure in some form. The House refused the extension, then stipulated that the policy end on March 4, the day Jefferson was to step down. A "sudden and unaccountable revolution of opinion, chiefly among the New England and New York members," had led to the experiment's demise, Jefferson remarked bitterly. Instead, Congress passed a weaker substitute, the Non-Intercourse Act, allowing exports to all countries except Britain and France and permitting a renewal of trade with whichever of the belligerents showed respect for neutral rights. An undisguised appeal to mercantile self-interest, the new policy virtually ensured that both Britain and France would obtain all they wanted of American goods, and that British goods would be smuggled with impunity across American borders. "Thus we were driven from the high and wise ground we had taken," Jefferson wrote.

Approaching the age of sixty-six and eager to retire to Monticello, Jefferson had firmly rejected supporters' entreaties that he seek a third term. Now he lacked the will to fight back over the embargo. But he battled hard to elect his secretary of state and political heir, James Madison, to the presidency. It was not a sure thing. John Randolph and other anti-administration Republicans persuaded James Monroe to allow his name to be placed before the Republican congressional nominating caucus as an alternative. Then Federalist state leaders, meeting secretly in a self-assembled conclave in New York, renominated their still-respected ticket of Charles Cotesworth Pinckney and Rufus King, claiming that they would restore the prosperity and national honor squandered by Jefferson's disastrous embargo. Younger Federalists, learning lessons from the Republicans and frustrated by their elders' antipolitical elitism, organized several state committees and geared up a disciplined electioneering machinery to promote their own brand of political elitism with populist trappings.

Finally, the ancient Vice President Clinton, nudged along by his up-and-coming nephew DeWitt, presented himself as a candidate for both president and vice president, strongly attacking the congressional caucus system for nominations. Jefferson unflinchingly stood by Madison, tried to convince Monroe to back off, and proved the chief of the Republican coalition, winning over skeptics such as William Duane and the *Aurora* group and forcing Clinton to accept the second spot. The Federalists' turn to popular electioneering, meanwhile, could not overcome the Republicans' political machinery, especially in the southern and middle states. Madison defeated Monroe with ease in the congressional nominating caucus (which the Quids did not even bother to attend), and he and Clinton crushed the Federalist ticket in the Electoral College. With his administration given a vote of confidence, and his legacy secured, Jefferson virtually handed over command at that moment, weary of the fight, knowing that his successor was in a terrible bind. "Our situation is truly difficult," he wrote in November. "We have been pressed by the belligerents to the very wall & all further retreat [is] impraticable."

On March 4, 1809, with the wounds from the embargo fight still bleeding, Jefferson declined Madison's offer to ride with him in his carriage to the inauguration ceremonies. Instead, he rode to the Capitol on horseback with his grandson, Thomas Jefferson Randolph, tied up his mount, and joined the assembly within. "[N]ever did [a] prisoner, released from his chains, feel such relief as I shall on shaking off the shackles of power," he wrote two days before. "[N]ature intended me for the tranquill pursuits of science, by rendering them my supreme delight. [B]ut the enormities of the times in which I have lived, have forced me to take a part in resisting them, and to commit myself on the boisterous ocean of political passions. I thank god for the opportunity of retiring from them without censure, and carrying with me the most consoling proofs of public approbation." A week later, after winding up some final pieces of personal business, he joined a small caravan of wagons and headed, at last, back to Monticello. Never again would Thomas Jefferson set foot in the city of Washington.

THOMAS JEFFERSON, JEFFERSONIAN DEMOCRACY, AND DEMOCRACY

The once-revered Jefferson and his presidency have suffered a long-term decline in historical reputation that would have delighted any conservative Federalist snob or fractious southern Quid. Historians have accused Jefferson of betraying his principles once he reached office by expanding federal power and outfederalizing the Federalists, chiefly through the Louisiana Purchase and the embargo. Others view Jefferson as a hopeless visionary who became entangled with great historical forces that he did not understand. Some have condemned Jefferson as a hypocrite who vaunted human equality and at the same time dispossessed Indians, owned slaves (and sired children with one of them), did nothing to benefit free blacks (while himself benefiting politically from the extra representation and electoral votes given the slave South), and held what have since become distasteful views about women. Still others depict him as a wild-eyed utopian revolutionist who (according to one variation on the theme) was a Jacobin fellow traveler and prototerrorist or (according to another) was a sentimental agrarian who tried to block America's destined transformation into a modern commercial society. Some of these critics wrench a handful of Jefferson's more intemperate or grandiose private remarks out of context in order to sustain the Federalist plotter Timothy Pickering's judgment that he was a "Parisian revolutionary monster." Others, with a preference for perfect consistency over political dexterity, turn Jefferson's virtues as a pragmatic leader into vices. Still others indict him as a foe of civil liberties.

These critics fail to recognize that Thomas Jefferson, although a fervent advocate of his principles, never thought he had to live up to some idealized abstraction of "Jeffersonian democracy" in the real political world. They seem to assume that time stood still from March 4, 1801, until March 4, 1809. The alleged grand inconsistencies of Jefferson's presidency were flexible responses to unforeseen events, responses to contingencies undertaken against fierce New England Federalist opposition—all the while in pursuit of ideals ranging from the enlargement of opportunities for the mass of ordinary, industrious Americans to the principled avoidance of war. The most significant of these, the Louisiana Purchase, was an outcome of luck more than design—but Jefferson smartly seized the opportunity.

Jefferson made serious blunders and miscalculations, especially in his anticlimactic second term. Ironies abounded, not least when Yankee Federalist obstruction of his boldest political experiment, the embargo, led the foremost champion of limiting federal power to try to impose federal power on almost every American community. And there were also victims of the Jeffersonians' success, quite apart from the Federalists. Although the great showdowns with the surviving eastern woodland tribes occurred after 1809, Jefferson's Indian treaties were predicated on his abiding faith that the white yeoman empire would—and should—supplant the Indians' hunting grounds. Regarding blacks, slave and free, Jefferson had abandoned the antislavery idealism of his youth as politically impractical. He believed that slavery was evil and that it was doomed—"interest," he wrote in 1805, "is really going over to the side of morality"—but he had no expectation that the end would come any time soon, and was ever fearful that precipitate emancipation would lead to race war and economic ruin. He had also reached the conclusion that blacks and whites could never peacefully inhabit the same country. His envisaged empire of liberty was for whites, with the inclusion of peaceable Indians who uplifted themselves and assimilated as idealized, virtuous yeomen farmers.

The fashion to demonize Jefferson and Jeffersonian democracy, however, badly distorts the record. On slavery, for example, Jefferson and his party left an ambiguous but largely positive legacy. His own evolving views were ambivalent, summed up in his later famous remark that he would go to great lengths to end slavery "in any practicable way." As things stood, he wrote, "we have the wolf by the ear, and we can neither hold him, nor safely let him go. [J]ustice is in one scale, and self-preservation in the other." If he became maddeningly circumspect about slavery, with the fear of black insurrection always in the back of his mind—and, with respect to Saint Domingue, in the front of his mind—Jefferson always considered racial bondage a threat to white liberty and equality, contrary to the growing view among slaveholders that slavery made white equality possible. And although issues connected to slavery did not bulk large in national politics during Jefferson's presidency, when they did arise, the Republicans divided against each other along sectional lines. Against strong opposition from Deep South slaveholders, Federalist and Republican, Jefferson backed the earliest possible closing of the transatlantic slave trade, with its "violations of human rights which have been so long continued on the unoffending inhabitants of Africa, and which the morality, the reputation, and the best interests of our country have long been eager to proscribe."

On other issues, ranging from the expansion of slavery into the western territories to slavery's future in the District of Columbia, northern Republicans, in and out of Congress, took outspoken antislavery positions on explicitly Jeffersonian grounds—proclaiming, in the words of one Massachusetts representative, that slavery negated "a proper respect for the rights of mankind." Basing his remarks on the Declaration of Independence and Paine's Common Sense, Abraham Bishop welcomed the insurrection in Saint Domingue and threw a challenge at his countrymen: "We have firmly asserted, that all men are free. Yet as soon as the poor blacks . . . cried out, It is enough, . . . we have been the first to assist in riveting their chains!" This northern Jeffersonian antislavery impulse would come into its own only after Jefferson left office. Yet even while Jefferson was president, antislavery Jeffersonians offered an alternative to Jefferson's own gloominess, discretion, and paralysis, and to the obdurate pro-slavery views of other southern Republicans. And Jefferson never tried to disown these antislavery men.

Nor, despite Jefferson's repeated paeans to rural life, were he and his party monolithic, unyielding agrarians. Even before he became president, Jefferson noted that the costs of the country's remaining "merely agricultural," and whether "such a state is more friendly to principles of virtue and liberty," were matters "yet to be solved." The embargo, and then the developments that led to the War of 1812, would finally settle the matter, causing Jefferson to change his mind and advocate great manufactories. Before then, the northern Republican press was more supportive of manufacturing than the Federalists, who eschewed both manufacturing and government support for it as violations of "free trade"—that is, the continued domination of ocean-borne commerce and mercantile interests in the northeastern economy.

It is extraordinary how much Jefferson and his collaborators did achieve in eight years. All of Jefferson's original legislative agenda became law. Thereafter, until the abandonment of the embargo in 1809, not a single important piece of Jeffersonian legislation failed to pass Congress. After 1801, the federal government ran a deficit in only one year before 1809, and accumulated a net surplus of more than $20 million. Although Jefferson resisted radical pressure to purge the government of Federalists and generally appointed accomplished men to office, he chose them on the basis of their records of intelligence and virtue, departing from the Federalists' preference for men of wealth and pedigree. Inside of four years, President Jefferson managed to turn the Republican majority of 1800–01—accompanying his own razor-thin victory—into the dominant force in national politics. He was the first American president to lead his party to triumph and, for nearly eight years, keep the momentum of that triumph going, while sustaining his immense personal reputation. (Even proud John Randolph, after his break with the administration, admitted that "[t]he colossal popularity of the President seemed to mock all opposition.") Jefferson is also the only national leader in history ever to achieve the vast expansion of his country—more than doubling its physical size—while at the same time professionalizing and curtailing its military. He accomplished all this while enduring the most venomous sorts of personal and political attacks, originating from inside his own party as well as from conservative Federalists.

The links among Jefferson, Republicanism, and democratic reform were less straightforward. By beating back Federalist presumption, the Jeffersonian ascendancy opened up the political system, encouraging and enabling self-made plebeians such as Simon Snyder to reach for and attain high political office. Here was the greatest political achievement of Jefferson's two presidencies. Against Federalism's immense condescension and determined obstructionism, Jefferson and his party vindicated the political equality of the mass of American citizens—those ordinary men whom Jefferson's supporter Bishop described, in a tart reply to Federalist taunts, as the "poor ragged democrats" who would no longer defer to "ye well-fed, well-dressed, chariot-lolling, caucus-keeping, levee-reveling federalists." In those regions and states, such as Bishop's Connecticut, where Republicanism initially was weakest, a substantial opposition arose and took the first steps toward democratic reform.

Popular participation in politics grew apace, in some places (especially in New England and the middle Atlantic states) exploding to levels unimaginable in the 1790s. In Massachusetts, the percentage of eligible white males who actually voted nearly doubled, reaching roughly 70 percent by 1808. In Pennsylvania, where turnouts of about 25 percent were typical for much of the 1790s, the proportion of free adult men voting for governor jumped from 56 percent in 1799 to 70 percent in 1808, a level not surpassed until after 1840. In some counties of North Carolina, turnouts reached beyond 80 percent. To be sure, voting for presidential electors still generally lagged behind that for state and local offices. (In Pennsylvania, for example, there was a 32 percent turnout for the presidential voting in 1808, less than half that for the governor's race.) But even these figures marked a substantial increase over the norm before Jefferson's election. And in some places—notably New Jersey, where more than 70 percent of eligible voters cast ballots for president in 1808—rising participation in national elections matched or even exceeded that in state and local elections. Only in states, especially in the South, where party competition was minimal, notably Virginia, did participation fall—although this may have been a factor of the unusual interest in the 1800 contest as well as the lack of a credible Federalist opposition. The heightened involvement elsewhere also mattered more as states began to shift from choosing presidential electors by legislative vote to direct elections by the voters. The filters on democracy created by the Framers were proving porous, while the suppression of democracy sought by the Federalists in the 1790s was thoroughly discredited.

Yet if democratic power and participation were expanding, politics and Republican Party affairs continued to operate at the national level largely from the top down. The congressional caucus held firm control over presidential and vice presidential nominations and the formulation of party policy. In the states where Republicanism was strongest, especially the South, reform was far less conspicuous than in other regions. Where reform did occur in the South, as in South Carolina, it paradoxically strengthened the power of the dominant slaveholder elite. If Federalism was badly weakened, the factions within the Republican coalition—urban radicals, rural Clodhoppers, schismatic Randolphite Quids, and dominant moderates—held very different views about democracy. The future of democratic reform depended on which of these Republican views prevailed.

That outcome in turn depended on the leadership of the new president, James Madison—exacting, self-effacing, and the greatest proponent of republican constitutionalism in the nation. Madison was a more rigorous political thinker than Jefferson, yet he lacked the intellectual breadth and the personal prestige that helped Jefferson hold together the querulous Republicans and sink Federalism into the abyss. He also lacked his old friend's disarming shrewdness and charm. On the evening of his inauguration, Madison attended a crowded celebration ball accompanied by his vivacious wife, Dolley. Jefferson, no longer in charge, arrived at the festivities buoyant but a little unsure of how he should act. He managed to corner John Quincy Adams—who, strikingly, had supported Jefferson over the Louisiana Purchase and the embargo, and had now broken with his party—for a learned and lively discussion of Homer, Virgil, and various minor later classical poets before making his polite farewells. Madison stayed on grimly, bored to distraction. Earlier in the day, he had mumbled through an unremarkable inauguration address, stating what he would repeat to visitors and friends in the coming weeks as his administration's basic posture in the wake of the embargo's failure: peace before war, war before submission.

Less than three years later, Madison would lead the country into the war that his predecessor had tried so hard, and at such great political cost, to avoid. The war's effects would startle the ultradoctrinaire Republicans, especially the surviving southern Quids, who assumed that military expenditures and wartime coercion inevitably destroyed public liberty. In some respects, in the ideologues' view, the war did just that. But in other ways, war generated fresh democratic forces with cruel ironies of their own.

5

NATIONALISM AND
THE WAR OF 1812

The coming of the war with Britain, and the war itself, permanently altered the structure of American politics. Internationally, the United States faced new tests of its will as a sovereign republic, secure in its rights to trade and sail the seas unencumbered. President Madison's exertions to find an honorable settlement short of war proved just as time-consuming and ineffective as had President Jefferson's. And domestic politics, connected as always to international politics, also remained troublesome, reopening debates over democracy and the scope of federal power.

On his first full day in office, the new president found himself not yet entangled either with Napoleon Bonaparte or British Foreign Secretary George Canning, but with a leading country democrat, the Clodhopper governor of Pennsylvania, Simon Snyder, and the Olmstead affair. The dispute involved a meandering court case dating back more than thirty years. One Captain Gideon Olmstead, having heroically commandeered a British sloop to Philadelphia during the Revolution, demanded his fair share of the prize money due him from the state of Pennsylvania. In early 1809, the U.S. Supreme Court ruled in Olmstead's favor and ordered Pennsylvania to pay. But Governor Snyder stood fast against what he called unjust federal interference and declared that he would call out the state militia to defy the Court's ruling. He was not bluffing. In late March, in Philadelphia, state troops, with bayonets fixed, forcibly prevented a U.S. marshal from serving the Court's writ.

Snyder quickly backed down after federal authorities intervened, and Olmstead eventually got his prize money. The militia commander and eight of his men were convicted for resisting the service of the writ, but swiftly pardoned by President Madison. The truly significant moment in the affair came when Snyder pleaded his case to Madison, railed against the Court's "usurpation of power and jurisdiction," and paraphrased the Virginia Resolutions of 1798 as if they endorsed the doctrine of state nullification. Madison's reply was at once conciliatory and firm, stating that the Constitution compelled him to enforce the Court's decree and suggesting that Snyder give way.

Few would recall for long the Olmstead affair, overtaken as it quickly was by momentous events at home and abroad. Yet Madison, in his handling of Governor Snyder, made it clear he did not believe that the Republicans' "Spirit of 1798" countenanced nullification—or any hint of state autarchy. As president, Madison would endorse a new and consistent but controversial Republican nationalism—too Republican to suit the persistent Federalists and too friendly to expanding federal power to suit many Republicans. In defending his position, Madison would eventually find himself leading the nation into war, while warding off domestic adversaries less pliable than Simon Snyder.

The war exposed the nation's internal rifts and military weaknesses. Although the Americans won some significant victories, they would be fortunate to conclude the conflict in a diplomatic impasse with the British. The war also pushed forward powerful paradoxes and omens about national development and democratic politics. Despite terrible embarrassments, Madison and the Republican nationalists, and their reconfiguration of Jeffersonian democracy, emerged politically supreme. Challenges to federal authority and even talk of secession abounded—but, ironically, these came chiefly from the erstwhile champions of strong central government, the New England Federalists. By sealing the fate of the Federalist Party as a national force, the conflict with Britain ended up affirming the Jeffersonian "revolution" of 1800–01, even though some Republicans thought that revolution had lost its way. Few democratic reforms of consequence occurred during Madison's presidency, but the war, by crushing Indian insurgencies in the South and Northwest, widened western expansionists' ambitions, which cleared the way for new permutations of American democracy. And the war's extraordinary final battle made a national hero out of a strange western slaveholding democrat who would dominate American politics over the decades to come.

THE RISE OF THE REPUBLICAN NATIONALISTS

The road to war ran unbroken from Jefferson's second administration. Instead of bringing Britain and France to heel, the Non-Intercourse Act irritated the British into sustaining the Orders in Council and impressing additional American sailors, and it led the French to seize American ships. In May 1810, the Republican-controlled Congress, trying to tether a drifting foreign policy, passed an act stating that should either of the belligerents cease violating neutral rights, the president could punish the other one by suspending trade. The French, contemptuous as ever of the Americans, ambiguously promised to lift their own decrees against American shipping if Washington broke off trade with London. Madison agreed. But Napoleon did not immediately call off his ship seizures, leaving Madison vulnerable to criticism from the British and Anglophile Federalists. By the autumn of 1811, the three-way estrangement of Britain, France, and the United States was complete, with Federalists opposing a war with Britain, Republicans favoring one, and Madison caught in the middle. For a time, it seemed that the

United States might enter an almost-certainly catastrophic triangular war with both of the great powers.

Two domestic factors tipped the balance toward war with Britain, and Britain alone, in 1812. The first was the emergence of a new generation of aggressive, anti-British Republican nationalists, who saw the spirit of 1776 endangered. The second was the appearance of a prophecy-driven Indian resistance to white encroachment.

During the first eighteen months of Madison's presidency, Republican faction fighting flared, all the more intensely now that Jefferson was no longer in charge. Divergent domestic and foreign policy aims defined the various camps. The leading city and country democrats, including William Duane and Simon Snyder, as well as some alienated moderate Jeffersonians from Virginia and Maryland, were furious at Madison's decision to retain Albert Gallatin as secretary of the Treasury, especially after they had scared Madison off from appointing Gallatin as secretary of state. Not only was Gallatin tied to the most moderate of Pennsylvania Republicans; under Jefferson, and even more under Madison, he became increasingly bold in calling for federal spending on canal- and road-building projects that the city and country democrats feared would favor the monied few. In direct conflict with Jefferson, although with Madison's tacit approval, Gallatin also prepared the way to gain, in 1811, a rechartering and enlargement of the Bank of the United States. To critics like Duane, these actions made Gallatin nothing less than "the evil genius of this nation, more pernicious and corrupt than Hamilton was and much more dangerous because insidious, frigid, and profound in artifice."

Duane and his fellow democrats were additionally enraged by Madison's foreign policy of commercial coercion—a policy they also blamed on Gallatin. When Jefferson's embargo failed, the democrats believed, the time had come for tougher measures, including preparations for a possible war against Great Britain. Gallatin—the "Genevan Secretary," Duane snorted—had unpatriotically intervened, counseling "base submission" to Britain's outrageous violations of American maritime rights to ensure that the treasury would continue to fatten on customs receipts. Only Gallatin's dismissal, and a new policy of armed neutrality and retaliation against the British, could vindicate the nation's honor and independence, Duane and the others declared.

Another group, consisting of John Randolph and the eternally discontented southern Old Republicans, abhorred the idea of a war with Britain but also disdained Gallatin, and harbored even deeper suspicions of the president, even though he was a Virginian. Randolph and his friends had long despised Madison for his involvement in framing, defending, and ratifying the Constitution. As president, Madison's acquiescence in Gallatin's banking and internal improvement schemes, and his supportive stance over rechartering the BUS in 1811, deepened their alienation. Worse, in 1810 and early 1811, what looked like the increasingly anti-British drift of administration policy offended planter ideologues who feared war and a consolidation of federal military power, and who, in any event, were devout Anglophiles. Madison tried to placate the Old Republicans in 1811 by naming the orthodox Jeffersonian James Monroe as his new secretary of state—but by 1812, even Monroe would begin looking unreliable to the Randolphites.

The younger Republican nationalists rejected what they considered Madison's appeasement of Britain as forcefully as did Duane. Yet to sustain, as historians have generally done, Randolph's polemical nickname for these nationalists, the "War Hawks," is to honor an eccentric source while reducing the group's outlook to bellicosity. Bellicose they were, especially toward Britain—but they also developed an expansive view of government and federal power, exceeding Madison's, that helped shape the nation's politics for the next forty years. Their foremost leader, now and later, was the young Kentucky lawyer Henry Clay.

Clay had come far since his reformist entry into Kentucky politics. After the pro-slavery Republicans' victory at the state constitutional convention in 1799, he tempered his egalitarianism and focused on his lucrative law practice. A gifted litigator, he gained special recognition for his talents in navigating Kentucky's arcane land-tenure laws and for his persuasive forensics in capital cases. He also married well, winning the daughter of one of Lexington's most prominent families. In 1803, Clay entered the state legislature, where he led the counterattack on the efforts by downstate yeomen to reform the state's court system. By 1805, Clay had become, at age twenty-eight, the leading spokesman for the Bluegrass Republicanism he had once battled so hard.

After he went to Washington (initially to serve out two other men's separate unexpired terms in the U.S. Senate), Clay made a strong impression there too, though not solely for his legislative skills. "He is a great favorite with the ladies . . . ," his fellow senator William Plumer remarked, "gambles much here—reads but little." Clay's unfeigned gregariousness helped make him a political powerhouse. During elections, he not only joined in the required stump-side fraternizing and drinking, he genuinely enjoyed it. A vivid conversationalist who could swear like a sailor, he would sit around for hours, with friends and voters, backslapping, joking, snorting snuff. John Quincy Adams, who did read much, thought Clay's public and private morals loose, yet he conceded that Clay had all the virtues required in a popular leader and was "a republican of the first fire." In 1810, his Kentucky fortune secure, Clay announced his candidacy for the House of Representatives, claiming to prefer the "turbulence" of the lower house to "the solemn stillness of the Senate Chamber."

Clay thought of himself as a devout Jeffersonian, and in some respects he still was. In the Senate, he staunchly opposed the pro-Gallatin moderate efforts to recharter the BUS, attacking the institution as a monopolistic, unconstitutional abomination, its stockholders mainly British and its officers and beneficiaries "a splendid association of favored individuals." Commerce and credit, he thought, were best expanded by local elites and the wildly proliferating state banks, most of them in the hands of friendly Republicans. Under his leadership, the Senate defeated the bank recharter bill.

But Clay's days as a mere local improver were nearly over. In

Washington, he declared that the West required nationally funded internal improvements and tariff protection. Just as urgently, he argued that the region needed the federal government to take firm action against Great Britain to ward off Indian attacks, Canadian competition, and naval interference with ships bearing western produce on the high seas. In 1810, he raised the roof of the Senate with a speech that pilloried the administration's policy of commercial coercion and called on "a new race of heroes" to vindicate the sacrifices of their patriot fathers. Clay's foreign policy pronouncements won him the most attention, but they were linked to a fresh view of American economic and political development, western in inspiration but national in its implications—the embryo of what would become known in later years as the American System.

A distinct but related southern pro-nationalism also arose in and around 1810, advanced most brilliantly by John Caldwell Calhoun of South Carolina. Born in 1782 to a successful Scots-Irish backcountry family, Calhoun was only thirteen when he lost his father, Patrick Calhoun, an immigrant who had played a leading role in South Carolina's variety of the early country democracy. Breaking off his formal education, John helped work his father's twelve-hundred-acre plantation (with about thirty slaves) for five years to support his mother. When his older brothers agreed to take over, Calhoun returned to school with a vengeance, mastering Latin and Greek at his brother-in-law Moses Waddell's soon-to-be-famous backwoods academy. He then headed north to Yale, where he enrolled as a junior in 1802 and where his intellectual exploits remain legendary to this day. After graduating, Calhoun attended Judge Tapping Reeve's law academy in Litchfield, Connecticut, then returned to South Carolina—not to the backcountry, but to aristocratic Charleston, where he read law in the office of the grandee Federalist attorney Henry William De Saussure. In 1808, he entered politics, winning election to the South Carolina House of Representatives. He arrived in the state capitol in Columbia in time to participate in revising the state constitution.

Calhoun's rise bespoke social changes as well as his personal achievements. With an iron will molded by his indomitable father and by his Presbyterian upbringing, he plotted his self-improvement precisely and became something of a celebrity wunderkind in South Carolina—severe, even priggish, and totally lacking a sense of humor, but with a correct and cultivated charm and a powerful mind. Calhoun's was a special case, but it was not an utterly isolated one. South Carolina, with its abundant waterways connecting hill piedmont to tidewater, was open to the spread of plantation agriculture to the backcountry, especially in the early years of the nineteenth century, when short-staple cotton cultivation became practicable thanks to Eli Whitney's invention of the cotton gin. In 1800, Governor John Drayton proclaimed the state's exploding cotton production, in the backcountry as well as the low country, "a matter of National joy." By 1808, even distant portions of the piedmont were absorbed into the plantation economy. With that absorption came the emergence of a unique statewide planter elite, composed increasingly of former outsiders like John Calhoun but united in its endorsement of established low-country interests, above all slavery.

The intermingling of South Carolina's backcountry and low-country slaveholders was a cultural and political as well as an economic phenomenon. Education was crucial: Moses Waddell's academy was one of several rural schools that arose after the Revolution to help prepare the sons of prosperous inlanders for the elite. Statewide improvements of bridges, ferries, and roads accelerated the backcountry cotton boom and lifted inland planters out of their social isolation from Charleston's high society. Intermarriage linked Charleston and piedmont fortunes. (In 1811, Calhoun married a low-country second cousin, Floride Colhoun, the daughter of a deceased Cooper River grandee and one-time U.S. Senator.) In state politics, the rising inland slaveholders, allied in national politics with the Republicans, eroded the Federalist low country's long-standing supremacy without threatening the solidarity of the slaveholders' regime—a process officially ratified by the reform of the state constitution in 1808.

Calhoun embodied the persisting divisions as well as the overriding unity of the evolving South Carolina slavocracy. Despite his prolonged sojourn in Charleston, his sense of propriety always made him uncomfortable with what he called the low country's "intemperance and debaucheries." After he established himself in politics, he resettled permanently at Fort Hill plantation, about twenty-five miles from his backcountry boyhood home. Yet Calhoun's support for internal improvements and his intensifying association with long-established political families helped him assimilate in the highest political circles. Yankee-trained, Calhoun was also more cosmopolitan than many of his better-born low-country peers. If his worldliness did not enamor him of New England politics, it helped make him a fervent nationalist during his early days in Columbia and, after his election to the House of Representatives in 1810, in Washington.

Anglophobia became for Calhoun, as for Clay, the chief initial outlet for his nationalist passions. British warships were blocking cotton shipments to Europe and had sent prices tumbling. Scorning both the Jeffersonian policy of peaceable coercion and the Yankee Federalists' friendliness to Great Britain, Calhoun concluded that the British had humiliated the new republic, and that only a rebirth of the old revolutionary spirit could vindicate the country. "It is the commence[ment] of a new era in our politicks," he wrote self-confidently shortly after his arrival in Congress, one that would end the "commercial arrangiments and negotiations" of the current regime, and dispel the chimera that the country could "avoid and remove difficulties by a sort of political management." That new era would advance deeper nationalist assumptions. "There is, sir, one principle necessary to make us a great people—," Calhoun declared, "to produce, not the form, but the real spirit of union, and that is to protect every citizen in the lawful pursuit of his business. . . . Protection and patriotism are reciprocal. This is the way which has led nations to greatness." Economic improvement with government backing had, in South Carolina, promoted statewide unity and prosperity. For Calhoun, it was essential to national unity and prosperity as well.

Henry Clay and John C. Calhoun, arrivistes from the West and the South, gravitated to each other shortly after they entered the House of Representatives. The elections had brought a reshuffling across the country, stemming from popular resentment at American acquiescence to Great Britain. When the new House finally assembled, in November 1811, almost half of its 140 old members had been replaced, leaving Republicans in charge by a margin of three to one, with younger militants in the forefront. Clay, having already won notice in the Senate, was immediately elected to fill the vacant House Speakership. After welcoming Calhoun to join his informal boardinghouse caucus, he helped arrange for the South Carolinian's appointment to the powerful Foreign Affairs Committee. Other young newly elected members with similar backgrounds shared their views, including Langdon Cheves and William Lowndes of South Carolina, and Clay's old antagonist, Felix Grundy, who, having moved to Tennessee and married a second cousin of Calhoun's, had become an outspoken advocate of western commercial expansion. Key northeastern congressmen were also sympathetic, including Calhoun's old associate from Yale and Reeve's academy, Peter B. Porter of New York, now chairman of the Foreign Affairs Committee, who hoped that with a quick thrust across the border, the United States might annex Upper Canada. All told, the militant younger men composed a bloc of around sixty representatives in the Twelfth Congress.

To John Randolph and the other die-hard Old Republican agrarians, the new-style nationalist Jeffersonian Republicans, with their love of tariffs and armies, came to look like neo-Federalists. But there were enormous differences between Federalism and the kind of pro-development Republicanism the younger men espoused. Federalists remained skeptical about rapid western settlement; the young Republicans promoted orderly growth and development of the West, linked to ambitious internal improvements. Federalists clung to their belief that American prosperity required close and special connections with Great Britain, but the young Republicans favored developing the nation's internal markets as well as its agricultural exports. Above all, the new Republicans advanced a more democratized conception of economic development, opening opportunity, as Calhoun put it, "to every capitalist, however inconsiderable."

On foreign affairs, the divergence between the younger nationalist Republicans and President Madison narrowed in 1810 and 1811. By the summer of 1811, Madison broadly agreed with Clay that war with Great Britain was almost inevitable. In November, the president greeted the new Twelfth Congress by announcing that it was time for "putting the United States into an armor and an attitude demanded by the crisis." He called for expanding the regular army and raising a volunteer corps.

HOSTILE INCURSIONS: THE PROPHET, TECUMSEH, AND INDIAN RESISTANCE

Fed by Madison's new militance, hatred of England mounted, spiked by the second key factor in leading America to war—a continuing political and spiritual revival among the displaced western Indian tribes. Although the Republicans entirely blamed the British, the insurgency was more a product of long-standing bitterness between the Indians and American settlers. It was led by a charismatic one-eyed Shawnee prophet who called himself Tenskwatawa, and his older brother, the warrior Tecumseh.

During Jefferson's second term, the governor of Indiana Territory, William Henry Harrison, a son of the Virginia Tidewater elite, wrote repeatedly to the president about an alarming new Indian cult and its shaman leader, the Prophet—"an engine set to work by the British for some bad purpose." Harrison insisted that sinister forces lay behind the spreading cult: "[T]he Prophet is a tool of British fears or British avarice, designed for the purpose of forming a combination of the Indians, which in case of war between that power and the United States may assist them in the defense of Canada." Jefferson, who considered the Indian seer merely a "transient enthusiasm," ordered Harrison to find some way to buy him off. Dismissive of the Indians' religion and wary of the British, both men reacted with the paternalism and the callousness that guided federal Indian policy.

In 1800, an estimated 600,000 Indians lived in what is now the continental United States, most of them west of the Mississippi. They were a mere remnant of the native American population, in excess of five million, before European arrivals brought devastating disease and displacement. The devastation had been particularly severe among the eastern woodland Indians, but the survivors still posed a problem for would-be American settlers. In the 1780s and early 1790s, raiding parties and combined forces of Shawnees, Ojibwas, and others successfully resisted American expansion into Ohio Territory. The decisive American victory at the Battle of Fallen Timbers in 1794 and the ensuing Treaty of Greenville gained the Americans enormous tracts of Indian land—and threw much of the Indian remnant, now pushed farther west, into demoralized poverty. Thereafter, Republican policy toward the survivors combined complaisant respect for the Indians' potential for uplift with resolve that they take up yeoman-style agriculture.

"I consider the business of hunting as already having become insufficient to furnish clothing and subsistence to the Indians," President Jefferson wrote to Benjamin Hawkins, his Indian agent for all of the tribes south of the Ohio River, in 1803. "The promotion of agriculture, therefore, and household manufacture"—by which Jefferson meant simple spinning and weaving—"are essential in their preservation, and I am disposed to aid and encourage it liberally." Jefferson projected an idyllic future yeoman republic in which "our settlements and theirs [would] meet and blend together, to intermix, and become one people." But Jeffersonian idealism about the Indians had a coercive side. One way to ensure that the natives would cede their hunting grounds on the cheap, Jefferson privately advised Governor Harrison, would be to ensnare them in debt for the cost of farming goods and other necessities. Active resistance could be punished by removal and resettlement across the Mississippi, as "an example to others, and a furtherance of our final consolidation."

Jefferson thus injected an ethos of uplift into his policy of manipulation. In the territories, other Americans—Indian-hating farmers, impatient land speculators, ambitious politicians—were less benevolent. Harrison served those more aggressive interests as much as he served Jefferson. Only twenty-seven when he became governor of Indiana Territory in 1800, Harrison had fought at Fallen Timbers and later served as a delegate from the Northwest Territory to Congress. Like his fellow gentry paternalist Jefferson, he bore no particular hatred toward the Indians. But as Jefferson's local lieutenant, he became the chief agent for the expropriation of Indian land, by means fair and foul. Between 1802 and 1805, he completed treaties with nearly a dozen tribes to gain title to southern Indiana, most of Illinois, and parts of Wisconsin and Missouri for two and a half cents or less per acre. Harrison was a sharp bargainer, bribing Indian leaders, striking side deals with renegade splinter groups, and plying negotiators with liquor. The treaties provoked protests from Indians caught up in the vicious cycle of distress, who charged, with reason, that they violated the Greenville Treaty. "The white people . . . ," one Shawnee chief complained, "destroyed all that God had given us for our support."

The Indians' discontent acquired powerful spiritual dimensions in 1805. A Shawnee healer named Lalawethika (or "the Rattle")—known among his fellows as a drunken idler—fell into a graphic dream-vision of the souls of the damned, their howls of suffering rising out of Eternity, "roaring like the falls of a river." Awakened, the healer swore off alcohol and began relating prophecies about the impending doom of the white invaders and sinful Indians. Americans, he declared, were children of the evil Great Serpent who had come from the sea to emasculate and conquer the Indians. To thwart them, Indians must ban alcohol, reduce their dependence on trade, and curtail social contacts with whites. From now on, he said, he would be known as Tenskwatawa (or "the Open Door"), the portal through which the regenerated Indians would gain salvation. By 1806, Tenkswatawa, also known as the Prophet, had enough of a following to build a new center for his religion—pointedly at Greenville, site of the despised treaty.

For decades, shamans of different eastern tribes had envisaged apocalyptic scenes and bid their fellows to repent. Tenskwatawa was special for two reasons. Although an ugly, off-putting man, he was eloquent in a trance, "expressive of a deep sense and solemn feeling of eternal things," according to a group of wandering American Shakers who witnessed one of his performances. And Tenkswatawa's brother Tecumseh (or "Shooting Star") would soon embark on efforts that gave the Shawnee prophet's warnings additional force.

Tecumseh had grown up in the Ohio River Valley to become an accomplished hunter and warrior. With his older brother, Chiksika, he participated in a number of bloody frontier raids in Kentucky and Tennessee in the late 1780s and early 1790s. He also fought at Fallen Timbers and, in its aftermath, refused to sign to the Treaty of Greenville. A respected chief by the time he reached his late twenties, Tecumseh led a small Shawnee band (including his wife and newborn son) to a permanent summer settlement in Indiana Territory in 1798. There he kept the peace and concentrated on the hunt.

During the uneasy winter of 1805–06, as Lalawethika spoke of the holy Open Door, Tecumseh changed his clothes and bearing. He abjured the beads and ribbons and linen shirts sold by American traders, donned the Shawnees' traditional simple deerskin suits, and renounced whiskey forever. Although not a thoroughgoing convert to the Prophet's religion, Tecumseh was strongly affected by the antisettler vision. He drew political conclusions. Much as his brother updated old religious themes, so Tecumseh drew on secular precedents, including Shawnee efforts at building an Indian confederacy that dated back to the 1740s. As members of far-flung tribes made their pilgrimage to Greenville to see Tenskwatawa—probably the greatest religious awakening among the woodland tribes to date—so Tecumseh's political, and military, plans grew more ambitious.

Heightened tensions between the British and Americans also pushed him. The British in Canada, defending a long and vulnerable border with the United States, were always looking for Indian support. The Americans, however, took any signs of goodwill between the British and the Indians—or, for that matter, of any change in Indian habits—as proof of an imminent Anglo-Indian offensive. Americans' fears worsened in the face of the Prophet's growing prominence. The senior British agent at Fort Malden, the chief British outpost in western Canada, could see clearly what was happening in 1806: "The discontent of the Indians arises principally from unfair purchases of their lands, but the Americans ascribe their dissatisfaction to the machinations of our government." In the late summer of 1807, President Jefferson, although still convinced that Tenskwatawa was more of a fool than a danger, ordered western governments to take military precautions.

The brothers Tecumseh and Tenskwatawa, hoping to consolidate their resources and preserve a fragile peace with both sides, retreated from Greenville with their people back into Indiana Territory in 1808, settled near the lush confluence of the Wabash and Tippecanoe rivers, and built a new village that the whites would come to call Prophetstown. With its two hundred bark houses set along neat rows and lanes, its council house and medicine lodge, and more than one hundred acres of cultivated fields, Prophetstown was an imposing, busy site, visited by white traders and travelers as well as by Indian pilgrims. For the Indians, it would be the headquarters for spiritual renewal. So powerful were the Prophet's visions that even Governor Harrison (with whom Tenkswatawa met in August 1808) temporarily revised his opinion and declared the cult a positive influence for reform and peace. Tecumseh dickered with the British as well as the Americans and shored up professions of mutual respect and nonaggression.

The calm proved illusory. West of Prophetstown, the situation remained disturbed, as old complaints and new ones against the Americans, chiefly from the Sac, Fox, and Winnebago tribes, led to a brief war scare in the spring of 1809. Governor Harrison, his ambitions fixed on gaining Indiana statehood, continued his inflammatory bargaining and obtained nearly three million more acres of Indian land at about one-third of a cent per acre. Criticized even by some local American land officials, Harrison's acquisitions enraged Tenkswatawa and Tecumseh. Wearing a British military uniform, Tecumseh threatened village chiefs with death for their accommodations. In 1810 and 1811, he organized an Indian confederation based on the doctrine of pantribal common land ownership, and leaned toward a formal alliance with the British.

"No difficulties deter him . . . ," Governor Harrison wrote of Tecumseh in 1811. "You see him today on the Wabash and in a short time you hear of him on the shores of Lake Erie or Michigan, or on the banks of the Mississippi, and wherever he goes he makes an impression favorable to his purposes." In fact, Tecumseh's aim extended far beyond the Great Lakes region, from New York all the way to Florida. Harrison recognized this and moved to check him. While Tecumseh, after a testy meeting with Harrison at Vincennes, was proselytizing among the Muskogees, Cherokees, and Chickasaws to the south in November 1811, Harrison made a decisive strike against Prophetstown.

In violation of President Madison's express orders to prepare for war but keep the peace, Harrison gathered a force of nearly one thousand regulars and militiamen, marched them north, and camped provocatively close to Prophetstown atop a high plateau. Assured by Tenkswatawa's visions of the Americans' gunpowder turning to sand and of the Indians becoming bulletproof, a force of between three and five hundred Indian converts—including Kickapoos and Winnebagos as well as Shawnees—attacked the Americans and inflicted heavy casualties in close-quarter combat. But the Open Door's visions came to naught. (He later blamed the failure on his wife's menstruation, which, he said, had weakened his spirit and sullied his medicine.) Despite heavy losses, Harrison's troops repelled the Indian attack. They then marched into Prophetstown, which the Indians had abandoned the night before, burned it to the ground, destroyed its food supplies, and opened and emptied Indian graves. Harrison claimed a great victory at what the Americans called the Battle of Tippecanoe.

In December 1811, five weeks after Prophetstown's destruction and shortly after Tecumseh completed his journey south, an enormous earthquake, centered in what is now northwestern Arkansas, shook Indian villages and American towns as far east as South Carolina. Thousands of severe aftershocks felt from Canada to the Gulf of Mexico followed over the next four months. Sand and water spewed as high as treetops, birds perched on people's heads, and the Mississippi River temporarily reversed its flow. Indians everywhere drew dire, even apocalyptic conclusions. In Ohio, an Indian told Moravian missionaries that the Great Spirit was sorely displeased by what had happened at Prophetstown. Among the Creeks, whom Tecumseh had recently visited, young prophets known as Red Sticks proclaimed the earthquake a sign of the Great Spirit's decree that land cessions had to stop and the tribes had to unite. There were reports that Tecumseh had predicted the devastation, and in some variants, that he had actually caused it by stamping the earth until it trembled.

Tecumseh was in Missouri, remarkably close to the quake's epicenter, making unsteady progress convincing local Shawnees and Delawares to join his confederation. In late January 1812, he returned to Prophetstown, which Tenkswatawa and the desolate survivors had reoccupied. While he tried to placate the Americans, Tecumseh edged ever closer to allying with the British. News of Harrison's attack arrived in Washington, to mixed reactions, just as the newly elected Twelfth Congress was assembling. John Randolph and the Anglophilic southern Old Republicans condemned the action as reckless. Western Federalists, thin though their ranks were, called Harrison a worthless busybody and condemned him for exceeding his orders and butchering the Indians purely to advance his personal ambitions. One Ohio Republican lamented the "melancholy affair" and wished it had never happened. Worse, reports began coming to Washington that contradicted Harrison's self-serving account of the battle and claimed that the general had won only because the Indians had staged a strategic retreat. But younger, belligerent Republicans, especially from the South and West, hailed Harrison as a hero.

The latter view prevailed at the Executive Mansion, at least initially. Madison sent a jubilant special message to Capitol Hill about the Battle of Tippecanoe, expressing his confidence that all "hostile incursions" would now cease. Over the coming months, he backed away from his enthusiasm, persuaded by reports that Harrison had attacked the Indians needlessly. But the administration acted hesitantly, and too late; Tippecanoe touched off further Indian attacks, and soon Tecumseh allied with the British, turning the belligerent Republicans' presumptions into self-fulfilled prophecy. The Indians' goal of checking American westward expansion became closely intertwined with the British goal of defending their interests in Canada. So long as American relations with Britain deteriorated, the likelihood of a full-scale war with the Indians grew. And the more the Indians resisted after Tippecanoe, the faster American relations with Britain deteriorated.

1812

As war fever intensified in America, opposition to the Orders in Council also mounted in Britain, chiefly among trade-starved manufacturers. But the dismissive British government only sent its haughty envoy, Sir Augustus John Foster, to lecture the Americans about the imperatives of imperial security. The victory of the U.S. ship *President* over a much weaker British sloop, *Little Belt*, off the Chesapeake coast in the spring of 1811 stimulated American outrage and overconfidence. "[F]orbearance has become a crime, and patience ceased to be a virtue," wrote the Baltimore editor Hezekiah Niles in his new *Weekly Register*. By January 1812, President Madison completely changed his mind about France presenting a greater threat to the republic than Britain. By April, he had decided for war.

The charge, endorsed by subsequent generations of historians, that Congress dragged a bumbling, weak-kneed Madison into war is highly overstated. Madison, to be sure, was a less effective president than his predecessor. He had spent his entire career, before 1809, either as a legislator or as a diplomat, and was better suited to backstairs committee work and negotiations than to any executive position. Colorless, shy, bookish, and prone to nervousness, he often seemed indecisive. Long after the Non-Intercourse Act proved a failure, Madison's continued, principled search for a diplomatic solution short of war, his naïveté in dealing with Napoleon, and his persistent underestimation of the British will made his administration look rudderless. The failure of the bank rechartering effort early in 1811 made it look as if it was sinking.

Yet Madison needed no prodding to change course and begin preparing resolutely for war. Like Jefferson, he rejected the Old World ideas of raison d'état and hated warfare, but he was no pacifist—especially so far as Great Britain was concerned. By the autumn of 1811, when he asked Congress for ten thousand additional troops, he began to see that no degree of commercial persuasion would force the British to back down. It was the supposedly warlike Congress, and not the White House, that then vacillated and avoided raising the taxes necessary to fulfill Madison's military requests until after war had actually been declared. Old Republicans and pro-British Federalists mocked the administration and the pro-war Republicans—"Go to war without money, without men, without a navy!" John Randolph sneered—which only stiffened the president's resolve. By the following spring, Madison was certain that the conservative British prime minister, Spencer Perceval, wanted war with the United States. "We have nothing left therefore, but to make ready for it," he wrote to Jefferson in early April 1812.

On April 1, Madison forced the issue by sending a terse one-sentence request to Congress asking for a new sixty-day embargo, which would give American ships time to return to port and await diplomatic news from Britain about the status of the Orders in

Council. The imperial dispatches stating that the Orders stood finally arrived in Washington on May 22. Nine days later, Madison sent a war message to Congress citing British impressment, goading of the Indians, blockades, and spurned diplomacy, and concluding that Britain was already "in a state of war against the United States." The House formally declared war by a decisive margin on June 4. The Senate concurred, by a much narrower majority, two weeks later.

Had the British and the Americans been better informed about each others' political situation—or had communications across the Atlantic simply been speedier—war might have been averted. Misreading Madison's early caution as passivity, the British ambassador did not recognize that by the time the Americans implemented their new embargo, they fully expected war would follow. Likewise, Foster's American counterpart in London, Jonathan Russell, could not see how British economic difficulties, beginning with a depression in late 1810 and exacerbated by Napoleon's blockade of Europe, were quickly sapping the Orders of political viability. Ironically, just as Madison was committing himself and the country to war, his peaceable coercion policies were beginning to hurt the British badly. Fate then intervened, to make war even less likely. On May 11, a madman in London assassinated Perceval. The new British ministry, headed by the Earl of Liverpool, put aside American affairs for several weeks, and by the time it recovered, Parliamentary opposition to the Orders prevailed. The Foreign Office reversed itself and announced that on June 23 the Orders would be suspended for one year. But by the time the news of that decision reached Washington in August, Congress had already declared war.

Even had the news arrived earlier, however, pro-war Republicans might have considered a one-year suspension of the Orders too little, too late. And well before they learned of the diplomatic paradox, New England Federalists and southern Old Republicans were outraged at the war vote. The Federalists, having undermined Jefferson's embargo, had tried to obstruct all subsequent efforts at peaceful coercion, and flatly endorsed British arguments, even over impressment. Pseudopatriotic Republicans, they claimed, were attempting to turn American ships into a refuge for low-life deserters from the Royal Navy. Jefferson's old foe Timothy Pickering wrote in all seriousness that he believed Napoleon Bonaparte himself had bribed the congressional majority. John Randolph denounced the pro-war Republicans as fools who lusted after Canada. "I know that we are on the brink of some dreadful scourge," he said.

In truth, the victorious majority represented the triumph of neither treachery nor cupidity, but the consolidation of the new nationalists, strongest in the West and the South, with crucial supporters from the middle Atlantic states. No single influence, political or economic, can explain this convergence. Economically, congressional support for the war tended to come from areas, now badly depressed, more involved in rural production for export than in the maritime transport trade. Anger at assumed British responsibility for Indian unrest—in which Americans conveniently overlooked their own mistreatment of the Indians—reinforced war fever in the West and Deep South. The pro-war Republicans' basic motives in seizing Canada were to deprive Britain of important naval bases and help quiet the Indians.

The crisis shows that, when push came to shove, the Republicans' shared patriotic fervor against the British Empire and concerns about Federalist treachery could overcome the factionalism of the Madison years. In the House, outside of the New York delegation (where anti-Madison feeling ran high), approximately nine out of ten Republicans voted in favor of war. In the Senate, where Federalists and Republicans were more evenly matched, a slender majority of members probably wished to avoid war. Ultimately, however, most of the wavering Republican Senate fell into line, including the veteran city democrat and longtime Madison antagonist Michael Leib of Philadelphia. So did the majority of country and city democrats outside Washington, their abiding contempt for Madison and Gallatin now put aside.

Fears that the republic was endangered bound the pro-war Republicans together. Ever since the completion of independence, they believed, the great ideal of republicanism had been threatened, by the British from without and the Federalists from within. The British, by exerting their naval might, had dominated the American economy and unjustly seized dozens of ships and thousands of American citizens. Those degrading arrangements might be tolerable for (mostly Federalist) Yankee shipmasters, who stood to make handsome profits under the British aegis and could write off the impressments as one of the costs of doing business. The arrangements might also be tolerable for anti-Jeffersonian Anglophiles. But they were anathema to economically stressed producers everywhere, who blamed their plight on the arrogant British and their loyal Yankee Federalist friends. Add to that the widespread belief that the British were responsible for subverting the Indians, and the fate of the republic seemed to be at stake. John Adams's son John Quincy—who, having quit his father's party, had become a new star of the Republican diplomatic corps, now as minister to St. Petersburg—contended that "something besides dollars and cents is concerned," and there was "no alternative left but war or the abandonment of our right as an independent nation."

As Madison prepared the country for combat, he also readied himself for his reelection campaign. Due to the war crisis, April passed without the customary nominating caucus of congressional Republicans. The president looked to be strongly positioned, though he still had powerful Republican opponents—above all, in Pennsylvania, William Duane, who hotly supported the war but preferred DeWitt Clinton of New York, the nephew of Madison's ailing vice president, George Clinton, to Madison. But Duane could not persuade Governor Simon Snyder and the Clodhopper country democrats, who on the eve of the Republican caucus announced their support for the president.

DeWitt Clinton, whose uncle finally died in mid-April, refused to give up. Long the leader of New York's Republicans and now the most powerful figure in the state's politics, Clinton, at age forty-three, was ready to carry on his family legacy, push aside the aging Revolutionary generation, and advance to national leadership. He and his fellow New York Republicans were also eager to challenge the Virginians' domination of their party. Shortly after Madison won the congressional caucus's endorsement, New York's Republican legislators nominated Clinton, who quickly accepted. Clinton then courted the Federalists, hoping to fuse them with the anti-Madisonian Republicans into a victorious coalition—what Duane, who had reconciled himself to Madison's reelection, called "a group more oddly consorted than the assemblage in the ark."

The early fighting against Britain improved Clinton's prospects. The war did not go well. American military strategy was straightforward: hit the British hard in Canada, gather support from anti-British Canadians (a group that amounted mostly to wishful thinking on the Americans' part), and seize the crucial river port of Montreal. But Madison had at his disposal only a small regular army scattered across the country, a larger but disorganized militia still under the official control of the individual states, a tiny navy, and virtually no military command structure whatsoever. In mid-August, the surrender of Detroit without a shot to a combined force of British troops and Indians by the frightened and quite possibly drug-addled General William Hull was a devastating military and emotional blow. Adding greatly to Hull's fear, and to the subsequent American disgrace, was the presence at Detroit of Tecumseh at the head of one thousand warriors.

By the end of 1812, the British controlled nearly half the Old Northwest. The small but stirring victory of the American ship *Constitution* (dubbed, thereafter, "Old Ironsides") over HMS *Guerrière* off the Massachusetts coast revived American spirits, as did, a few weeks later, the news that Captain Stephen Decatur's *United States* had captured the British frigate *Macedonian* off the coast of Africa. Even some of the most sanguine hawks were worried, though. "Our executive officers are most incompetent," John C. Calhoun despaired to a friend.

Amid the setbacks, Federalist organizers, especially the

younger men, continued to retool the Republican techniques they had once maligned. Federalist state delegates from around the country met in New York at a "peace convention," a rudimentary version of a national nominating convention. Unable to agree on a candidate, the group decided to leave the way open for state Federalist parties to support Clinton. Most of them did so; but even more important, local and national organizations (led by scores of "popular" groups called Washington Benevolent Societies) arose to campaign, at times rambunctiously, for Federalist candidates, and to make sure that supporters got to the polls. In New England, pro-Clinton Federalists proclaimed that their man was a peace candidate; their counterparts in the middle Atlantic states and the South suggested that Clinton would conduct the war with greater skill and fortitude than Madison; and everywhere, Federalist partisans denounced Madison's Republicans as complacent officeholding elitists—lackeys of Napoleon Bonaparte who cared nothing about the well-being of the American people.

By late summer, although Clinton had his hands full creating his bipartisan coalition, Madison's reelection was no longer guaranteed. Four years earlier, Madison had won all but five of the seventeen states, and the Republicans retained two-thirds of the House. In the off-year balloting for Congress in 1810, the Republicans actually picked up seats, cutting the size of the Federalist House caucus in half. But under the strain of a divisive war—with New York Republicans chafing under the domination of the Virginians, and Federalists learning the virtues of grassroots political organization—Madison became vulnerable. Assured of solid support from New England (apart from Republican Vermont), Clinton needed only to hold on to his home state's electoral votes and win Pennsylvania's to gain the White House.

New York did stay loyal to Clinton, largely (and, in retrospect, ironically) because of the labors of a young upstate legislator, Martin Van Buren. The son of a tavern-keeper from the sleepy Hudson River Valley town of Kinderhook, Van Buren, at age thirty, had enjoyed a swift rise. Admitted to the New York State bar in 1803, he became known as the ablest Republican lawyer in rural, Federalist Columbia County, and in 1812, with Clinton's support, he narrowly won election to the state senate. Van Buren took up his seat in Albany as the new legislature decided to whom it would award the state's twenty-nine electoral votes. He was torn, he later recalled, between his personal loyalty to Clinton and his desire to support "a vigorous prosecution of the War." What tipped him was the legislature's earlier endorsement of his patron Clinton and "the wishes of my immediate constituents." Already Van Buren was an effective backstairs politician, crafting and then helping to ram through the senate a resolution binding the caucus to an exclusively Clintonian electoral ticket. The state assembly, where the Federalists were strong, followed suit. Van Buren had won New York for his patron, rather than his president.

Pennsylvania saved Madison's presidency. The Clintonians inundated the state with propaganda pitched directly at nominal Republicans. They appealed much more quietly to Pennsylvania Federalists. Clinton, it appears, styled himself in Federalist circles an "American Federalist," who, as president, would make immediate peace with Britain. But among most Republicans, patriotic unity over the war outstripped the abiding distrust of President Madison. When news of Clinton's negotiations with the Federalists leaked out, lukewarm Republicans, offended, turned against him. Despite the persistent factionalism, the president still won a large statewide victory, which gave him, barely, the electoral margin he needed to win reelection.

The politics of 1812 are supposed to have brought a continued rejuvenation and democratization of the Federalist Party—what one historian has described as nothing less than "a revolution of American conservatism." The claims are inflated. Outside New England and portions of New York, Federalism was too weak to accomplish much of anything, let alone revolutionize conservatism. DeWitt Clinton was a fusion candidate, not a Federalist, and his supporters made sure to call him a pro-war man wherever it would gain him votes. Many of Clinton's key backers, from

Michael Leib to Martin Van Buren, were not conservatives and certainly not Federalists. Federalist candidates did sweep congressional districts in New England and upstate New York, doubling their strength in the new Congress. But that still left them with only one-third of the total membership in the House, roughly what they had in 1809—and that membership, more than ever, hailed from a small portion of the Northeast, chiefly Massachusetts and Connecticut. Federalists in 1812 were a narrow sectional party, powerless outside their surviving strongholds. Younger conservatives may have started to come to terms with democratic politics, but they could not complete that revolution until they had abandoned Federalism.

The politics of 1812 instead highlighted the shifting dynamics within the Republican Party. Potentially damaging divisions persisted, but the younger militant nationalists, now allied with Madison, had won the political initiative. A new generation of Republican moderates had come to the fore—friendly to government-backed economic development, opposed to Federalist political principles, and eager for war with Britain. Simultaneously, up-and-comers like Martin Van Buren were staking out their own political careers, firmly within the Republicans' ranks. The war itself would prove extremely difficult, and stir heated dissent in New England. Finally, though, it would solidify the nationalist Republicans' control of national politics—and their ascendancy over the contending forces within their own party, including southern Quids, country Clodhoppers, pro-Clinton schismatics, and fiery urban democrats like William Duane.

WAR, POLITICS, AND THE FEDERALISTS IN DISSENT

In 1813, Britain's exasperated reaction to Congress's declaration of war turned into outrage as the war against Napoleon reached its climactic phase. New England Federalists' attacks turned accordingly vitriolic, at once sympathetic to the British and contemptuous of their own government's unfortunate early war efforts. "Utterly astonished at the declaration of war, I have been surprised at nothing since," observed the freshman representative Daniel Webster, elected to Congress in the Federalists' New England sweep of 1812. "Unless all history deceives me, I saw how it would be prosecuted when I saw how it was begun. There is in the nature of things an unchangeable relation between rash counsels and feeble execution."

So long as Britain remained chiefly concerned with France, the Americans did not suffer as greatly as they might have. (Thanks to the British, New England merchants suffered the least of all. At the end of 1812, the Royal Navy clamped down a blockade that would eventually stretch from New York to New Orleans—but the friendly New Englanders were permitted maritime access to the lucrative Canada trade they had cultivated during the embargo and nonimportation.) Neither side was able to break through against the other in 1813. Indeed, the Americans could actually claim some important victories. American naval forces under Commodore Isaac Chauncey deployed enough warships on Lake Erie, the crucial waterway of the northern theater of action, to keep the British from capturing it. In September, a small newly built American fleet, under Captain Oliver Hazard Perry, defeated the enemy off South Bass Island at the lake's western end in the deadliest naval battle of the entire conflict. Perry's success opened the way for William Henry Harrison, now the senior American officer in the Northwest, to prosecute one of the most important campaigns of the war.

For nearly a year, Harrison had tried and failed to break the British and their Indians allies' hold on the land approaches to Detroit. Once he received word of Perry's victory, Harrison shipped twenty-seven hundred troops westward from Ohio across Lake Erie. This compelled the British and the Indians to withdraw their main force, including fifteen hundred Indians under Tecumseh, from Fort Malden, near Detroit. The British brigadier marched his men eastward toward Niagara; the Americans—most of them militiamen from Kentucky—pursued on horseback and finally caught up with them on October 5 at a Canadian settlement along the Thames River. Losing only twelve dead and nineteen wounded, Harrison's troops killed or wounded forty-eight of the British and Canadian soldiers, captured six hundred, and killed thirty-three Indians. The British retreated ingloriously, never again to threaten from the Northwest. And among the dead Indian warriors in the riverside brush was Harrison's nemesis, Tecumseh.

Nearly forgotten today, the Battle of the Thames had an enduring significance only slightly smaller than that of the renowned Battle of New Orleans fifteen months later. Harrison's triumph added not an acre of conquered land to the American dominion. Its chief immediate result was a grisly rampage of Indian hating. (The Kentuckians reportedly skinned the bodies of Indian victims and tanned the skin into leather for trophies.) But the battle's long-term effects were manifold. Harrison's triumph virtually settled the northwestern boundary and Indian questions. With Tecumseh dead and the major Indian opposition crushed, American settlers could now safely move into all of Indiana and Michigan Territories and farther west. The British would soon abandon their idea, first broached in the 1770s, of creating an Indian buffer state between the United States and Canada.

None of these larger results could have materialized had the United States lost the war, which at times in 1814 seemed genuinely possible. In April, after his disastrous retreat from Moscow and more than a year of crushing reversals, Napoleon abdicated his throne. Battle-tested British troops now came to America. Out to avenge the setbacks of the previous year, they planned to retake the key northern lakes and rivers and hand Michigan Territory over to the Indians. They also hoped to seize enough of the Maine district to secure Canada's southeastern border. Between July and September, the British occupied coastal Maine, where many antiwar locals reportedly welcomed them with open arms.

In July, British Major General Robert Ross, commanding forty-five hundred veterans of the Napoleonic wars, joined forces with Vice Admiral Alexander Cochrane in Bermuda. Cochrane's assignment was to distract the Americans and exact retribution short of killing civilians. He sailed north to hit the Chesapeake. After chasing a small American naval force up the Patuxent River, the British dispersed a combined force of competent regular artillery and poorly trained militia, reached Washington, and set fire to the Capitol. President and Mrs. Madison fled the White House just before the arrival of local looters and His Majesty's army, leaving behind, one memoirist wrote, "an elegant and sumptuous past and a table set for forty." The British commanding officers, Ross and Admiral George Cockburn, entered the executive residence with their hungry men and enjoyed the presidential meal. Cockburn, who despised America and Americans, raised a facetious toast to Madison, swiped a cushion and one of the president's hats, and delivered ribald remarks about the country and its First Family. Then the two commanders personally set fire to the Executive Mansion. The next morning, British troops burned the building housing the State, War, and Navy Departments, as well as all nonmilitary public buildings except for the combined General Post Office and Patent Office. After departing Washington, the mud-splattered exiles of the Madison administration regrouped as best they could across the Potomac at the Reverend William Moffit's estate in Little Falls, Virginia, four miles from the city, which for a night became the closest thing there was to a capital of the United States.

The destruction in Washington and the temporary removal of the government proved more a psychological than a military setback for the Americans. Washington was strategically valueless: the British abandoned the city as soon as they had burned it. Because the Americans' chain of command remained dispersed, with considerable discretion still left to state militias, the gutting of the national capital did not unduly interfere with their military capabilities. Two weeks after they set fire to Washington, the self-confident British, under Cochrane, Ross, and Cockburn, attacked Baltimore and were repulsed by the heavily entrenched Maryland militia. An intense British rocket bombardment on Fort McHenry in Baltimore harbor failed utterly, inspiring the Maryland lawyer and eyewitness Francis Scott Key to write his defiant anthem, "The Star Spangled Banner." Then, in early September, American naval forces under Captain Thomas Macdonough thrashed a major enemy offensive near Lake Champlain, decisively checking the latest British effort to grab American territories on the northern front and sending the redcoats scurrying back to Canada.

The British could not vanquish the Americans, and the Americans could not vanquish the British. Neither the Madison administration (which returned to what was left of Washington) nor Congress could expect to accomplish any of the high-flown war aims proclaimed two years earlier. In January 1814, Madison entered diplomatic negotiations, and in early August, in the Flemish town of Ghent, an American delegation that included John Quincy Adams and Henry Clay met the British. The British initially took a hard line, demanding concessions that included the creation of an Indian nation north of the Ohio River. The American envoys threatened to break off negotiations if the British did not drop their Indian demands. Thereafter, both sides moved closer to a peace agreement, if only because neither side had much hunger to prolong the war.

For the American delegation, ending the war was imperative. Embittered New Englanders had detached from the rest of the country more than at any time since Jefferson's election. By December 1814, obdurate New England Federalists were talking openly of secession and a separate peace with the British, and popular unrest had sporadically turned violent. The dissent, among secessionists and nonsecessionists alike, focused on foreign affairs but was rooted in the Yankee Federalists' undiminished resistance to Jeffersonian ideas and politics. In Connecticut, Rhode Island, and, especially, Massachusetts, the war offered the Federalists a new lease on political life. Massachusetts Republicans, alarmingly, had taken control of the General Court in 1806 and won the governorship. But outrage at the embargo, the enforcement acts, and the war drove a successful Federalist resurgence.

In 1812, Congress's declaration of war immediately led the newly reelected Federalist Massachusetts governor, Caleb Strong, to call for a public fast to express outrage about the conflict, in sympathy with "the nation from which we are descended." Strong later refused to call up the state's militia to serve, as did three other New England Federalist governors. President Madison's difficult reelection, and the British occupation of Maine in 1814, deepened dissent. One round of memorials, collected from at least forty towns early in 1814, called for a New England antiwar convention, to seek remedies for the federal government's unconstitutional abuses. Some carried plain seccessionist implications. "The history of the late administration of the national Government," wrote the townsmen of Wendell, in words that both sarcastically and ominously paraphrased Jefferson's Declaration of Independence, is "a history of repeated injuries and usurpations, having a direct tendency to the Establishment of an Absolute Tyranny over these States."

The politics of the Massachusetts Federalist leadership, like those of the rest of the region, varied from the hatred of democracy spewed by the self-described "raving" Fisher Ames and the hard-line Essex Junto, to the more practical elitism of the elegant Bostonian Harrison Gray Otis. Their differences of tone and strategy did not disrupt the Federalists' basic unity over fundamental principles. Old and young, secessionist and antisecessionist—all agreed that the Revolution had been won to replace the British monarchy with a natural American aristocracy of moral, well-educated property holders, the rightful governors over a licentious and disorderly populace. They shared an a priori respect for the past, upholding "the good old school" of their fathers against "the insidious encroachments of innovation." Since the Revolution, supposedly, agrarian Virginia Jacobin slaveholders had taken advantage of the Constitution's three-fifths rule and stirred up the ignorant democratic populace (including hateful recent immigrants), thus undermining balance and order. In 1801, they seized the reins of national government. Once in power, the levelers attacked all that was sound and conservative, and despoiled the mercantile interests of New England. "From the peace to this time," Stephen Higginson wrote in 1803, "it has been [Virginia's] main object, to depress the northern States, to secure the influence & safety of the south." New England Federalists argued the same points even more fervently after more than a decade of Jeffersonian democracy.

Curiously, it has become fashionable in more recent times to cast the Federalists' apprehensions and antiwar protests as part of a broader Federalist antislavery humanitarianism—one that was egalitarian when compared to the glaring contradictions of the Republican slaveholders, Jefferson above all, about human liberty. By these lights, opposition to the War Hawks was in part an effort to halt the growth of slavery. Rarely has any group of Americans done so little to deserve such praise. Several members of the older Federalist cohort could boast of authentic antislavery activities in the 1770s and 1780s (along with, it should be added, some northern Republicans). Through the 1820s some Yankee Federalist lawmakers and clergymen expressed sincere moral repugnance at human bondage. But the antislavery currents in Federalism were always restrained, and they virtually dried up after 1800. The Federalists' chief aim was the removal of the three-fifths clause, without any true representation for blacks— that is, the political aggrandizement of northern Federalism. Although public attacks on the planters for their immorality and hypocrisy added to the Yankee Federalists' treasury of moral virtue, those attacks often expressed little concern about the slaves, or about slavery as an institution. The Federalists did not hate the Jeffersonians out of antislavery conviction; rather, they sometimes took antislavery positions because they hated the "Jacobin" Jeffersonians.

Beneath the surface, the Federalists' views on the South and slavery were perfectly in keeping with their broader antidemocratic politics and their partisan interests. To have any right to interfere with southern institutions and property would have contradicted their own insistence on property's inviolability and their region's rights to freedom from outside interference. It also would have killed off what remained of southern Federalism, which was positively pro-slavery, foreclosing any possibility that the party could regain a national presence, let alone national power. Charging the Jeffersonians with duplicity, on the other hand, permitted the Federalists to evade the fact that northeastern Republicans had greatly increased their strength from 1800 through 1809, thanks largely to city and country democrats who had no stake in slavery and whose ranks included many outspoken antislavery men. It also cloaked how traditionalist ideas about order and station left open no room to equality for freed slaves. Even authentically antislavery Federalist clerics bid northern blacks to "be contented," as Jedidiah Morse put it, "in the humble station in which Providence has placed you."

In the end, the war's democratic repercussions contradicted the Federalists' antidemocratic assumptions and accentuated their political isolation from the rest of the country. Those repercussions originated not in politics but in how the Americans fought the war. For better and for worse, the Jeffersonians' long-standing opposition to a large standing army meant that militiamen and volunteers bore much of the burden of fighting on land after 1812. Barely trained and poorly supplied, the militias earned a reputation among the officer corps for uselessness. Yet some outfits acquitted themselves as gunmen, creating a myth of the brave and patriotic citizen-soldier. The imagery stimulated demands for widening the franchise, above all in Virginia, where property qualifications remained steep. Across the state, militiamen mustered into the service signed petitions protesting their disenfranchisement. At the war's end, the exclusion seemed all the more outrageous. How, some democrats asked, could men be expected to fight and die for their country if they could not vote? "A Representative Democracy is the Ordinance of God," declared one protest meeting of backcountry democrats and militia veterans that gathered in Harrisonburg in June 1815.

The war also produced a new crop of military heroes whose authentic and invented glory became a democratic political resource waiting to be tapped. During and after the Revolution, most of this sort of political capital had flowed to the austere Federalist George Washington. But during the War of 1812, when military leadership was more fragmented, many more commanders gained renown for the respect they had earned from the rank and file of ordinary soldiers as well as for their triumphs in the field. The politically ambitious victor of the Battle of the Thames, William Henry Harrison, was one of these commanders; so, in a smaller way, was Colonel Richard Mentor Johnson of Kentucky, who would later claim, dubiously but to great effect, that he had personally slain Tecumseh. And among the new heroes was a general barely known to the citizenry before the war—Andrew Jackson of Tennessee.

None of the new popular military men were Federalists, and none came from New England. And so the War of 1812 further hastened the Federalists' final crisis, in ways that even the gloomiest among them could not have fully anticipated. In retrospect, the ironies are poignant, even painful. In their own minds, the Federalists were bravely defending the political spirit and substance of 1776 against southern planters and the deluded democratic hordes. Yet with their antiwar activities, they turned their political movement—originally organized by some of the most determined anti-British and anti-Tory leaders in America—into a pro-British American Tory party. The sons of New Englanders who had once defied the British Empire now seemed, at best, equivocal in the face of British coercion. The confident, nationalist party of Washington, Hamilton, and Adams had shriveled into the phobic sectional party of Otis, Pickering, and Ames. And the Federalists themselves dealt their party its coup de grace.

The end would come suddenly and, for the Federalists, by surprise. In 1814, New England Federalism was still riding high. In the Massachusetts governor's race, the incumbent Caleb Strong ridiculed complaints about his indiscriminate opposition to the war and won roughly 55 percent of the vote. In the legislative elections, the Federalists gained control over the lower house with a gargantuan majority. Federalist leaders remained on the antiwar barricades in the autumn, as the British blockade of the

coast, now expanded to include New England, remained unbroken. Governor Strong ordered the Massachusetts General Court
to consider what steps to take amid the crisis. In mid-October,
both houses of the Court approved a report, written by a joint
committee chaired by Harrison Gray Otis, summoning a convention of delegates from the New England states to consider the
expediency of proposing "a radical reform in the national compact." Connecticut and Rhode Island heeded the call and chose
delegations, as did a handful of commercial Connecticut River
Valley counties in New Hampshire and Vermont. On December
15, twenty-six eminent Federalists, mostly lawyers, convened at
the State House in Hartford, Connecticut.

By assembling in an extralegal convention, the Federalists at
once underscored their self-conscious links to the Revolution
and built on their own more recent partisan precedents, including the thinly veiled pro-Clinton "peace convention" of 1812.
Various plans were afoot. One group (including Noah Webster)
in Hampshire County, Massachusetts, revived Webster's proposal for a convention to recommend amendments to the Constitution. Hard-liners demanded even bolder action. John Low, a
representative from coastal Maine, called for a deputation of
Massachusetts leaders to travel to Washington, inform President
Madison of New England's displeasure, and demand that he
resign. Another dissenter devised a plan to prohibit collection of
federal internal duties. But the relatively moderate complexion of
the Hartford group—which, within New England Federalism,
was more a matter of degree than philosophy—portended a cali-
brated outcome, mild in its rhetoric if not its final intentions.
Under the control of practical party men like Harrison Gray Otis,
the convention included none of the most prominent Federalist
recalcitrants like Fisher Ames or Timothy Pickering. On the eve
of the gathering, Josiah Quincy asked George Cabot, who had
been named the convention's president, to predict what would
happen. Cabot replied that he knew exactly what the result
would be: "A GREAT PAMPHLET!" He proved correct.

On January 3, after nearly a month of disputation behind

closed doors, the convention adopted its final report, largely the work of Otis. The report began with the convention's hope to reconcile everyone "to a course of moderation and firmness." Yet what, to Otis, seemed moderate still represented a drastic program. A section on the South was meant to sound conciliatory, predicting that a new nationalist solidarity would soon arise, but only with the disappearance of the South's "visionary theorists"— old Federalist code words for the Jeffersonian democrats. The bulk of the writing recited New England's familiar wartime grievances—the conscription of state militiamen, the inequitable political power of the slaveholding states—and proposed seven "essential" constitutional amendments as nonnegotiable demands. These included the repeal of the three-fifths clause, a requirement that two-thirds of both houses of Congress agree before any new state could be admitted to the Union, limits on the length of embargoes, and the outlawing of the election of a president from the same state to successive terms, clearly aimed at the Virginians. Finally, the report authorized future conventions. Although the delegates endorsed neither New England secession nor the pursuit of a separate peace with Britain, they did not foreclose either should the war drag on and their resolutions fail.

From a Federalist angle, it all looked like a triumph of prudent but stern good sense. Some of the "warm bloods" grumbled, but most Connecticut and Massachusetts partisans—including the normally irreconcilable Pickering—praised the report for what Pickering called its "high character of wisdom, fairness, and dignity." Federalist newspapers from New Hampshire to New York extolled the document. For all of January, Federalists were optimistic that they might at last have some effect again on national policy. With the approval of his legislature, Governor Strong of Massachusetts appointed a three-man commission to present the gist of the convention's grievances, in his state's name, to President Madison. The trio left Boston on February 3. Only on February 14, the day after they arrived in Washington, did the commissioners learn, with the rest of the capital, that the negotiators at Ghent had signed a peace treaty six weeks earlier, on Christmas Eve.

At Ghent, American bargaining depended largely on the disposition of Henry Clay. Madison had included Clay in the peace delegation not because of his negotiating prowess—Clay was known as a fearsome debater and organizer, not a suave diplomat—but because he could be counted on to defend western interests and because he had enormous influence in Congress. At the peace table, Clay's directness of speech, along with his taste for rambling late-night conversations and card-playing sessions featuring plenty of liquor and cheap cigars, surprised his British counterparts and offended his American colleague, the correct professional John Quincy Adams. More than the other Americans, Clay remained brightly optimistic about his country's fortunes in the field and in the negotiations. He dismissed the rising dissent in New England as "a game of swaggering and gasconade." He also encouraged his fellow Americans, as the negotiations wore on, to adopt a cardsharp's calculating spirit of "brag"—what is known today as bluffing. "He asked me if I knew how to play *brag*," Adams wrote in his diary. "I had forgotten how. He said the art of it was to beat your adversary by holding your hand with a solemn and confident phiz, and out bragging him."

Clay nearly overdid it. Once news of the American victories in Baltimore and upstate New York reached Ghent, the British backed off from their tough demands and followed up an American suggestion that a treaty be negotiated based on the complete restoration of the status quo as of July 1812. Clay would have liked to get more out of the enemy, but he checked his disappointment and agreed to go along—only to put his foot down, to Adams's consternation, over the matter of British navigation rights on the Mississippi River. James Bayard, one of the American delegates, despaired at Clay's stubborness and accused him of "bragging a million against a cent." Fortunately for the negotiations, all sides eventually agreed to omit the Mississippi question from the treaty, leaving it, along with several other outstanding issues, to be settled at some future date. Otherwise, the prewar status was restored.

Intrepid gambler though he was, it would require even more of Clay's bluffing skills to make the Treaty of Ghent look like a great American victory. After two and a half years of war, the United States was left with a few heroes such as Harrison, Perry, and Johnson, a few disgraces such as William Hull, a government with its finances in disarray, a federal capital that partially lay in ashes, and nearly seven thousand killed or wounded—almost two-thirds the number of casualties incurred during the Revolutionary War, which had lasted nearly three times as long. The republic had survived, a patriotic vindication. Otherwise, the best that could be said was that American military triumphs of late summer had staved off defeat and helped push the British into serious negotiations—a genuine, but modest, achievement.

At year's end, in Ghent, Clay, ignorant of events back home, was assembling his arguments to prove that the diplomatic stalemate was in fact a glorious affirmation of American independence. In frigid Hartford, Harrison Gray Otis was drafting the Federalist manifesto whose sentiments would later be officially delivered to James Madison. And nearly fifteen hundred miles to the southwest, in the parlor of a makeshift headquarters on Royal Street in New Orleans, an American general, Andrew Jackson, was scrambling to thwart a British invasion—an engagement whose outcome would cinch Clay's brag and complete the Federalists' ruin.

VENGEANCE AND GLORY: THE EMERGENCE OF JACKSON

Jackson looked like a man cut away from the stake, erect but gaunt and pallid after more than a year of nearly continuous combat, capped by repeated attacks of dysentery. At age forty-seven, he was wrinkled and his auburn hair gone gray. His head and left fingers bore jagged livid reminders of a sword blow struck by a British officer during the Revolution, when he was a boy.

Jackson had been in New Orleans for three weeks, pulling

together the city's defenses and awaiting an enormous British expeditionary force. Early on the afternoon of December 23, three Creole gentlemen appeared with important information. The visitors, sweaty and winded from a hard ride, were duly ushered in to see the general. One of them, a young M. Villère, stammered that the British had just encamped at his family's plantation nine miles away. Jackson invited his guests to share a glass of wine. "I will smash them, so help me God!" Jackson supposedly said of his old enemy.

Jackson was a skilled general, not a great one. Although he had built a career in the military, it was not his first profession. His father, also named Andrew, arrived in the Carolina backcountry from Ireland with his wife Elizabeth and their two sons in 1765. Subsistence farmers, the Jacksons settled along the disputed border between the two Carolinas in the Waxhaw area, near Elizabeth's five married sisters and another family of in-laws. Andrew built a small log cabin and cleared enough land to support Elizabeth and the boys, but in the late winter of 1767, he died— killed, according to one account, by a falling log while he was clearing timber. A few days later, with the clan deep in mourning, Elizabeth gave birth to her third son, whom she named in honor of her dead husband.

Elizabeth, a pious Presbyterian, wanted young Andrew to train for the ministry, one of the chief paths to social advancement for a poor Scots-Irish boy. She put aside enough money to provide him with the best possible schooling with local ministers, which by Waxhaw standards was exceptional. But the Revolution and its chance for patriotic adventure intervened. At age thirteen, Andrew joined in ferocious irregular backwoods fighting against the British. One of his brothers died of exposure after the Battle of Stono Ferry in 1779; Andrew and his surviving brother, Robert, were betrayed by a Waxhaw Tory and captured. When Andrew refused to polish a British officer's boots, the officer slashed him, scarring him for life. Jailed in Camden, the brothers contracted smallpox, whereupon Elizabeth arranged to have them released as part of a prisoner exchange. Robert died; Andrew's fever broke;

and (before Andrew fully recovered) Elizabeth journeyed to British-occupied Charleston to nurse two nephews held on a disease-ridden prison ship. There she died of cholera, her body placed in an unmarked grave. "I felt utterly alone," Jackson recalled years later, "and tried to recall her last words to me."

Jackson fell back on the largess of his Waxhaw kinfolk, but found them, to one degree or another, disagreeable. They found him obstreperous. He took work as a saddler's helper, then traveled on his own to liberated Charleston to receive a four-hundred-pound inheritance from one of his Irish grandfathers. Only fifteen, he remained in Charleston and acted out the role of a high-living, low-country gentleman, squandering his inheritance on a binge of drinking, gambling, and women. He returned to the Waxhaw district, shamed and somewhat chastened, taught school, went back to work for the saddler, and saved his wages. In 1784, he left for good and traveled north to Salisbury, North Carolina, a growing county seat, to study law. He could not persuade the best lawyer in town to take him on as a clerk, but he picked up enough training from local attorneys to qualify for the bar in 1787. When the position of first public prosecutor in newly settled middle Tennessee opened up, Jackson got the job. On his way west, he fought the first of what would be several duels (this one bloodless) and purchased his first slave—minimum requirements for any true southern gentleman. Lawyer Jackson arrived in Nashville in October 1788. He was only twenty-one.

There has been, in recent decades, abundant psychological theorizing on how Jackson's youthful traumas accounted for his later vengeful personality. The prenatal loss of his father, his "abandonment" by his mother, his testy relations with his Waxhaw kin—all could well have accounted for the grown man's propensity for violent language (and violent actions), his abrupt mood swings, and a "slobbering" speech impediment that curtailed his ability to address crowds. A drawback to these arguments is that there is no evidence whatsoever that Jackson harbored any resentments toward either of his parents. The estrangement between Jackson and the rest of his family was

hardly unusual for ambitious young men in the insular backcountry. But whatever the familial sources of his rage may have been,
two important and exhaustively documented facets of that rage
plainly resulted from Jackson's boyhood tribulations. One was a
mighty drive to gain honor and respect, according to the prickly
mores of southern manhood. The other, rooted in his Scots-Irish
heritage but scorched into his body and soul by the Revolution,
was his hatred of the British and their empire.

Jackson's rapid rise had social and political as well as personal
origins, not unlike Henry Clay's in Kentucky and John C. Calhoun's in South Carolina. The uprooting of the old Tory elite of
the colonial North Carolina bench and bar had opened up a
vocation much better suited to Jackson's talents and tastes than
the ministry or saddle making. Among the first lawyers to arrive
in the Cumberland River region, Jackson quickly became one of
Nashville's leading citizens in the years before Tennessee statehood. His marriage in 1791 to Rachel Donelson, from a prominent local family, added to his political stature, which then
helped elect him as a delegate to the state constitutional convention in 1795 and, the following year, as the new state's first congressman. In Philadelphia, Congressman Jackson aligned himself
with the backcountry opposition, supporting western military
preparedness, opposing direct federal taxation, and voting against
an effusive House resolution in praise of the departing President
Washington. But Jackson had no patience for the backstairs plotting and purely rhetorical combat of national politics. Soon after
being elevated to the Senate, he resigned, spent a few years as a
circuit-riding justice on the Tennessee Supreme Court, and then
quit government affairs, apparently forever, in favor of moneymaking and a career in the military.

The moneymaking was a matter of utmost necessity. While
advancing in law and politics, Jackson had also plowed his ener-
gies into planting, merchandising, and land speculation, only to
lose nearly everything when a business associate whose notes he
had endorsed went bankrupt. Forced to start over outside
Nashville, Jackson recouped his losses by buying slaves and cash-

ing in on the boom market for short-staple cotton. In time, his new enterprise, the Hermitage, would become one of the most successful plantations in Tennessee. But the master (who always referred to the Hermitage as his "farm") would permanently harbor a raging distrust of debt, banks, and the entire paper-money credit system.

Jackson's passion for the military reignited soon after he arrived in the Cumberland region, when he joined fellow settlers' counterattacks against Muskogee and Chickamauga raiding parties. He angled for the post of commander of the Tennessee militia, a job he captured in 1802. Thereafter, his political involvement dwindled to nothing and his military ambitions soared, though there were new frustrations. For ten years, he leaped at the first sign that war might be declared, if not against the British, then against their allies, the Spanish and the Indians. (Jackson took a kinder view of Britain's greatest enemies, the French, including Napoleon, whom he admired for his bravura and energy.) But there was little need for Jackson's military services. In 1806, he fell in with the wandering adventurer Aaron Burr and played a direct if minor role in provisioning Burr's western conspiracy (only to discover to his horror that at least some of the conspirators were plotting treason). Jackson returned to the Hermitage, purchased more land and slaves, gambled on his gamecocks and racehorses, and endlessly quarreled with his detractors, at times with pistols drawn: a self-made southern planter, restlessly awaiting a war.

When war finally came, it was against Jackson's mightiest enemies, the British, along with the major fifth column in the southern theater, the rebellious Muskogee Indians of the upper Alabama region around the Coosa and Tallapoosa rivers. "*Who are we? and for what are we going to fight,*" Jackson proclaimed in a handwritten call for enlistments. "[A]re we the titled Slaves of George the third? the military conscripts of Napoleon the great? or the frozen peasants of the Russian Czar? No—we are the free born sons of america; the citizens of the only republick now existing in the world."

After he led his troops on a mission (eventually aborted by Secretary of War John Armstrong) to defend the lower Mississippi Valley, Commander Jackson's troops, in recognition of his toughness, gave him the nickname "Hickory," which soon became "Old Hickory." In the autumn of 1813, he received another chance at glory when ordered to clear up a persisting Indian threat in northern Alabama Territory. Upwards of four thousand discontented Muskogees (called "Creeks" by the Americans, because of their skill in navigating and settling in their heavily creek-crossed terrain) emerged as the southern branch of Tecumseh's pantribal confederacy. Led by the half-Creek, half-Scots chief Red Eagle—called, in English, William Weatherford—these Red Sticks (they painted their bodies and war clubs bright red) alienated both the neighboring Chickasaws and a large faction of their fellow Creeks, thus precipitating a civil war.

News that the Red Sticks had massacred hundreds of white Americans, adults and children, at the fortified Alabama River home of a part-Creek, part-white merchant, Samuel Mims, led Jackson and the Americans to intervene directly. The Fort Mims massacre struck all of Jackson's sore points about rebellious Indians, gallant southern manhood, and (through the Red Sticks' connection to Tecumseh) the perfidious British. Ordered by Tennessee's governor to go on the offensive, Jackson assured friendly Creeks and their leaders that he would defend them, but vowed personal revenge against all others, and swore to his own troops that he would fight by their side. At a hostile Creek village south of Huntsville, Alabama, one thousand of Jackson's soldiers encircled nearly two hundred Creek fighters, killed every one of them, and took the women and children as captives. (American losses totaled only five dead and forty-one wounded.) "We have retaliated for the destruction of Fort Mims," Jackson reported curtly to Tennessee governor Willie Blount. "We shot them like dogs," a then-obscure Tennessee soldier and marksman named David Crockett later recollected.

After another smashing victory in November at the village of Talladega, Jackson's fortunes soured when his supplies ran low and his men threatened to desert. Only the fortuitous arrival of replacements permitted him to remain in the field. At the end of March 1814, the augmented forces, now numbering close to four thousand men including friendly Creeks and Cherokees, overwhelmed nearly a thousand Red Sticks at Horseshoe Bend, in another lopsided bloodbath. Three weeks later, Red Eagle surrendered, and virtually the entire Creek Nation submitted to Jackson's authority.

As the price of peace, Jackson imposed a treaty that ceded twenty-three million acres of Creek land to the United States—more than half of the Creeks' total holdings, representing approximately three-fifths of present-day Alabama and one-fifth of Georgia. The forfeited lands included territories held by friendly Creeks who had fought alongside Jackson as well as territories held by Red Sticks. Jackson forced his allies, as well as those he had defeated, to submit. In doing so, he completed a land grab that opened up immense tracts of fertile land to speculators and settlers, and foreclosed the doom of the entire Creek Nation. Although the rigors of the campaign permanently broke his already damaged health—struck down by his chronic dysentery and unable to digest food, he sometimes subsisted on diluted gin—Jackson was rewarded with a commission as major general in the U.S. Army.

In strictly military terms, his reputation was exaggerated. The enemy, although formidable, was far less so than the British army and navy. Lacking ordnance and sufficient musketry, the rebels could not match the Americans' firepower. Jackson did perform well on the field for an inexperienced commander, designing simple but effective stratagems for confusing the Creeks, deploying his men skillfully, and redeploying them swiftly. His indomitable will, displayed both in suppressing mutiny among the militia and in dictating peace to the surrendering Creek chiefs, overcame his own torments. Given the delicate balance of American wins and losses in the War of 1812, his victories made him look like a military genius. But the reality was more prosaic: Jackson, when aroused, was an accomplished and unforgiving killer.

Jackson turned his fury against his greatest foe of all. "I owe to Britain a debt of retaliatory vengeance," he wrote to his wife. "[S]hould our forces meet I trust I shall pay the debt." After repulsing a British attack on Mobile, he made war on the Spanish in West Florida, who with the British (he told Rachel) were "arming the hostile Indians to butcher our women & children." The only snag in his plan was the inconvenient fact that the United States was not formally at war with Spain. Jackson, caring little for technicalities, threatened to invade Florida, provoking the Spanish governor to invite the British to land at Pensacola, a clear violation of Spanish neutrality. Fully justified in his own mind, Jackson invaded in October 1814, seized Pensacola from a combined force of Spanish, British, and Indians, and then handed the town, rendered militarily useless, back to its Spanish governor. A week later, while still in Pensacola, Jackson learned that the British had launched an enormous invasion from Jamaica— sixty ships carrying more than ten thousand troops—aimed at New Orleans, and that he had been ordered to crush it.

New Orleans was the gateway to what Thomas Jefferson had envisaged as the empire of liberty. If the British could seize it, they would control the entire lower Mississippi Valley and, once joined by forces sent from Canada, effectively control all of what was then the American West. Since the British had never formally recognized the Spanish retrocession of western lands to the French in 1800, there would have been strong grounds for them to claim that the Louisiana Purchase was illegitimate and, by right of conquest, the entire area would belong to them. Even short of such schemes, possession of New Orleans was vital to the outcome of the current fighting. Should the Americans lose the city, everyone realized, they would almost certainly lose the war. Although New Orleans, surrounded by lakes and bayous, enjoyed daunting natural protections against invasion, the British had the navy and the men.

Louisiana had been admitted to the Union in 1812, but the state's loyalties and those of its city were uncertain. In New Orleans, the long-resident Creole French and Spanish populations could not be counted on to support the American cause. South of the city, the bayous around Barataria Bay belonged to a large band of well-armed privateers and smugglers commanded by a fiercely independent, Haitian-born former blacksmith, Jean Lafitte. There were also fears of slave unrest. In January 1811, the territorial governor had savagely suppressed a rebellion of five hundred slaves, who burned several sugar-cane plantations north of New Orleans and briefly menaced the city itself. Now, with a British armada at Louisiana's doorstep, there was every reason to fear that the invaders would try to mobilize the slaves.

Jackson arrived with his troops on December 1, and with his slim force (numbering, at best, seven hundred), he hastily pieced together an auxiliary army and navy. He had insulted Lafitte and the Baratarians as "hellish banditti," but now he struck a deal that secured their supplies and skills (including their expertise at cannoneering). Over the objections of skittish slaveholders, Jackson also organized two battalions of free black soldiers, ordering one reluctant assistant district paymaster to respect all of the enlistees on the muster rolls "without inquiring whether the troops are white, black or tea." Finally, in late December, contingents from Tennessee, Kentucky, and Mississippi arrived, brought by General John Coffee, General William Carroll, and Major Thomas Hinds. Although still outnumbered, the swarming Americans at least resembled a credible fighting force.

Once he had learned that the British were closing in, Jackson redeployed his main force behind an old millrace five miles outside the city and dug in behind mud ramparts reinforced with cotton bales and wooden platforms. There, for three weeks, the Americans withstood repeated bombardments and ground attacks. By January 8, with four thousand men on his frontline and another thousand in reserve, Jackson faced, less than a mile to the east, ten thousand British, most of them veterans of the Napoleonic wars, under the command of Lieutenant General Sir Edward Pakenham. At dawn, the British began an all-out assault on the Americans.

Pakenham's original plan of attack had called for widening a canal to allow British-controlled barges to ferry troops across the Mississippi and blister the Americans with crossfire. Fortune wound up favoring the Americans. A hastily built British dam containing the river collapsed, delaying and nearly ruining the canal effort. The next morning, a British regiment was supposed to spearhead the British attack using ladders and sugar-cane bundles to bridge the ditches that lay in front of the American position, and then to scale Jackson's breastworks. Only when the men were in attack position did they realize that they had left the ladders and cane bundles to the rear. By the time they retrieved their equipment, the battle was well underway. Protected behind their barricades, the Americans poured volley after volley of grape, canister, and rifle fire into the advancing British line.*

By eight in the morning, the shooting had stopped. Jackson walked from position to position, congratulating the soldiers, as the army's band (which had been playing "Yankee Doodle" throughout the battle) struck up "Hail Columbia." The men cheered for General Jackson. Then the Americans climbed up and over their embankments to see what they had done.

Not even the most gruesome scenes of backwoods Indian fighting could prepare them for the aftermath of this kind of battle, fought with a heavy complement of cannons against thousands of uniformed troops. The British dead and wounded lay in scarlet heaps that stretched out unbroken for as far as a quarter mile. Maimed soldiers crawled and lurched about. Eerily, while the battle smoke cleared off, there was a stirring among the slain soldiers, as dazed redcoats who had used their comrades' bodies as shields arose and surrendered to the Americans. Jackson, who had seen hard combat and not flinched, was shaken: "I never had

---

* The British might also have gained an advantage when, despite the canal fiasco, five hundred troops managed to cross to the opposite banks of the Mississippi. Easily dispersing the token American defense force—a major deployment error by Jackson—the men rushed to the American batteries where they could rake Jackson's men undisturbed. But the detachment had landed well south of where it intended, and by the time the men were ready to unleash their crossfire, the main British assault had become a shambles.

so grand and awful an idea of the resurrection as on that day," he later recalled. In two hours of combat (and, perhaps, only five minutes of truly decisive shooting) the British had lost, by their own accounting, almost three hundred killed, over a thousand wounded, and almost five hundred captured or missing—roughly 40 percent of their main attack force of five thousand. American casualties totaled only thirteen killed, thirty-nine wounded, and nineteen missing. It was a stunning disparity, greater than even the most one-sided of Jackson's triumphs over the Creeks.

If the battle's scale was difficult to comprehend, the outcome was still in many ways a typical Jackson victory, brutal, lucky, and finally overwhelming. Two weeks later, all of the British sailed away. Then began the exaltation of Andrew Jackson. President Madison sent a special commendation. Congress unanimously passed a lengthy resolution of thanks and ordered a gold medal struck. The city of Washington, still recovering from the fires of August, erupted with delight, as did Philadelphia and New York. Newspapers ran encomiums from Jackson's men talking of his shrewd leadership and his bravery under fire. Parades were organized, songs and fiddle tunes composed, illuminations lit.

Jackson did nothing to discourage the ecstatic homage. "[T]he 8th of January," he wrote to one associate a month after the battle, "will be ever recollected by the British nation, and always hailed by every true american." Vengeance and glory were his.

THE WAR OF 1812 AND THE TRANSFORMATION OF AMERICAN POLITICS

When the news from Ghent came just over a week after the news from New Orleans, Washington's jubilation redoubled—but three visitors from Boston walked glumly past the throngs of revelers. Harrison Gray Otis, Thomas H. Perkins, and William Sullivan, the Massachusetts commission sent to relay the Yankee Federalist complaints to President Madison, knew their effort was now pointless. Perkins and Thompson did drop in at the president's lodgings, a large house formerly occupied by the French minister, where they paid their respects to Madison. Otis, embittered, stood on ceremony and refused to enter because he and his delegation had received no formal invitation. Otis also reported that Madison was now claiming that the New Englanders' efforts had been bound to fail all along, no matter the circumstances. "I believe however we should have succeeded," the unrepentant Otis wrote to his wife, "and that the little Pigmy shook in his shoes at our approach."

The pygmy was now elated. The undertaking begun at Hartford, so mild and purposeful in the Federalists' own minds, had placed not just Otis and his colleagues but Federalists everywhere in an awkward position that lent itself cruelly to ridicule. In New England, self-righteousness died hard: there alone, Federalism persisted as a credible force over the coming years, especially in Massachusetts, where Federalists retained control of the state government until 1823. Elsewhere, Federalists finally fell outside the ken of respectability, reviled as disloyalists who had wanted to end the war on Britain's terms, and lumped together with the traitorous "blue-lights" who had signaled at night to British warships anchored off the Connecticut shore. The quasi–Federalist Republican jurist Joseph Story enthused to a friend that the war's conclusion presented a "glorious opportunity for the Republican party to place themselves permanently in power."

Posterity's judgment on the War of 1812 has been more severe. Ever since Henry Adams wrote his enormous and misunderstood study of the Jefferson and Madison administrations, the war has generally been viewed as a needless and costly conflict, instigated by predatory War Hawk Republicans and bungled by an inept president. Such accounts usually minimize the British offenses to American independence, and not just to commercial interests. Impressments, above all, struck at the lowest and most vulnerable of free Americans, and even such ex-Federalists as John Quincy Adams viewed them as intolerable. The critics often slight the active and purposeful efforts by the New England Federalists to undermine the war effort while New England merchants cheerfully traded with British and American forces alike. They slight Madison's remarkable calm in the face of those efforts. They disregard how, simply by fighting the Royal Navy to a standoff, the American navy performed better than any of Britain's other foes of the era. They dwell on how the war's expenses deranged the country's public finances—true enough—but they neglect how (thanks to bonds floated by Gallatin's protégé and successor, Alexander J. Dallas) the U.S. Treasury, at the end of 1815, boasted the largest credit balance in the young nation's history. They miss the fact that apart from the symbolic embarrassment at Washington, the worst American defeats came early in the war—and that, by mid-1814, Madison had found generals like Jackson who measured up to their assignments. They forget that although the Treaty of Ghent failed to end impressment, it did stipulate the repatriation of nearly four thousand Americans, classified as prisoners of war, who had been press-ganged into the British service.

Even without Jackson's victory, Madison and the Republicans could have mounted the strained but plausible case that they had defied the dire early predictions of the Federalists and the Old Republicans. At the very least, they would have ceded nothing to the mighty British. On the eve of the signing of the Ghent Treaty, John Quincy Adams wrote to his wife that he had had the privilege of helping in "redeeming our union." His fellow negotiator, James Bayard, spoke of how Europeans regarded the Americans with a newfound respect. But with the Battle of New Orleans, what had ended as a kind of proud stalemate had the look and feel of an enormous American victory.

The United States was the war's emblematic winner, but there were also very real losers in America. The biggest losses of all were suffered by Indians, North and South, whose power to resist expansion east of the ninety-fifth meridian was forever destroyed. Next came the disgraced New England Federalists, and then the southern Quids and the city and country democrats (including fervently pro-war democrats) who, for different reasons, had opposed the moderate Republicanism of the Jefferson years and, later, the nationalist Republicanism advanced by Henry Clay and John C. Calhoun. "Let us extend the national authority over the whole extent of power given by the Constitution," Joseph Story exclaimed. "Let us have great military and naval schools; an adequate regular army; the broad foundations laid of a permanent navy; a national bank." What had begun as the congressional nationalist faction in 1811, a pro-war version of moderate Republicanism, now commanded a seemingly unbeatable Republican Party.

The war's end also marked a watershed in the rise of American democracy. Between 1801 and 1815, a Jeffersonian democracy that had once rightly feared for its own existence became the nation's preeminent political power. Presumptions about the natural superiority of well-born and well-bred gentlemen, challenged during the American Revolution, now fell. A new generation of Republicans, including men of humble origins, attained high government and military office. The proportion of eligible voters who participated in American elections grew substantially, as did (though less substantially) the proportion of American men who were eligible to vote. Party competition was the major reason, as political involvement grew most intense and widespread in areas where the rivalry between Republican and Federalists sharpened most, above all in the middle Atlantic states. Republican political organization, foreshadowed by the Democratic-Republican societies of the 1790s, had become increasingly sophisticated, producing statewide organizations that, again chiefly in the middle Atlantic states, opened up more participation by the rank-and-file party faithful and moved away from the top-down organization through state caucuses. These democratic alterations forced the more realistic of the Federalists to adapt to increasingly democratic American realities. Yet despite those adjustments, the Federalist realists could not sustain Federalism. The truly dynamic force in American politics after 1809 was not a rejuvenated Federalism, learning from the Jeffersonians' successes and exploiting their mistakes. It was a nationalist Republicanism, promoted by westerners and southerners who rejected the Federalists' political ideas and their Anglophilic economics as inimical to the character of the country.

Compared to the American polity of the founding era, the change was, in retrospect, extraordinary. When the country and city organizers of the Democratic-Republican societies of the 1790s dared to speak out, between elections, on sensitive public issues, the president of the United States and the U.S. Senate (and, nearly, the House of Representatives too) formally censured them as fomenters of disorder and tyranny. Even the societies' friends in the early Republican opposition did not quite know what to make of the rambunctious, undeferential democrats. At the end of the War of 1812, this kind of hauteur and such confusion were unimaginable outside the most hidebound conservative circles. In one of the greatest paradoxes of all, the most inflammatory criticisms of the government during the war had came from conservative New England Federalists—with no Sedition Law raining down on their heads.

The pressures for democratic reform had not come even close to exhausting themselves in 1815. "The spirit of our country is doubtless more democratic than the form of our government," the Massachusetts Federalist George Cabot ruefully acknowledged after Thomas Jefferson's election in 1801. Fifteen years later, although much had changed, the form had still not kept pace with the growing spirit. Despite Federalism's retreat, there were powerful Americans who wanted to restrain that change, and keep the boisterous influence of popular politics to a minimum. Even within the triumphant Republican coalition, the congressional caucus system, although under increasing pressure, still governed the selection of national candidates and the formulation of programs. And even among Republicans, there remained fundamental differences, cloaked during the war, about the definition of democratic government.

Despite the wishful thinking of some Republican leaders, the end of Federalism as a national power did not bring the end of fundamental political conflicts. Affirming the republic's independence in the war against Britain actually had the unforeseen effect of spurring action among ordinary Americans for even wider democracy—action that would meet with resistance from quondam Federalists and some Republicans alike. Those conflicts would become intertwined with divisions at the political top that, within a decade, would shatter the deceptive harmony and single-party ascendancy of the immediate postwar years. One of those divisions, over the future of American slavery, would set northern and southern Republicans—and the constituencies they represented—on a fateful collision course. The other major division, over the proper instruments and democratic direction of national development, would pit both Clay and Calhoun against a new—and, to many, frightening—popular political force. At the head of that force would stand Andrew Jackson.

SELECTED FURTHER READING

This list of suggested readings is far from exhaustive. Readers interested in exploring particular topics in greater depth, especially concerning local and state politics, may wish to consult the relevant endnotes in the full one-volume Norton edition of *The Rise of American Democracy*, available in paperback.

Henry Adams, *History of the United States during the Administrations of Thomas Jefferson and James Madison* (1889–91; New York, 1986).

Joyce O. Appleby, *Capitalism and a New Social Order: The Republican Vision of the 1790s* (New York, 1984).

James M. Banner Jr., *To the Hartford Convention: Federalists and the Origins of Party Politics in Massachusetts, 1789–1815* (New York, 1970).

Lance Banning, *The Sacred Fire of Liberty: James Madison and the Founding of the Federal Republic* (Ithaca, 1995).

R. B. Bernstein, *Thomas Jefferson* (New York, 2003).

Irving Brant, *James Madison* (Indianapolis, 1941–68).

Saul Cornell, *The Other Founders: Anti-Federalism and the Dissenting Tradition in America, 1788–1828* (Chapel Hill, 2000).

Noble E. Cunningham Jr., *The Jeffersonian Republicans in Power: Party Operations 1801–1809* (Chapel Hill, 1963).

———, *The Jeffersonian Republicans: The Formation of Party Organization: 1789–1801* (Chapel Hill, 1957).

———, *The Pursuit of Reason: The Life of Thomas Jefferson* (Baton Rouge, 1987).

David Brion Davis, *The Problem of Slavery in the Age of Revolution, 1770–1823* (Ithaca, 1975).

Gregory Evans Dowd, *A Spirited Resistance: The North Ameri-*

can Indian Struggle for Unity, 1745–1815 (Baltimore, 1992).

Stanley Elkins and Eric L. McKitrick, *The Age of Federalism: The Early American Republic, 1788–1800* (New York, 1993).

Richard E. Ellis, *The Jeffersonian Crisis: Courts and Politics in the Young Republic* (New York, 1971).

John Ferling, *John Adams: A Life* (Knoxville, 1992).

———, *Adams vs. Jefferson: The Tumultuous Election of 1800* (New York, 2004).

David Hackett Fischer, *The Revolution of American Conservatism: The Federalist Party in the Era of Jeffersonian Democracy* (New York, 1965).

Sylvia R. Frey, *Water from the Rock: Black Resistance in a Revolutionary Age* (Princeton, 1991).

Donald R. Hickey, *The War of 1812: A Forgotten Conflict* (Urbana, 1989).

Richard Hofstadter, *The Idea of a Party System: The Rise of Legitimate Opposition in the United States, 1780–1840* (Berkeley, 1969).

Linda K. Kerber, *Federalists in Dissent: Imagery and Ideology in Jeffersonian America* (Ithaca, 1970).

Alexander Keyssar, *The Right to Vote: The Contested History of Democracy in the United States* (New York, 2001).

Dumas Malone, *Jefferson and His Time* (New York, 1948–81).

Forrest McDonald, *The Presidency of Thomas Jefferson* (Lawrence, 1976).

Edmund S. Morgan, *Inventing the People: The Rise of Popular Sovereignty in Britain and America* (New York, 1988).

Bradford Perkins, *Prologue to War: England and the United States, 1805–1812* (Berkeley, 1961).

Merrill Peterson, *Thomas Jefferson and the New Nation* (New York, 1970).

Robert V. Remini, *The Battle of New Orleans* (New York, 1999).

Norman K. Risjord, *The Old Republicans: Southern Conservatives in the Age of Jefferson* (New York, 1965).

Robert A. Rutland, *The Presidency of James Madison* (Lawrence, 1990).

Jean Edward Smith, *John Marshall: Definer of a Nation* (New York, 1996).

J. C. A. Stagg, *Mr. Madison's War: Politics, Diplomacy, and Warfare in the Early American Republic, 1783–1830* (Princeton, 1983).

John Sugden, *Tecumseh: A Life* (New York, 1998).

Gordon S. Wood, *The Creation of the American Republic, 1776–1787* (Chapel Hill, 1969).

————, *The Radicalism of the American Revolution* (New York, 1992).

James Morton Smith, *Freedom's Fetters: The Alien and Sedition Laws and American Civil Liberties* (Ithaca, 1956).

Arthur Zilversmit, *The First Emancipation: The Abolition of Slavery in the North* (Chicago, 1967).

ACKNOWLEDGMENTS

I am deeply grateful to the John Simon Guggenheim Memorial Foundation and the American Council of Learned Societies for their financial support. An intellectually challenging fellowship year at the Woodrow Wilson International Center for Scholars in 1998–99 transformed my understanding of American democracy, for which I am indebted to the Center and its excellent staff. I am equally indebted to the Princeton University Research Board, the Shelby Cullom Davis Center for Historical Studies, and the Princeton University History Department for their generosity over many years.

Gerald Howard, then of W. W. Norton & Company, showed faith in this book and its author when he signed me up long ago, and he remains a steadfast ally. At Norton, I have been blessed to work with Drake McFeely, a friend for more than two decades and a wise editor, who also possesses the patience and fortitude of a saint. His assistant, Brendan Curry, offered me his energy, encouragement, and shrewd expertise. Mary Babcock's superb copyediting improved my prose and pushed me to omit large amounts of extraneous material. Thanks go as well to Starling Lawrence and Jeannie Luciano for their support. During the final stages, Nancy Palmquist, Anna Oler, Gina Webster, Don Rifkin, Bill Rusin, Louise Brockett, Elizabeth Riley, Sally Anne McCartin, and their staffs performed splendidly in turning out the finished book.

Tom Wallace of T. C. Wallace, Ltd., and Andrew Wylie of the Wylie Agency handled business matters with sagacity and efficiency.

Judith Ferszt, the manager of the Program in American Studies at Princeton, has helped me in matters large and small nearly every day for the past dozen years and given me the gifts of her singular intelligence and good cheer.

Amanda Ameer and Samantha Williamson put in many hard hours checking footnotes and quotations.

Numerous friends, loved ones, colleagues, students, teachers, librarians, research assistants, technical wizards, counselors, and confessors have helped me beyond measure, in everything from suggesting sources, locating documents, and reading drafts to making allowances for my exasperating distraction. To praise them here as they deserve would add many more pages to an already long book. I have thanked them, and will continue to thank them, personally. Above all, thanks go to my beloved and forbearing family, who make me wish I could have been a poet instead of a historian and said it all much better and quicker.

The dedication is a toast to essential companions and decades of companionship—and to decades more, through thick and thin.

CREDITS

1. The Granger Collection, New York
2. The Granger Collection, New York
3. Princeton University. Bequest of Charles A. Munn, Class of 1881. Photo Credit: Bruce M. White
4. The Granger Collection, New York
5. National Gallery of Art, Washington. Andrew W. Mellon Collection. Image © Board of Trustees, National Gallery of Art, Washington, DC
6. The Granger Collection, New York
7. Independence National Historical Park
8. The Granger Collection, New York
9. Kilroe Collection, Rare Books and Manuscripts Library, Columbia University
10. Library of Congress
11. The Granger Collection, New York
12. William Loughton Smith (1758–1812) by Gilbert Stuart (1755–1828). Oil on canvas, Gibbes Museum of Art / Carolina Art Association, 1883.01.03
13. National Gallery of Art, Washington, DC. Andrew W. Mellon Collection. Image © Board of Trustees, National Gallery of Art, Washington, DC
14. National Archives and Records Administration
15. Library of Congress
16. © The New Haven Colony Historical Society
17. The Granger Collection, New York
18. Library of Congress
19. © American Antiquarian Society
20. Library of Congress
21. Library of Congress
22. The Granger Collection, New York
23. Library of Congress
24. The Granger Collection, New York

INDEX